D0914666

WORLDVIEW
and the
Communication
of the Gospel

The William Carey Library Series on Applied Cultural Anthropology

William A. Smalley, Editor

Becoming Bilingual: A Guide to Language Learning by Donald N. Larson and William A. Smalley, 425 pages, $5.95x

Bibliography for Cross-Cultural Workers compiled by Alan R. Tippett, 256 pages, $4.95

Christopaganism or Indigenous Christianity? edited by Tetsunao Yamamori and Charles R. Taber, 264 pages, $5.95

The Church and Cultures: An Applied Anthropology for the Religious Worker by Louis J. Luzbetak, 448 pages, $5.95x

Culture and Human Values: Christian Intervention in Anthropological Perspective, articles by Jacob Loewen, edited by William A. Smalley, 464 pages, $5.95x

Customs and Cultures: Anthropology for Christian Missions by Eugene A. Nida, 320 pages, $3.95x

Manual of Articulatory Phonetics by William A. Smalley, 522 pages, $5.95x

Message and Mission: The Communication of the Christian Faith by Eugene A. Nida, 272 pages, $3.95x

Readings in Missionary Anthropology II edited by William A. Smalley, 944 pages, $9.95x

Solomon Islands Christianity: A Study in Growth and Obstruction by Alan R. Tippett, 428 pages, $5.95

Tips on Taping: Language Recording in the Social Sciences by Wayne and Lonna Dickerson, 208 pages, $4.95x

Understanding Latin Americans with Special Reference to Religious Values and Movements by Eugene A. Nida, 176 pages, $3.95

Worldview and Communication of the Gospel: A Nigerian Case Study by Marguerite G. Kraft, 240 pages, $7.95

WORLDVIEW
and the
Communication of the Gospel

A Nigerian case study

Marguerite Kraft

William Carey Library

533 HERMOSA STREET • SOUTH PASADENA, CALIFORNIA 91030

Library of Congress Cataloging in Publication Data

Kraft, Marguerite G
   Worldview and the communication of the Gospel.

   Originally presented as the author's thesis, Fuller
Theological Seminary.
   Bibliography: p.
   Includes index.
   1. Missions to Kamwes (African people)
2. Kamwes (African people) 3. Communication (Theology)
I. Title.
BV3630.K35K7 1978   266'.009669'5   78-10196
ISBN 0-87808-324-3

BV
3630
.K35
K 7
1978

Copyright © 1978 by Marguerite G. Kraft

Published by the William Carey Library
            1705 N. Sierra Bonita Avenue
            Pasadena, California 91104
            Telephone (213) 798-0819

In accord with some of the most recent thinking in the academic
press, the William Carey Library is pleased to present this
scholarly book which has been prepared from an author-edited
and author-prepared camera ready copy.

PRINTED IN THE UNITED STATES OF AMERICA

Contents

Figures and Tables

Foreword

In this lucid study, Meg Kraft leads us to the heart of the mission task – the communication of the Gospel within the context of another culture. In the first place, she makes us aware of the fact that this process is not so simple as many would have us believe. It is not enough simply to declare the message of God in our own terms. The message must be translated into forms that the people understand and are willing to trust. There must be the translation from one language to another, from one set of social structures to another, and from one form of communication to another. But even this is not enough. At the deepest level, in missions the Gospel must be translated into a new worldview if the church is to become truly indigenous. But this is often threatening. On the one hand, there is the real danger of syncretism, particularly if we are not careful to preserve the essence of the Gospel. On the other hand, in an attempt to avoid such syncretism, we may tie the Gospel so closely to our own cultural expressions of Christianity, or to our own theological interpretations which have arisen as we read the Scriptures from the perspective of our own culture and times, that it remains totally foreign to the people we serve. However, in doing so, we, in effect, close to them the door of salvation, not because they reject the Word, but because we have added so heavy a cultural load to the requirements for becoming a Christian.

In the second place, Kraft provides us with an excellent case study of how the Gospel can be translated into another culture. There are many who, when faced with an awareness of the difficulties of cross-cultural communication, throw up their hands in

despair that the task can ever be done. Kraft here skillfully
takes us into the worldview of the Kamwə and shows us how the
Gospel can be translated into forms that the Kamwə understand.
And she does so not only on the level of language and communication, but also in social structures and conceptual frameworks.
Enroute, she makes us aware of the fact that we too have received the Gospel within a set of cultural forms, and that our
understanding and application of the Scriptures is incomplete.
As we see the Gospel at work in the Kamwə context, we realize
that in some ways they understand the message of the Bible better than we. We need a stronger theology of family, of corporate responsibility, of worship, and of the forces of evil against
which we contend. God has, indeed, given His Spirit to His
people throughout the world, and has given to them unique understandings of Himself. And we have much to gain if we listen to
one another and share the insights God has given us.

But this book is more than a case study. It is a model that
can be used in other mission contexts. Kraft makes explicit
the theoretical framework she is using, and shows us how it can
be practically applied to real life situations. This wedding of
theory and reality makes the study valuable not only to those
studying missions, but also those involved in it. Not all will
agree with her conclusions at every point, but everyone in missions should come to grips with the questions she has raised
and consider seriously the insights she shares. Today in a post-
colonial era, more than ever before the church must be deeply
aware of the intercultural nature of its mission, and must explore what that has to say about the nature of the church itself.
We have the beginnings of an answer in this book, but a great
many more serious studies of missions like this one are needed
to give us an understanding of the church around the world today.

Paul G. Hiebert
Associate Professor of Anthropology
      and South Asian Studies
School of World Mission, Pasadena

Preface

Dr. Kraft's study of the Kamwə worldview is of great value to both anthropology and missiology, and something quite new in the area between those two disciplines. It shows how much anthropology may learn from missiology and vice versa.

Here we meet many key concepts of anthropology--group awareness, the notion of the family as the basic unit, and the interdependence of groups and persons (tradesmen and commoners, young and old, male and female) and we are shown how these features hold the society in equilibrium.

Dr. Kraft uses the techniques of ethnoscience to ascertain the dominant linguistic (and therefore cultural) components of the society. This causes her to focus on four dynamic themes in the Kamwə worldview--the mountain orientation, the guinea corn complex, the ideal person and the supernatural with its practitioners, paraphernalia and performances.

This valuable assembly of anthropological information forms the background for her missiology and missiological strategy. How is the Christian gospel communicated to people with such a worldview? This question brings her into communication theory and indigenous theology, two fields in which she has some considerable knowledge.

The Kamwə worldview becomes her point of reference for a study of church planting and growth, which naturally requires some time depth for analysis. For this Dr. Kraft arranges her data on an ethnohistorical structure of the cultural continuum type, probing her data at three points of time--the mid-1950's, the mid-1960's and mid-1970's--thus providing three synchronic levels for analysis in a diachronic sequence.

Methodologically this is a real breakthrough in missiological research at two significant points: 1) it demonstrates the cultural continuum approach to be an appropriate model for church planting and growth studies over the life span of a missionary researcher who can return to the field at 10 year intervals, and 2) it shows that a reconstruction of a pre-Christian worldview by using the methods of ethnoscience is likewise a good model for analysing the cross-cultural communication of the gospel and the cultural changes due to conversion side by side with those indigenous values which persist through change--cultural tarriance as it has been called.

In this way Dr. Kraft is able to provide a church-planting strategy which makes allowance for music, dancing, drama and oral arts, together with new innovative communication techniques, which are appropriate to both the traditional worldview and the new value system which comes with Christianity.

This all makes a highly competent piece of anthropological research into a valuable missiological study. One certainly hopes it will become an inspiration and model for other missiologists. For non-missiological readers in theology and the social sciences it will serve to indicate the kind of dissertation coverage expected at the School of World Mission, at the Fuller Theological Seminary, Pasadena for the degree of Doctor of Missiology.

A. R. Tippett
Senior Professor of Anthropology
and Oceanic Studies
School of World Mission, Pasadena

Acknowledgments

The Kamwə people of northeastern Nigeria, particularly the people of the Mbororo and Micika area, have been adding to my understanding of life and mission work for a number of years now. It would be impossible to include all who should be recognized in this brief acknowledgment. I am indebted to Daniel, Bugi, Vandi, Nggari, Nggida, Zira, Wampana, Dali, David Vandi, Kwatiri, Zira Dya, Yohanna, the people of Lughwi, and (to say it in the Kamwə way) the wife of Yohanna, the wife of John Guli, and especially the wife of Daniel. While doing my research in 1974 these and many others were most cooperative and helpful in teaching me about their beliefs and customs. I wish to thank Joseph who allowed my husband and me to live in his home while doing the 1974 part of this research. My special thanks go to John Guli who made this book possible by patiently giving many hours for interviewing and discussion in the Micika setting and also in Pasadena when he was studying at the School of World Mission.

Special thanks go to the Brethren Church and the Church of the Brethren Mission who first put me in touch with the Kamwə people. I am greatly indebted to Daystar Communications and to Dr. Kenneth Taylor of Living Bibles International for the opportunity to go to the field for research in 1974. I am also indebted to the Missions Department at Biola which has encouraged me in this writing and helped finance the final typing. Library studies were carried out at McAlister Library at Fuller Theological Seminary, the U.C.L.A. Research Library in Los Angeles, and the library at the University of Southern California.

I would like to give special thanks to Dr. Alan R. Tippett, who directed my research and guided my writing. His vital suggestions and appreciative comments, as he read chapter after chapter, provided continual inspiration and encouragement. At the School of World Mission, Drs. Glasser, Wagner, Winter and McGavran have contributed greatly to my understanding of the issues involved in this disseration. Dr. Lloyd Kwast and Dr. Betty Sue Brewster, who served on my doctoral committee, were most helpful in their suggestions for the final draft.

I would also like to acknowledge my husband, Dr. Charles H. Kraft, without whose encouragement and inspiration this disseration would not have been written. My change in role from wife to scholar has not been an easy one for any of the members of my family, and I have needed much support and help. My daughter, Karen, has also been very supportive in assuming some of the responsibilities for keeping the household running smoothly. I also wish to thank Joyce Showalter, who has kept the chapters typed as I've moved along, and Joy Young, who faithfully typed the final draft. I feel that this has been a group venture. Thank you all.

PART I
Introduction

1

Methodology

The perceptive British anthropologist, R. R. Marett, when his contemporaries were mostly speculating on the origin of religion at the turn of the century, was struggling with the idea of a religion which has to be "danced and felt" rather than explained. In his book, *The Threshold of Religion* (1909), he was entering an area of awareness that African and Western forms and experiences were not acted out in the same frame of reference. Marett used missionary data, especially that of R. H. Codrington, who introduced him to such concepts as mana and taboo. Codrington in Melanesia, Henri Junod in South Africa, and a little earlier Lorimer Fison in Fiji, were missionary anthropologists who recognized the significance of what we now call worldview for cross-cultural communication. Yet although this perception goes back a century, we still badly need case studies to demonstrate its great importance for the cross-cultural communication of the Gospel and the planting of indigenous Christianity. In this presentation I focus on the Higi or Kamwə[1] people of Nigeria and attempt to relieve this deficiency.

---

[1] See Appendix B for a description of Kamwə orthography used throughout this document.

The purpose of this study is to examine the worldview of the Kamwə. It is my premise that a people's concepts, basic presuppositions, and experiences affect the way the message of Christianity is heard and interpreted. Understanding the worldview is a necessary basis for effective hearer-oriented communication. It is the basis also for strategizing for presenting the Gospel as well as effectively nurturing the Christians.

Worldview Definition

Every culture has its own worldview, the central governing set of concepts and presuppositions that its society lives by. Robert Redfield described the worldview of a people as "the way a people characteristically look outward upon the universe...how everything looks to a people" (1953:85). Worldview involves the idea of self, distinction of in-group and out-group, a person's relationship to the non-human in his surroundings, his attitude toward the universe, his spatial and temporal orientation, his values and norms. People are not always consciously aware of their worldview even though these ideas, values, and assumptions underlie their actions and give them meaning.

Worldview serves a function very similar to that of religion. The distinction between the two is that "a worldview provides people with their basic assumptions about reality. Religion provides them with the specific content of this reality" (Hiebert 1976:371).

Worldview is learned unconsciously early in life and it is not readily changed. As a child learns how to interact with his surroundings in a socially acceptable way, he is developing a worldview which will influence his actions the rest of his life. This will be the integrating core at the center of his perspective on reality. Worldview bridges the gap between the objective reality around him and the culturally agreed upon perception of that reality within him. This integrated core that is learned provides the framework for accepting or rejecting new elements in life. As he comes into contact with new ideas and elements, they are borrowed only if they fit into his worldview or if they can be recut or recolored to fit. Charles Kraft (1974a) lists five functions of worldview:

1. *Explanatory Function* - it explains why and how things got to be as they are and why and how they continue that way.

2. *Validating Function* - it sanctions the goals, institutions, and values of a society and provides them with a means for evaluating all outside influences as well as activities and attitudes within the society. It gives one a perspective on life.

3. *Reinforcement Function* - it provides psychological reinforcement for the group at points of anxiety or crisis in life providing security and support for the behavior of the group. One's worldview gives encouragement to go on or stimulus to take other action. It prescribes the form of action to take for sickness, death, initiation, etc.

4. *Integrating Function* - it systematizes and orders the perceptions of reality into an overall design with everything fitting into place. This system makes it possible for a people to conceptualize what reality should be like and to understand and interpret all that happens day by day in this framework.

5. *Adaptational Function* - it is resilient and reconciles differences between the old understandings and the new in order to maintain a state of equilibrium. It may be necessary to reinterpret values, to adjust origin myths, to alter beliefs about the supernatural, etc. Worldview has built into it this ability which makes it possible to adapt with culture change (see Malinowski 1925 for a similar analysis of religion).

Before the end of the 19th Century, Lorimer Fison, a missionary and anthropologist working in the South Pacific, wrote about the "mind world". By this he referred to what anthropologists later would call worldview. He recognized that the concepts, values, and presuppositions of the Fijians formed a valid system for understanding and operating in their surroundings. Their daily reactions and behaviour reflected their mind world. He used lexical data to get into the Fijian thought system and then classified his data on such subjects as land tenure, the personality of the cannibal, and kinship structure according to the Fijian terms.

The Approach of Ethnoscience

The outsider cannot see ideas, presuppositions and values. Insiders often cannot verbalize the worldview because it is not necessarily explicit in their own minds. Since worldview is largely acquired unconsciously, the insider takes it for granted and often does not question it or examine it. But language reflects and reveals a people's concepts and values. I have looked to the language to better understand the thoughts and perceptions of the Kamwə. Benjamin Lee Whorf discussed the relationship of language to the thought processes and the perception of the surrounding world. Language segments reality and influences the way man understands his environment. Whorf illustrates this:

> in word reference we deal with size by breaking it into
> size classes--small, medium, large, immense, etc.--but
> size objectively is not divided into classes, but is
> pure continuum of relativity. Yet we think of size con-
> stantly as a set of classes because language has seg-
> mented and named the experience in this way (Carroll
> 1956:259).

The frame of reference I have used in understanding worldview
is the approach of ethnoscience. Ethnoscience builds on the
assumption that the things and events in a people's conceptual
world will be mirrored in the semantic categories of the language.
By looking into how things are labeled and grouped, what is distinctive in assigned meanings, and how the people feel about
specific words and phrases, I have gained insights into their
worldview. Perchonock and Werner describe this methodology:

> Ethnoscience is concerned solely with classificatory
> principles as they are expressed by native speakers
> of the language, not as they are determined through
> anthropological observation. Ethnoscientists are
> interested in the speaker's knowledge of the various
> domains within his culture, not in his actual beha-
> vior in these domains (1969:229).

Goodenough (1957) viewed culture as not consisting of things,
people, behavior, or emotions, but as the forms or organization
of these in the minds of people. He advocated giving a central
place to the cognitive processes in order to obtain reliable cultural data for a description of culture that states what one must
know in order to generate culturally acceptable acts and utter-
ances appropriate to a given sociocultural context. By focusing
on the Kamwə terms and what they mean to the native speaker, I
myself have gained insights into the way the native speaker feels
about and sees the world around him. Anthropological observation
and participation in the culture for three years has given me the
insights and basis for generating questions about the native
speaker's perspective. But the organization of my materials and
the method of research is that of ethnoscience.

The analytical process I used for determining the meaning of
individual lexical items is known as componential analysis. Nida
noted that:

> there is no meaning apart from significant differ-
> ences...[words] have meaning only in terms of sys-
> tematic contrasts with other words which share cer-
> tain features with them but contrast with them in
> respect to other features (1975:32).

This process involves lumping together lexical items that have
features in common, separating out those that are distinct from
one another, determining the basis for such grouping, and classifying the material accordingly. The result is an intimate knowledge of how the native speaker feels about that particular lexical
item. An illustration of the insights gained through this method
is seen in the terms used to refer to Kamwə religious ceremonies.
In Figure 1 below, the three columns represent three different
ceremonies. Numbers 1-4 under each represent the common components and the other components are distinguishing components.
Ethnoscience refers to these as a paradigm relationship.
Lounsbury defines a paradigm as:

> any set of linguistic forms wherein (a) the meaning
> of every form has a feature in ·common with the mean-
> ings of all other forms of the set, and (b) the mean-
> ing of every form differs from that of every other
> form of the set by one or more additional features
> (Tyler 1969:193).

By examining these components, the difference between these various religious ceremonies becomes clear.

Componential analysis was particularly useful in understanding
the role of the various Kamwə practitioners, in comprehending the
meaning of the various Kamwə terms for "come" and "go," and in
gaining a knowledge of the meaning of the personal values. It
also proved useful for comparing the meaning of concepts at different periods in time, i.e., defining "riches" in the early days
and at the present time, in order to better understand worldview
change.

Working with lexical items in this way reinforces the fact that
there are several kinds of meaning: 1) <u>referential</u> - the particular symbol used to designate a specific entity, event, etc.,
2) <u>conceptual</u> - the concepts people have about objects, events,
relations, etc., and 3) <u>emotive</u> - the degree of emotional reaction
brought about by the use of the symbol. The below described d̄a
məlyə ceremony refers to the ritual performance that takes place
in the home. The conceptual meaning for this ceremony includes
the fact that a family member has a very real need that cannot be
met by man alone. So the unseen are called on for assistance.
God's power is recognized. It is important for the entire family
(excluding the daughters who have married out into another family
and are no longer family members) to be present and to participate. The ceremonial eating served by the household head reaf-
firms each person's place in the family unit. Man's offering a
sacrifice recognizes the order felt between man and God. The
emotive meaning in this event involves a satisfaction that all

ɗa mɛlyɛ	sareka	kelengi
1) God is addressed	1) God is addressed	1) God is addressed
2) Sacrifice involved	2) Sacrifice involved	2) Sacrifice involved
3) Expression of unity of group	3) Expression of unity of group	3) Expression of unity of group
4) Response to specific need	4) Response to specific need	4) Response to specific need
5) Appeal for help from God or appease the spirits	5) Appeal for help from God or appease the spirits	5) Appeal for help from God
6) Called for and performed by household head	6) Called for by chief or elders, carried out by household head	6) Called for and carried out by elders
7) Household unit only is present	7) Whole community participates	7) Elders only present but act on behalf of community
8) Held at the place of the special pot mɛlyɛ	8) Held outside of homes but sacrifice may be at crossing of paths	8) Held at special sacred place near village
9) For sickness, barren woman, harvest, planting	9) For drought, epidemic, harvesting, planting	9) For warfare, epidemic, marriage, harvest
10) May be prescribed by medium	10) May be prescribed by medium	10) Not prescribed by medium

Figure 1. Componential Analysis of Ceremonies

will be well--their sacrifice will be honored, the entire family
group has experienced the individual need or hurt, solidarity and
security is reaffirmed in the family group, etc.

> The semantic structure reveals more clearly than any
> other part of language a people's world view...in the
> semantic structure one finds the manner in which exper-
> ience tends to be classified...and that classification
> is indicative of the way in which people tend to view
> experience... (Coseriu 1975:177).

Another helpful analytic process I used for a better understanding of the cognitive world of the native speaker was arranging
lexical items in taxonomies. Describing lexical items according
to hierarchical relationship divides them into two dimensions:
a horizontal one of discrimination (paradigms as illustrated above
with the religious ceremonies) and a vertical one of generalization. This procedure integrates individual terms into the system
with the categories at any one level being included in the cate-
gory next higher. Taxonomic organization shortens the procedure
for defining individual lexical items. This was particularly
helpful in coming to an understanding of the spirit world and also
the history of the people. To illustrate, the organization of the
Kamwə tribe is made clear by taxonomic arrangement. All Kamwə
trace their origin to one place, Mcakili. Each level can be described simply: level 1 - dialect groups (see map on page 22),
level 2 - geographical groups (independent mountain-centered
groups), level 3 - the family groupings, level 4 - the basic
family units (see Figure 2).

A member of one of the family units, <u>kata</u>, of the Gapa group is
also a member of Ka Mwicika, Ka Nkafa, and the Kamwə. Every Kamwə
person is a meaningful part of a level 4 family group and his
identity can be traced through each level of this taxonomy.

The most effective means of eliciting materials was the <u>ques-
tion-answer method</u>. By asking culturally appropriate and relevant questions, culturally appropriate and relevant answers were
given. Using the Kamwə terms resulted in a very relaxed explanation and discussion. To help with taxonomic organization I used
the <u>card-sorting method</u> in which individual lexical items appear
on each card and the native speaker groups them as he sees fit.
Then we discussed reasons for putting each group together. This
method has limitations though because of literacy being required.
I also used the <u>linguistic frame method</u> where a sentence is given
and the native speaker is asked to fill in the blank with what-
ever to his thinking best fits in that slot. I also used proverbs
for discussion because much teaching of values is given in this
way.

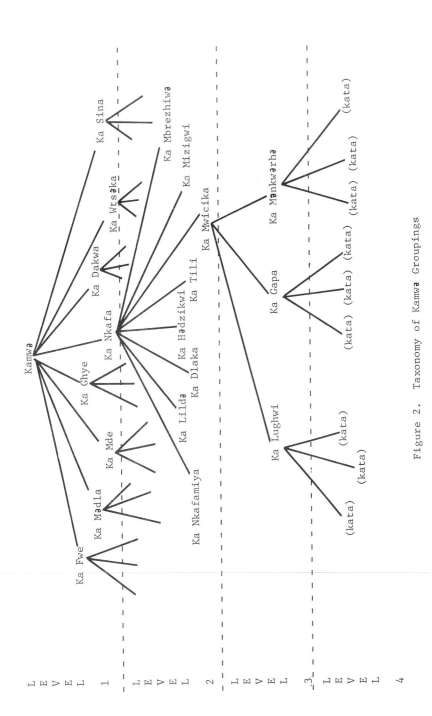

Figure 2. Taxonomy of Kamwə Groupings

I am aware that though the "emic" viewpoint was my goal, it was necessary to use "etic" terms on occasion in my writing. The terms emic and etic come from the field of linguistics. Kenneth Pike (1956-58) first applied these terms to nonverbal human behavior. An emic perspective refers to the manner in which native participants (cultural insiders) react and refer to their own behavior and to the behavior of their colleagues. An etic perspective is the outsider's point of view. There were times in my diagramming when, through the study of the culture as expressed in language, I became very aware of an important phase of the worldview, but there was no Kamwə term to use to represent it on the diagram. For example, the words for "go" and "come" and the locational prepositions are in six or more Kamwə terms depending on the location of the speaker in relation to the mountain. This I labeled from an etic perspective "mountain proximity".

Ethnoscience has its limitations. One difficulty lies in the assumption that the cognitive categories are conscious elements in the native speaker's mind. People are assumed to be aware of the categories they use to order their behavior and these categories are discoverable in the terms (words, labels) they use to discuss their behavior. Hunter and Foley warn about these limitations:

> Some evidence exists that people can be--in fact
> are--aware of domains of experience for which they
> do not have a simple label or term. Harold Conklin
> (1955) found that the Hanunoo, shifting rice culti-
> vators living in the Philippine jungle, understand
> that things have colors but do not have the equiva-
> lent term (or concept) of our general term color.
> This suggests that in order to find out all the
> cognitive categories of a particular society one
> must do more than merely study their language. All
> aspects of their behavior must be examined in order
> to find out if they are patterning their behavior--
> making choices--in terms of cognitive categories that
> are only minimally encoded in their speech (1976:136).

Resources

The sources for this study include written materials as well as personal interviews. The amount of published material on the Kamwə and neighboring tribes is quite limited. It has all been done by outsiders looking in--the missionary, the traveler, the anthropologist. The value of each piece of writing depends on the author's social status (in both the eyes of the Kamwə and in his own society), his training, culture consciousness, knowledge of the Kamwə, and understanding and depth of penetration into the Kamwə thought patterns. Kwast discusses the problems of documentary interpretation:

> Not all sources, even primary sources, are of equal
> value or reliability. One has to be continually on
> his guard. He needs to approach his documents with
> an adequate chronology and biography so that in pro-
> jecting himself into the past he does not also assume
> knowledge of the present on the part of his sources.
> He needs to remember that all sources have their biases
> and become more valuable when the bias is understood
> (Tippett 1973:298).

He goes on to enumerate a number of specific problems involving
authenticity, reliability, textual inconsistency, meaning, and
personal bias. These were considered in my studying these materials.

I also used unpublished material that was written by four
Kamwə men in 1967 when I was living in Jos, Nigeria. After reading descriptions of other Nigerian cultures, they were asked to
describe their own culture in a similar way. Various topics were
suggested, i.e., gods, spirits, death, marriage, etc., and they
were encouraged to add any other ideas they could think of to explain how their people related to the world around them. The men
who wrote these materials are: 1) Joseph Takwale, in his early
20s and with secondary school education, 2) Tumba Nggida, around
20 and in his fourth year of teacher training beyond seven years
of elementary school, 3) John Guli, in his mid 20s, with four
years of Bible School and in his second year of a four-year Theological College, and 4) Zira Dya - in his mid 20s, with four
years of Bible School and in his second year of a four-year Theological College. These men were encouraged to interview the older
men in the Kamwə villages whenever things were not clear in their
own minds. This served as a valuable corrective. Each of these
men grew up in a traditional home where the Kamwə language
(Vəcəmwə) was the language of the home. This body of writing con-
tains their personal descriptions, recollections and analyses with
the recollections of village elders intertwined throughout the
materials. Their contact with Western ideas was mostly through
their schooling and church experience. It was necessary to keep
this in mind lest acculturation affect the data. It is good to
have material like this from more than one source so the data can
be compared.

Further intensive interviewing and checking concerning the
worldview was done in my three-week return work visit to the
Kamwə while I was putting this presentation together. At that
time I worked with many elderly people, usually in their homes,
farms, or villages. A few came to my hut to be interviewed. I
wrote notes and also recorded most of the data on tape noting the

informant's name, age, occupation, and residence, and also noting
details on the situation of the interview, etc. People were very
trusting and cooperative since I had lived in the area for three
years previously. I also took with me a well-known church worker
on all occasions.

At this time I also had opportunity to question and interact
with Roger Mohrlang, an American-born Wycliffe Bible Translator
who lived in a Kamwə home for six years while he was reducing the
language to writing and translating the New Testament into Vəcəmwə.
The majority of the proverbs that I used for discussion and illustration are from his collection.

The leader of the Kamwə Church, John Guli, was a very valuable
help to me while he was studying recently for fifteen months at
Fuller Theological Seminary, Pasadena. He is now in his mid-30s
and recently spent several years as co-translator of the Kamwə
New Testament. I interviewed him regularly, and this gave opportunity for checking the other collected materials. He was studying anthropology as part of his missions course, so he understood
very quickly my frame of reference and goals. Since he has had
more experience than any other Kamwə in working with the written
form of his language, he was able to help write some of these concepts that have never before been recorded.

An Overview

In this research of Kamwə worldview the all-important and dom-
inating factor that constantly appeared was the very significant
meaning of the family unit. The patrilineal family group, kata,
which traces back to a single ancestor through the male line is
the important unit. In my questioning it became evident that the
Kamwə person, according to tradition, has no identity apart from
his family--he reflects his family, he is obligated to his family,
and he depends on his family for help in time of need. Because
of this emphasis, I have dealt with group awareness in Chapter 2.

As I attempted to understand how the Kamwə sees, feels toward,
values, and understands the world about him, four main conceptual
domains became evident for gaining this understanding. In Part II
I have dealt with each of these domains in a separate chapter
(Chapters 3 through 6). My aim is to give insights into how the
Kamwə sees the world about him. These four domains are: 1) the
mountain orientation, 2) the guinea corn complex, 3) belief in
the supernatural, and 4) the ideal person. At the end of each of
these chapters there is a diagram that shows the important components of each of these domains. The family unit is the "glasses"
through which the world is seen. By focusing on these four significant domains, the integrated system takes shape (see Figure 3).

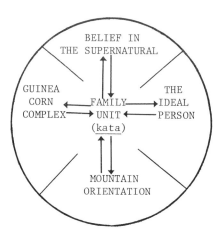

Figure 3. Kamwə Worldview

After presenting the traditional worldview, I will deal with the
influence of contemporary culture change on their worldview.

   In Part III (Chapters 8 through 11) I seek to define and describe communication by examining (in Chapter 8) the three essential components of communication: the communicator, his message,
and the receptor. Communication is a dynamic process and I deal
with the specific areas where there may be breakdown in the
process. Some principles of communication are then discussed
(Chapter 9) with hopes for a clearer understanding of the communication process.

   In order to see how worldview is related to communicating the
Gospel, I examine (in Chapter 10) three different worldviews: the
American worldview, the worldviews of Scripture, and the Kamwə
worldview in relation to the commandment, "honor your father and
your mother," and also in relation to the use of music. Scripture
quoted in this document is from the New American Standard Version
of the Bible. Chapter 11, then, focuses on the communication
results from understanding worldviews in relation to the receptor,
the communicator, the message, communication forms, worship forms,
church structure, and leadership roles.

   The final section (Part IV) involves a brief historical "cultural continuum" analysis of the Kamwə Church (Chapter 12). I
deal with three synchronic layers in a diachronic analysis in
order to better understand the present Church situation. Using

the Kamwə worldview as a basis, I then explore strategy for the
Church (Chapters 13 through 16) suggesting specific ways to have
a Church that is relevant and meaningful. Chapter 17 is a con-
cluding summary.

By examining the conceptual divisions mirrored in the language,
it is possible to begin to more clearly understand life as a Kamwə
sees it, to understand his values and basic presuppositions, and
to better understand the organization of his experiential world.
These insights will hopefully be the basis for much more effective
communication for the cross-cultural Christian worker and for the
local church leaders concerned with reaching out and ministering
to all of the Kamwə people. These are times of a great number of
changes in the area including economic, political, religious,
social, and technical change. After describing the traditional
worldview of the Kamwə, I will be looking at the influence of
these changing times on Kamwə worldview. But first we must get
a clearer picture of who the Kamwə are and where they get their
identity.

2

Kamwə Group Awareness

In my investigation of the Kamwə worldview I was continually
confronted with a fact that affects every aspect of Kamwə life.
This fact was the tight-knit relationship that an individual feels
with the family group. The individual is only seen as a functioning part of a family. Further investigation might indicate that
this aspect of Kamwə culture would better be handled as one of the
major domains of the worldview, but at this point in my research
it seems to be an all-encompassing factor that provides the matrix
for understanding the worldview. For this reason I am treating
it in a chapter by itself as preparation for understanding the
worldview.

In order to understand the cognitive world of the Kamwə we
must understand the man-group relationship. Authority is in the
family ancestors and elders. Land for farming and building a
house is obtained (leased) through the family. Interpersonal
unity is conceived of in terms of extended family relationships.
One's family is seen as his most valuable possession. One's daily
relationships with the family are paramount. It is as a family
group that one relates to other groups and to the outside world.
Order is seen as family based. The family is seen as the ideal
of beauty and security, without which there would be no meaning
in life. The family is the basic economic unit, the significant
group for relating to the unseen, the basic political unit, and
the center of social life and obligations. Analytically, it is
impossible to abstract this larger family unit out in an ethno-
semantic way because in the worldview there is no alternative
envisioned.

History and Location

The Kamwə live in the Mandara Hill area of Northern Nigeria and the adjacent Cameroon Republic. They are a group of around 200,000 people who have been called "Higi" by a neighboring tribe. They refer to themselves, however, as Kamwə, "the people of the mountain,"[1] and prefer to be called the Kamwə. They presently occupy an area from the Mandara Hills on the east to the Yedzeram River on the west between the towns of Madagali on the north and Uba on the south. The Kamwə trace their origins to Mcakili which is in the Cameroons to the north of the present Kamwə area (some say near present-day Kirawa). Several of the neighboring tribes, or at least sections of the tribes trace their roots to this place as well. According to origin myths there were several possible reasons for the emigration of the Kamwə: shortage of farmland, shortage of water supply, disagreements (sometimes isolation due to breaking the traditional law). The people were mountain people and the Mandara Hills provide many hills 1,000 to 2,000 feet high for habitation. So when there was a reason to move on, the leader would move to another hill and his family would settle there. Each group was independent of the other but had similar laws and ways of living.

Often the place names are the names of the traditional founders. A detailed example of place names that are names of the founders is found in the origin of the Bazza Clan (see Appendix C) where Kamale and Bazza were brothers. This is reflected today in a feeling of closeness between the groups and in the language itself (for the Bazza dialect is closer to the Kamale dialect but different from the intervening Nkafa dialect).

Other place names are derived from impressive historical events:

1. *Ghumci* - "good-bye forever" - when a younger brother was not treated fairly by his brothers (see Appendix C).

2. *Metla* - "falling mountain" - at the time the people were settling there and building their compounds there were constant landslides.

---

[1] There is an alternate theory of the meaning of Kamwə, as "mwə" means either mountain or a vine grown by the people specifically to be used for tying around their waists as part of the ritual at the time of death. This vine shows who are the ones related to the deceased. This is a Kamwə custom throughout the area.

3. *Muncika* (Micika) - "stalking mountain" - any person who came to this mountain must be stalked because there were many enemies from different groups of people--Marghi, Bazza, Nkafa.

4. *Kashigete* - "people on the end" - land given to people of the chief's family by the people of Kamale.

In an article on Higi (Kamwə) warfare, Otterbein refers to the "political community" (1968:195), He defines the political community as a group of people organized into a single unit managing its affairs independently of external control. These people would be from the same clan and living in close proximity to each other. He differentiates between internal conflict (fighting with clubs and sticks within the political community in order to provide social control) and warfare (combat with bows and arrows occurring between political communities). The internal conflict took place when the chief and elders were not successful in settling the dispute and also in the presence of the chief and elders. Warfare is usually with the neighboring political communities or in the case of communities on the fringe of the Kamwə area with neighboring tribes, e.g., Marghi, Fali, Gude.

The early migrations of Fulani pastoralists into this area were peaceful. The Fulani who lived in Micika sometimes married Kamwə women and were protected by the Kamwə when the Kanuri attacked them (Takwale 1967). Later in the 19th Century, the Fulani became a threat to the cultural identity of the Kamwə and neighboring tribes (Vaughan 1964). At this point they attempted to rule and were expected to send a quota of slaves to Sokoto. This caused tension between the Fulani and the other tribes. The Kamwə were expected to pay tribute and donate labor on the orders of the ruling Fulani. In those days the tribute was in the form of slaves, animals, farm products, clothes, or iron bars (a form of money). Usually the tribute was paid before the Kamwə could plant their farms and again before they could harvest their crops. Not everyone in a village would have to pay, but if no one from the village paid, the Fulani would prevent them from planting or harvesting. The Fulani could only enforce this on the flatlands. The Kamwə were never conquered by the Fulanis since they could be safe in the hills. But the relationship through the years became strained, and the Kamwə began to feel that to rule, one had to "become Fulani." Becoming Fulani implies a greater or lesser degree of conversion from Kamwə to Fulani culture and Muslim religion. It is symbolized by association with those who are ethnically Fulani. The idea of becoming Fulani was offensive to most Kamwə, but for various reasons some changed from allegiance to Kamwə culture to allegiance to Fulani culture. Takwale (1967) lists some of the reasons:

1. Being sold to the Fulanis as slaves.

2. Having been cast out by their clan as a result of their bad character or possessing the (vwə) spirit, etc.

3. Young people running from their masters because of bad treatment.

4. Marrying a Fulani man.

5. Marrying a Fulani girl because the "brideprice" was very small.

6. The availability of prostitutes among the Fulani (not available among the Kamwə).

7. Captured by the Fulani.

8. Jobs available among the Fulani.

In the early part of the 20th Century, German and British colonial administration was felt in Kamwə country. The Kamwə were made submissive first to German, then to British colonial administrations. When, after World War I, the British took charge of the area, they set up "indirect rule" giving the Fulani rulers in the area political power. It wasn't until 1936 when the Kamwə Native Court was formed that the Kamwə started to enjoy political rights and to feel like real citizens. The first Native Court was made up of five Kamwə chiefs, their five assistants and three lesser chiefs. By the late 1950s there were fifty qualified Kamwə chiefs who had the right to join the Native Court. Also in the 1950s, some Kamwə were elected to higher government positions (e.g., House of Representatives in Lagos and the Kaduna House of Chiefs). Since Nigerian independence in 1960, there have been more government positions open to the Kamwə. Gradually schools were built in this area, beginning in the late 1920s. But in the early days people felt they lost their children when they sent them to school. They sent them to school so that they might learn much and come back and help, but they often found that the school children became like strangers and only criticized the way the parents lived. When they finished school they no longer wanted to help at home.

Divisions of the Kamwə

There are eight dialect areas in the Kamwə region:

1. *Ghye* - this area is on the Cameroon border. According to tradition, Ghye is the name of one of the early settlers from Mcakili.

2. *Sina* - this area is on the Cameroon border just north of Ghye and is also said to be one of the early settlements from Mcakili.

3. *Wtsəka* - this area is on the Cameroon border. Its founder, so they say, came from Mcakili in search of farmland.

4. *Dakwa* - this is the southern part of the Kamwə area. These people are related more closely to Ka Wstəka (ka means "people from"). Their founder, Dakwa, was a brother to Wstəka (see Appendix C, "Origin of Bazza Clan"). They left Mcakili, according to legend, in search of farmland.

5. *Mde* - this area is on the Cameroon border and the people there trace their heritage through Ghye.

6. *Fwe* - the people of this area trace their origin through Sukur which is north of the Kamwə area and was an early settlement from Mcakili as well.

7. *Mədla* - there is evidence of the origin of the people of this area tracing their heritage through either Ghye or Sukur.

8. *Nkafa* - this area is the largest at present and is located away from the Cameroon border. These people trace their heritage through Ghye.

These various groups first settled on specific hills. Many villages are now located on the plains but these are always associated with hills or hill villages with which the people identify.

The largest dialect area is Nkafa. Since this is the area where my research was done, I will be discussing worldview from the perspective of the Kamwə from this area. The Nkafa include eight exogamous groups:

1. Ka Mbrezhiwə	5. Ka Nkafamiya
2. Ka Lidle	6. Ka Dlaka
3. Ka Hədzikwi	7. Ka Tili
4. Ka Mizigwi	8. Ka Micika

Even though these all speak the same dialect, they are independent groups. Each group traces its origin back to a common ancestor who settled on a mountain. There was definite hostility and frequent wars between groups. The plains between their hills were used as battlefields. These wars were fought with bows and arrows.

Causes for war between these groups were: 1) wife stealing,
2) quarrels about farmland, 3) a means of showing bravery, 4) a
means of releasing anger when something happened to an important
person, 5) animal stealing. With the British rule of Nigeria the
wars were stopped and slowly the people began moving to the plains
to live and farm. Some of these exogamous units have "initiation
rites," others do not. For some the birth of one child cancels
the "brideprice," but for others two children are required. After
the required number of children, a wife is free to leave the marriage, and often the parents encourage this so that they can collect more "brideprice." As a result, the husband must give gifts
to the in-laws when another child is born to keep them happy and
satisfied.

Each of these exogamous groups functions as a socio-political
unit under its own laws with a chief and elders in charge. Traditionally the chief served merely as a unifying agent and did
not have executive power. He was closer to the supernatural than
to the commoner. The people felt that to offend the chief was
to offend the gods he served and to endanger the public welfare
(Meek 1931:254-255). Most groups bury their chiefs in charcoal,
but some do not.

The Ka Micika area represents three family groups: Lughwi who
call themselves Kwaɓe, Gapa who call themselves Kwaga, and
Mənkwərhə who call themselves Kwace. Each of these family groups
consists of several <u>kata</u>. In the Kamwə language <u>kata</u> refers to
those who have a single known ancestor. Within the <u>kata</u> one cannot
intermarry or fight with arrows in traditional warfare. If fighting occurs it must be with clubs only. The <u>kata</u> must approve the
marriage choice, provide farmland for each member, help at ceremonial times, i.e., wedding and burial, and be responsible for
each member's behavior. All of the Ka Micika are buried in a common burial ground. There is one chief for the combined three
family groups. Thus it will be seen that each of the social groups
is a tight-knit homogeneous unit.

The map that follows (Figure 4) shows: 1) the dialect areas,
2) the major mountains, the Cameroon border and the Yedzeram River
that are important markers for understanding the east-west bound-
aries of the Kamwə, and 3) the motor roads that pass through the
area.

The Basic Unit: The Family

The Kamwə are a patrilineal and a patrilocal society. The
bride leaves her clan of birth and becomes a part of her husband's
clan. A baby daughter is referred to as <u>kakye</u>, "stranger" or
outsider," and a baby boy is referred to as <u>mdi məlimi</u> (literally
"man of the town"), a member of the core group. All girls get

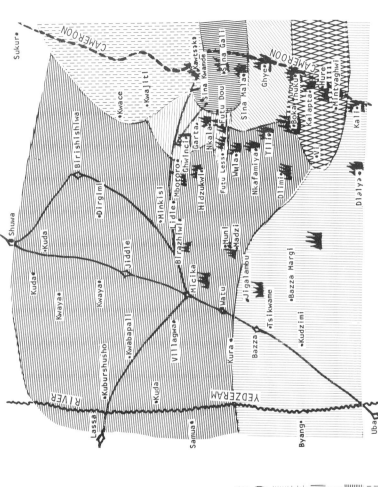

Figure 4. Map of Kamwə Area

MOUNTAINS
RIVER
ROADS
LARGE TOWNS
BOUNDARY
DIALECT AREAS:

Ka Ghye
Ka Mde
Ka Mədlə
Ka Fwe
Ka Sina
Ka Dakwa
Ka Nkafa
Ka Wtsəkə

married in Kamwə society so the time in the clan of birth is for
only a few years. The family is very important in arranging for
marriages and in seeing that a new home is properly established.
The marriage partners are expected to reflect the characteristics
of their families and this is considered important when arranging
a marriage for one's offspring. "Brideprice" and dowry are
required. These show the commitment of one family to another and
provide much support for a successful marriage. There is a special word in the language for daughter-in-law, makwa. This word
signifies the responsibility the groom's parents take on when a
son marries. The wife has left her clan of birth and is a new
member in her husband's family. His parents are now responsible
for her well-being. Another term məkwe refers to a man's mother-
in-law, father-in-law, or son-in-law, but the responsibility is
very little and almost casual to persons in this relationship.
The bride, however, does not use this term for her husband's
parents. Instead, she uses the term taraza (father of my husband)
and maraza (mother of my husband), again showing her responsibility to them as her new father and mother.

The relationship of brothers is very important. The term for
father, ta, refers to both the biological father and all his
brothers. The words for brother show two different relationships:
dəgwəma, brothers born of the same mother and dəgwəta, brothers
born of the same father (but of different mothers). However, the
latter term includes sons of the father's brother as well. The
words for sister, wzarma and wzarta have the same distinction
with the latter term referring as well to the father's brother's
daughters. The terms used for son, zigwi and daughter, wza, are
used for the sons and daughters of all whom one refers to as
dəgwəta or dəgwəma. This indicates the close relationship and
responsibility one feels for the core group of the clan. The
levirate is practiced with brothers inheriting the wives of the
deceased. The wife and children belong to the clan.

Brothers and their wives, their sons and their sons' wives,
etc. are buried traditionally at a family burial ground. Brothers
and their sons must help one another with family needs--such as
school fees, "brideprice," farmland--and must furnish food for
wedding celebrations as well as goats for funerals of any of its
members. Brothers share their possessions also. Brothers are
responsible for an orphan or a widow in the family.

The single term, wtsəgə, refers to the relatives on the
mother's side as well as the children of daughters who have
married out of the clan. They have the privilege of appearing
at feast times and participating and the obligation of digging
the grave when one dies! They are seen as takers, not givers, and
they have no obligation to contribute.

A special relationship seems to exist between grandparent and grandchild. In the language the same term is used for both of these, <u>shi</u>. It is interesting to note that there is no sex distinction in this term as in most of the other kinship terms. I suspect that this may have to do with productivity. Since the focus is on the non-productive time of life, the implications of the term are lumped together. This needs further research, however. At any rate, the grandparent sees in the grandchild the means of carrying on the lineage and values that are dear and significant. The grandchild is often in the care of the grandparent so that this projection of self is very realistic.

Interdependence

In traditional Kamwə society there is much interdependence. This is evident in the caste structure, the division between men's and women's communities, and the relationship of the young and old.

Tradesman and Commoner

There are two castes: the tradesman, <u>lighe</u>, and the commoner, <u>mələ</u>. Every clan has its own tradesmen who serve them. The tradesmen are actually only a small percentage of the total Kamwə population. In the one village I checked there were seven tradesmen's homes out of thirty homes in the village. Even this percentage may be a bit high, however, as a general rule. Takwale (1967) states that only two percent of the Kamwə are tradesmen. According to a Kamwə myth (see Appendix C) the tradesmen came from within the society. The tradesmen are the makers of hoes, bows, arrows, spears, knives, machetes, musical instruments, women's clothing (made of metal and hides), baby carriers, etc., as well as being the undertakers, the barbers, the housebuilders, and the musicians. The wives of the tradesmen make clay pots, decorate calabashes, and do the women's barbering and the scarification on the girls. They also are the mid-wives. All of these services are essential for life. The tradesmen are dependent on the commoners for food because their farms are very small. They are not ashamed to ask for things they need.

The commoner mələ is a farmer. He pays for the services of the tradesmen with produce and supplies them with the charcoal, skins, and metal for their work. The cost of the tradesman's services varies according to the wealth of the farmer. When a tradesman who has served the farmer comes asking for guinea corn, he is given it even if it is the last he has because without the tradesmen there would be no implements for farming. When a member of a tradesman's family dies, all the people in the area collect guinea corn for them.

The chief of the tradesmen works in a complementary way with the chief of the commoners who has the greater authority. One of the important roles of the chief of the tradesmen is to be the spokesman for the chief of the commoners. He informs the people when there is a call for community action and on occasion he represents the community in offering a sacrifice on their behalf.

The tradesmen and the commoners do not intermarry, neither do they eat together. The tradesmen eat foods that the commoners do not, i.e., donkey, monkey, horse, cat, crocodile. According to legend, the tradesmen originated from within the Kamwə when a man was greedy. He stole the meat at a death ceremony. After this happened several times the people caught him and decided that he should prepare the goat and make the loincloth for the corpse so he could earn his way and have the meat. The tradesmen are looked down upon by the commoner because of the "unclean" foods that they eat and their untidy homes, but they are also highly respected because no community can exist without them.

en and Women

The relationship of men and women in Kamwə society shows much interdependence. The compound is divided into the men's side and the women's side. The men and boys over six to eight years of age sit together apart from the women. The men sit together in the evening and chat. They gather often for drinking beer which seems to be a symbol of friendship, oneness, and acceptability. The division of labor is very clear. The men represent the family for community matters, are responsible for the spiritual activities in the home, arrange for and pay for the services of the tradesmen, and provide the guinea corn, meat, and salt for their households. The women are responsible for the daily care of the household, preparing the food, the gathering of firewood, and carrying of water to the compound, and providing vegetables for eating. Both men and women may own animals but only women care for the chickens, and only men care for the sheep, goats, donkeys, and cattle. This structuring makes it necessary for every Kamwə person to marry.

ung and Old

The old and the young in Kamwə society depend on each other also. The most important goal that the Kamwə have in life is to provide for their families. Children are a man's or woman's most valuable possession for his/her importance is dependent on how many children he has. Children are named according to the order of their birth--Tizhe, the first born, if a boy; Kuve, the first born, if a girl; Zira, the second born, if a boy; Masi, the second born, if a girl, etc.[1] It is the repsonsibility of the elders to teach the children the traditions and values of the society. Parents teach their children what they need to know as adults--the care of animals, how to repair the huts, how to prepar food, farming, etc. Children who do not listen to their parents are regarded as without sense, but those who do listen and heed what the parents teach are said to be of good character and with good sense.

Children must treat older people with respect and it is a very serious matter (even requiring ritual to make things right again) when a younger person does not listen and follow the advice of his elder. If an edler person dies without the younger person being in his good favor, the young person will supposedly suffer much harm thereafter. Small children share food from their hunting with the grandparents. Sons take care of their parents in their old age. It is definitely essential for one to help the person who gave you birth. The old need the young and the young need the old in Kamwə society.

The importance of age and the interdependent groups shown is in the traditional length of the funeral ceremony. When a child dies he/she is buried in one day, a woman is buried after one and one half days, a young man after two days, a chief after three or more days, and the head tradesman after seven days. The longer the ceremony the greater the honor. There is continual dancing, cryin and singing during this period of ceremony for the deceased.

These homogeneous social units, then, maintain their social cohesion by the interdependence of opposites--tradesman and commoner, male and female, the elder and the youth.

---

[1]A complete list of the Kamwə names include:

	male	female		male	female
3rd	Tumba	Kwaramba	8th	Kwada	Kwada
4th	Vandi	Kwanye	9th	Drembi	Drembi
5th	Kwaji	Kwaji	10th	Kwatari	Kwartari
6th	Teri	Kwata	11th	Tihale	Kuvehale
7th	Sini	Kwasini	12th	Zirahale	Masihale

PART II
Kamwə Worldview

3

Kamwə Mountain Orientation

The Kamwə see themselves as the people of the mountain and the mountain area is where they feel secure. Living on the plains in safety was made possible by colonial government control. Previous to that the people lived in the mountains and began to farm some on the plains near to the mountain. However, in the early days, and even today, one found terraced farming on the mountainsides.

Protection

As has been explained, each mountain represents a homogeneous group (a lineage group), and intergroup fighting was frequent between different mountain groups. The people living on a single mountain were an exogamous group often sharing the same water supply and depending on each other for protection. The size of the group is very important since they must provide their own defense. The number of fighters is crucial in bow and arrow warfare. To fail to have children is a serious matter for the homogeneous group one represents because the number of fighters makes a significant difference in strength in battle. Thus the power of a lineage is directly related to its numerical size.

In precolonial days there was much warfare between the various independent clans. Otterbein lists several purposes for the Kamwə wars: 1) to avenge grievances arising from disputes over women and custody of the children, 2) to relieve grief, 3) to retain control of the fields, 4) to achieve status as warriors, 5) to acquire captives for ransoming, and 6) to avenge raids and stealing (Otterbein 1968:208). Since women marry into the clan

and the brideprice is repaid by the birth of two children, a man's
parents-in-law are apt to arrange another marriage for a man's wife
in another political community after she has given birth to two
children. Raiding parties can be used to carry out these plans.
When an important man in one clan dies, there used to be the alle-
viating of grief by killing someone in another political community.

The compounds were built in inaccessible places and were sur-
rounded with high stone walls and thick cactus hedges. In the past
it was a challenge to the Kamwə man's bravery and skill to creep
in and steal an animal or a wife from enemy territory, If successful he clearly demonstrated his bravery. The security that
the people feel in the mountain is expressed in the concept, "The
mountain has protected the people" (wuri mwə kə yate mbəlyi).

When the Fulani came in to conquer with horses, the mountain
was refuge for the Kamwə and the mountain prevented their being
overtaken. It provided an advantage for locating the approach of
the attackers and also in fighting off the opponent. During the
reign of Haman Yaji, a powerful post World War I Fulani ruler,
many Kamwə were caught and either made slaves or killed. At this
time especially, the caves in the mountains were used for hiding
in safety.

Tradition

The mountain is a special place because of tradition, wsi wshi -
"a thing of the ancestors." The style of house that the ancestors
built and that many Kamwə live in today requires supplies
from the mountain for building. Grass for thatching the roof and
stones for the base of the granary and for the protective fence
around the outside of the compound come from the mountain. The
grinding stone comes from the mountain area as does firewood--
both essential for daily living. Certain herbs used for medicines
come from the mountain also.

Each homogeneous lineage group had its own burial grounds, nkwa
məkulə, which were located on their mountains. Even today when
many Kamwə live on the plains, many burial grounds are on the
mountains. The corpse may have to be carried nine or ten miles
to the clan burial grounds on the ancestral mountain. The ancestral mountain very clearly speaks of history, tradition and the
ancestors. It is the original homeland of the lineage group and
it is where the individual is placed in death before entering the
spirit world.

The position of the mountain is considered in the building of
a compound. Each compound has two parts: the up-side of the
compound, nkwa mə thala, where the men and granaries are, and the

down-side of the compound, tərənkwə, where the women live and work
on food preparations. This speaks of the war days when the man
has an advantage to be on the up-side--to be able to see the enemy,
on the one hand, and to be closer to God, on the other hand.

Association with the Supernatural

It seems that the Kamwə also feel that the mountain is a place
that is closer to God. God is envisioned as a God of the sky and
it is only natural that the mountain is the closest place to God's
place. In the Scriptures, the mountain is significant and meaningful also, i.e., Moses receiving the stone tablets from God,
Elijah and his confrontation with the prophets of Baal, the crucifixion, the ascension, etc. In Kamwə land when there is a drought
the whole community feasts and a sacrifice is made, then the young
people and adults go up the mountain to dance. The tradesmen
musicians beat the drums and play other instruments, too. The
people feel that they are attracting God's attention to their need
and also pleasing Him.

Reflected in the Language

The language reflects the significance of the mountain in the
thinking of the people. In order to express "come from" a specific
place, or "go to" a specific place, the relation to the mountain
must be considered (of course this is unconscious for the Kamwə).
These terms are diagramed in Figures 5 and 6 which follow. There
is a general term which can be used, however, for any direction
if no specific place is indicated:

> wuri njə kə səkə.   He came.

> wuri njə kə dzəgə.   He went.

There are three words for "come" when referring to an area within
calling distance: 1) sha meaning come down, used if coming from
the mountainside toward the speaker; 2) satə meaning come up, used
if coming toward the speaker and from the opposite direction from
the mountain; 3) shalyi meaning come over, used when parallel to
the speaker and the mountain. The comparable words for go are:
1) ja--go down; 2) dzatə--go up; 3) jalyi--go over. This means
that when calling to a person "Come here." the term used (one of
the three) depends on where the person is in relation to the
speaker and the mountain.

Another set of words for come and go are used if the distance
is far from the speaker. These include: 1) səkwa meaning come
far down, used when referring to coming from a place on the mountainside; 2) səmə meaning come up far, used when coming from the

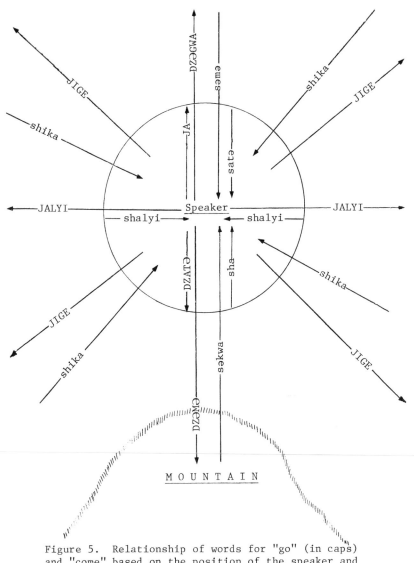

Figure 5. Relationship of words for "go" (in caps)
and "come" based on the position of the speaker and
the mountain.

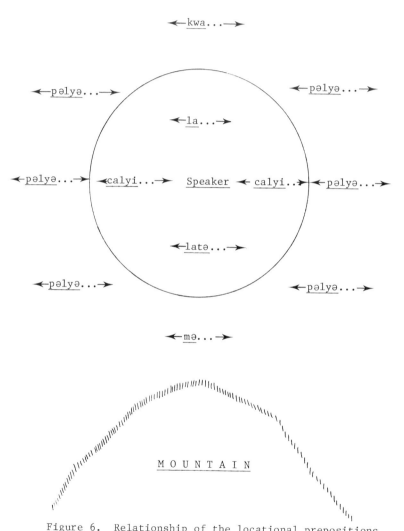

Figure 6. Relationship of the locational prepositions to the speaker and the mountain.

opposite direction from the mountain; 3) shilyə meaning come over
from far used when parallel to the speaker and the mountain. The
comparable words for go are: 1) dzəgwa--go down far; 2) dzəmə--
go up far; 3) jilyə--go over far. Shilyə and jilyə are now used
more often for come/go into or out of (across a border). There
is one more rather general term used for coming inside, or coming
from the farm or bush, into the village: shika. The comparable
term for go is jigə.

   Locational prepositions also reflect this mountain relationship. When saying things like "on the ground", "at home", "in...",
"from...", the following set of words are used:

   1. la...a place down close

   2. latə...a place up close

   3. calyi...a place over close parallel to mountain

   4. kwa...a place down far

   5. mə...a place up far

   6. pəlyə...a place far parallel to mountain/outside bounda:

To illustrate the use of these, if one wanted to say "inside the
hut" it could be said in various ways depending on the location of
the hut in relation to the speaker and the mountain--mə mpya "in
the hut up far", kwa mpya "in the hut down far", latə mpya "in the
hut close by and up", pəlyə mpya "in the hut which is outside, far
calyi mpya "in the hut which is horizontal to the mountain and
close by", la mpya "in the hut close by and down from the mountain"

   Investigating the use of these words, the importance of the
higher hills along the Cameroon border becomes evident. From
Kamale one goes down to Micika, from Sina one goes down to Garta,
from Mbororo one goes up to Futu, etc. The preceding diagrams
show the orientation to the mountain as is reflected in the terms
of go (appearing in capital letters), the terms for come (in small
letters), and the locational prepositions (underlined and followed
by...). The hyphenated circle represents an area around the
speaker close--perhaps within calling distance.

Summary

Location, direction and movement are thus all related to the mountain. Yet the meaning has deeper roots than just position. We are sharing in an "orientation to the mountain" that first springs from the origin stories that located the homogeneous units in their respective mountain habitats, and then provided their social cohesion and sense of security which guarantee their ethnic perpetuity. In other words, we are being drawn into their own frame of reference, which we have called the "worldview." The mountain orientation can be diagrammed as follows in Figure 7:

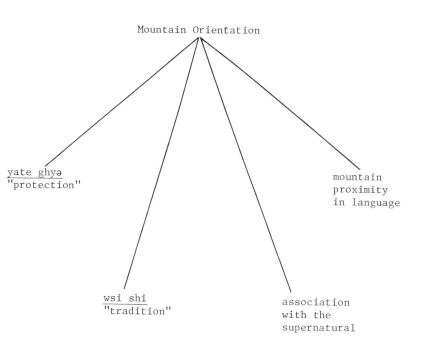

Figure 7. Mountain Orientation

4

Kamwə Guinea Corn Complex

A saying you hear among the Kamwə is "Why are you making your-self so important? Do you think you are guinea corn?" This reflects the idea that guinea corn is of supreme importance be-cause it is the symbol of life (Takwale 1967). When western foreigners first began to live in Kamwəland, some Kamwə considered them supernatural beings since they did not eat guinea corn daily. They thought that a human being could not live without it. In this chapter we are dealing with the significance of guinea corn to the Kamwə.

Essential for Life

The Kamwə have the saying that guinea corn keeps people alive, "Ha wsi kə mbə nkwa." Mush made out of guinea corn flour is the staple food eaten twice a day. Before eating, the household head takes a small portion of the food and throws it to the wind to recognize the supernatural. Each family must have a sufficient supply of guinea corn. The head of the household is responsible for providing it, storing it, and portioning it out as needed by the family. It is considered necessary that every Kamwə man see to it that enough guinea corn is grown for his family. The man who buys guinea corn is thought of as lazy, an embarrassment to the society. The whole family works together on the farm and considers it a privilege to cultivate the land and grow this all-important crop.

Another indication of the importance the people attach to guinea corn is indicated by the fact that there are no less than twenty-six terms used for it in the language. These various terms express the color, the length of growing time required, the quality, the hardness, etc.

According to legend guinea corn was given to them by God. Before they received it they ate leaves and fruit from trees and bushes. They were not strong and energetic. But after the dog with guinea corn on its tail came, the people began planting and eating guinea corn. People then became strong and active (see Appendix C for the whole legend).

The year is traditionally divided according to the phases of the growing of guinea corn. The first month is May when it is planted. January is the ninth month or harvesting moon, February is the threshing moon, March the taboo moon as the granary is not to be opened. April is the warning moon as everybody is talking about farming again and is busy getting the farms cleared and ready to plant when the rain comes.

The Kamwə attitude toward guinea corn is much like that of the Navajo toward their corn. Redfield (1947:304) illustrates the personifying of foodstuffs from W. W. Hill's research on the Navajo. Corn is like a child lost and starving. Thus, when you see some on the path you pick it up. It is holier than a human being, the cornfield is a holy place, and agriculture is a holy occupation. The Kamwə feel much the same. They say that guinea corn is like a baby, one doesn't play around with it but gives it special care. When guinea corn is seen on the path, one must kneel down and get some lest the guinea corn thinks you have ignored it. In the past no one would steal guinea corn because if he did, guinea corn would get angry with him.

Pounding and winnowing the grain is serious business. On threshing day a special soup made of sheanut oil and beans is cooked. A certain red grass and a certain type of guinea corn are tied to a cornstalk and placed in the area. Workers must take off their shoes when approaching the threshing place. A gourd with guinea corn flour, water, and herbs in it is placed at the threshing floor when one is working there. No whistling is allowed in the guinea corn field and certain songs must not be sung. No talking is allowed when putting grain in or taking it out of the granary. All of these taboos teach children the significance of guinea corn in their lives. The household head is the only one who can speak from the granary and even he cannot shout--showing his respect for the guinea corn. If a cock should crow from on top of the granary, it results in his sudden death and chicken stew for he has usurped the place of the man of the house.

Use for Personal Relationships

The concept "peace and unity", debəghi, is very important to
Kamwə clans. When there is friction and fighting and no peace
between people, a special ceremony called tsawhi must take place.
At this time there is confession and prayer. A grain of guinea
corn is taken by each person present and chewed, then spat out as
a symbol of getting rid of all hard feelings. Peace is restored.
Before going to war there must be peace among those fighting together, so this ceremony takes place. This form of prayer and
ritual chewing guinea corn is performed for forgiveness, for
restoring peace, and for recovery in illness which has resulted
from a lack of peace.

Before a bride leaves her home there is a special tsawhi ceremony called pisi malə. For this ceremony, guinea corn flour and
water are used and spat on the ground. The representatives from
the groom's home who have come to get her are present with her
family for this ceremony. At the time of the wedding, the groom's
parents perform the same ceremony. The symbolism here seems to
be to restore harmony and remove any discord before a person moves
out of one clan into another.

Ritual Use

Guinea corn is associated with numerous ritual performances.
In this way it is used to draw on supernatural power. The ceremonies involved are for the household, the community, and the
ancestors.

Household Ceremony

Each household has a special pot, məlyə, located near the hut
of the household head. This is where he performs the ceremony,
ɗa məlyə, and makes requests of God for the well-being of his
family. These ceremonies are only for those inside the compound,
mbəlyi hankə. Married daughters or outsiders are not allowed to be
present. The occasions for which this ceremony is performed are
to save a life in case of illness, to help a barren woman bear a
child, for good luck in marriage, and for good health for the family.
The diviner, when consulted, instructs the household head in what
kind of sacrifice to make. It may be a blood sacrifice or tya
(sweet drink) sacrifice, or simply a bean soup and mush sacrifice.
In case of a ceremony at the pot for planting or harvesting, the
household head decides what kind of sacrifice to make.

Community Ceremony

Another form of ceremony involves the whole community. This is called saraka. At this time food is cooked, a sacrifice is made and guinea corn beer is drunk ceremonially by the men. An individual family who has had a member get well after a long, serious illness may call a saraka celebration. On this occasion they furnish the food and beer, and thankfulness to God is expressed by the elder. Sometimes when one goes to the specialist to find out what is wrong, he is told to have a saraka for the community. Again, he and his family must furnish the food and/or beer. When there is drought or epidemic and before planting and harvesting, the chief and the elders call for saraka. The people are all told what to cook, and often a blood sacrifice is required.

The elder of each family sees that the sacrifice is ready and makes it at the prescribed spot, often where paths cross. In the case of a blood sacrifice, when the animal is killed, blood is sprinkled on the sacred place. Sometimes some of the entrails are left also. Then after the animal is cooked, a small amount of guinea corn mush and soup/gravy is put at the place of sacrifice. Before the food is eaten in a ritual meal, a little is served to each person ceremonially by the elder. Beer is also prepared and a small amount put at the place of sacrifice before it is drunk ceremonially by the men. For ceremonial beer drinking, a guest or an outsider serves the men in order, from the oldest down to the youngest. The saraka ceremony is either to appease the spirits causing the trouble, or to beg God to help and bless in the peoples' work. Prayer is always involved.

Ceremony of the Elders

Another kind of group ceremony is called kələngi. Only the elders are involved in this one. They call for it and it is held at the sacred place known as kələngi. This is a place near the village where there are special pots. Each family is represented by the household head and combined sacrifice is made in the sacred place. The elders prepare the food and sacrifice. Women and children are not allowed to be present. This ceremony is performed to bring good will to the village or as preparation for war.

Ceremony for the Ancestor

Burial rites are very important because they assure the deceased of a good place in the spirit world and also provide a means for the living to be assured that the spirit of the deceased will not harm them. A sweet (non-fermented) drink, tya, is made from germ-

inating the dry shoots of guinea corn, then cooking them.[1] A week
or so after the death of a person of ten years or older, this
drink must be used for the libation ceremony, shikǝkulǝ. This
libation ceremony is essential so that the spirit of the dead can
move into the world of the spirits. Then again, after the period
of mourning, shikǝkulǝ is performed.

   In the above ceremonies, guinea corn is important. It may be
used in the form of local beer (made of guinea corn). The oldest
man takes some, saying a prayer to God and making special requests,
pouring some on the ground. At a sarǝka some is left at the
crossroads. Guinea corn may be used for ceremony in the form of
mush eaten ceremonially with the required sacrifice.

Summary

   In summary, although guinea corn is used as daily food, as a
necessary and much respected part of life, it is also the essential component in the ceremonies used in times of trouble or
thanksgiving and for softening hard feelings and restoring peaceful relationships.

   The guinea corn is thus not merely essential as food for the
body, but it is associated with numerous ritual performances. The
guinea corn myth indicates its divine origin. It serves as the
fruit of the earth by which the Kamwǝ draw on supernatural power
in rites of passage and all kinds of ritual bearing on the maintenance and restoration of peace, unity, reconciliation and the overall harmony and cohesion of the social unit. It operates functionally to bring the real social behavior more into line with the
accepted social ideal. As God gave guinea corn and man cultivates
it, what better cooperative component could there be for indicating
the oneness of the supernatural and the human? Thus, the guinea
corn complex is a symbolic focus of the restoration and maintenance
of harmony and homogeneity for the ethnic unit. It is a focus of
Kamwǝ worldview. As it has been discussed in this chapter, it can
be summarized in the following diagram in Figure 8.

---

[1]This is a drink that women and children drink (at other times)
 instead of the fermented beer. Sometimes this sweet drink is
 used for sacrifice at the special pot in the home. It used to
 be made mainly at the time of marriage or death.

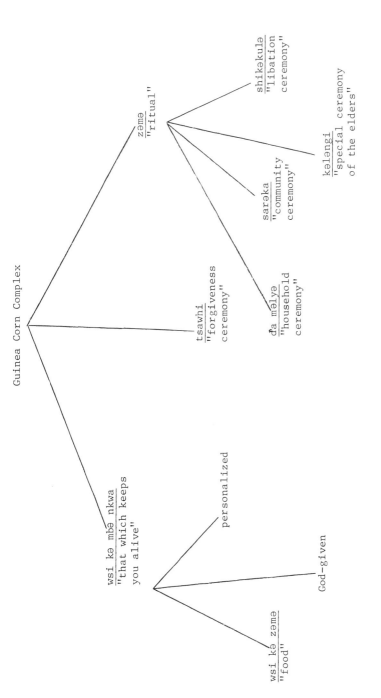

Figure 8. Guinea Corn Complex

5

Kamwə Belief in the Supernatural

The Kamwə are very aware of active supernatural forces at work in everyday life. Man is not only a part of a functioning tight-knit family, but also on a larger scale a functioning part of the total universe. The universe includes visible forces and invisible forces interacting together. The Kamwə person sees his survival dependent on maintaining an equilibrium between these forces. The invisible forces are the cause of trouble and sickness, yet man is the cause also because of his behavior toward or relationships with the invisible forces. In this chapter I will describe the invisible beings, focus on the various practitioners who guide in maintaining the equilibrium, and elaborate the causes of illness and protective measures taken to keep things in balance.

The Unseen

The invisible forces that are active in daily life are referred to as "the unseen," wsha ndəma nata gwa - "Something you can't see." Included in the unseen are God (Hyalatəmwə), spirits which cause both good and evil (hyala), spirits that live in people (vwə), and ancestor spirits (mbəlyi kwahye). The Kamwə worldview sees the blessing of the supernatural as essential if one is to become important and wealthy. This dimension of a man's success is called pi, "the blessing of the unseen."

God

God as the Kamwə perceive him is the creator of all things: man, nature, spirits, animals, etc. He used to be very near to men, legend says, but because of an accident on man's part, God went far away, and he is still far away. His place of abode is far up in the sky (məɓatamwə). The Kamwə word for God means "the spirit who never dies." Since God made everything, all is ulti- mately in his control. He is often involved in the origin myths, e.g., the guinea corn that God sent to the Kamwə on the tail of a dog, the first death, the first marriage (see Appendix C). God is seen as the source of the laws of the ancestors, their traditions. He is seen as a just God, and if the laws of the ancestors are not kept, he will justly punish. The payment required is twice that of the offence. If a person kills a man (outside of war) two of his children will die in some way or other by divine retribution.

The Kamwə see God as a person, one who gives, sees, walks, acts. They have a saying that sums up their feeling toward God – Hyalatəmwə-ra ya ra, "my God protects me." He is a very kind person and is not blamed when evil comes to man. However, since God is so important and so far away, the Kamwə try to manage their own affairs as much as possible. God never interferes with the work of the people. He exists far away and should be called on only in desperate need. The people know that God will not let them down. When man has tried every possible solution to his problems and has failed, then he goes to God for help.

God is called on not only in times of great need: planting, marriage, birth, sickness, etc., but also in times of great thank- fulness: harvest, health and recovery after a long illness, etc. This ritual of thanksgiving may be by the household unit under the leadership of the head of the household or by the community group under the leadership of the chief and the elders. God's name is also mentioned often when an appeasement sacrifice is made to the evil spirits or the ancestor spirits. This may be a recognition of the importance of God, the order he has made in the universe and the subjection of the lesser dieties to him.

Good and Evil Spirits

The good and evil spirits, hyala, reside in certain big trees, rivers, stones, mountains, caves, and pools. The local people know where these spirits live. One must be very careful not to touch anything close to their dwelling place. Spirits often appear in the form of very old men, big snakes, tiny babies, or white mice. They appear unexpectedly and disappear quickly as well. The Kamwə say that if a person is not frightened on these occasions, he will be blessed by the spirit. Or he may have mis- fortune as a result of seeing the spirit. A person does not want to see a spirit because of the trouble that may result in his life. The basic attitude seems to be that although seeing a spirit might result in good, the fear that it may result in evil causes the Kamwə to prefer not to chance it. When ones sees a spirit he must

collect all kinds of things that man eats, uses, and plants, and
place them at the place where he saw the spirit. He may see the
spirit again later in a dream.

There are various names for spirits, especially the ones that
are likely to cause harm. Ⅾiɗiwi refers to a spirit that lives
in the forest. It is especially dangerous for people to step on
the footprint of ɗiɗiwi. Ntuntuli is a spirit that can harm a
person at any time of the day. Shetari is another spirit that is
active both night and day causing trouble. The name and possibly
the concept seems to have been borrowed. Quarrels are caused by
Shetari. When he is causing quarrels, the elders can decide the
reconciliation that is necessary to settle the matter.

When an evil spirit causes an illness the patient is instructed
to make a specific sacrifice of appeasement at a specific place in
order to get well. If he is too afraid or sick to go to the place
the specialist for getting rid of spirits or a relative may go in
his place.

The Vwə Spirit

The vwə spirit is distinct from the other unseen forces because
it lives only in people. One is born with this spirit, inheriting
it through the maternal line. This spirit is with a person all
his life. This is one reason why a very careful check is made
into the bride-to-be's mother's line before the marriage is final-
ized. No one admits he has a vwə spirit, but the people who have
it are believed to know they have it. People are very careful how
they treat a person who is suspected of having a vwə spirit. They
are careful not to offend such people. If a person suspected of
possessing a vwə spirit comes upon people who are eating, the latter share what they are eating with that person or hide it so it
won't be seen. People avoid such suspected persons whenever possible. They might also get medicine to protect them from being th
recipients of the vwə spirit's actions. When a person is sick for
a long time, he may be informed that the cause of his illness is
the vwə spirit. The specialist who informs him does not give him
the name of the person who has the spirit. He, rather, gives a
general description of the person. He may suggest that that person lives in the compound next door, is a short person, is a very
black person, etc. The family of the sick person then determines
who the culprit is and goes to that person and accuses him. They
threaten to tell the whole community if he doesn't release the
soul of the sick person. In the early days some people with the
vwə spirit were burned to death or beaten. It is said that if one
has such a spirit it can be controlled. If one doesn't hurt other
with it, it will protect him and his children. A vwə spirit can
be used for good.

Ancestor Spirits

Ancestor spirits, <u>mbəlyi kwahye</u>, reside in the afterworld which
is located deep inside the earth. The spirit of a person who dies
<u>(məmbali)</u> is believed to remain near his home and grave and must
be fed food and drink along with the family for several days. The
<u>tya</u> libation ceremony takes place seven to nine days after burial.
As the <u>tya</u> drink is poured on the grave, other spirits come to
welcome the new ancestor spirit into the place of the spirits of
the dead. These spirits may communicate with the living in dreams
and may return in the form of <u>ntuntuli</u> (see above) or <u>mtə mə jige</u>
(the dead who live in the red guinea corn) and cause evil. When
one has a problem, the medium may inform him that he is not following the advice his father gave him. A ceremony at the grave of
the father will clear up this matter.

The language gives insight into the way the Kamwə see life after
physical death. Death is referred to as:

1. "He went home to see the ancestors" - <u>wuri njə kə li jəge
    ta mbəlyi kukuli</u>.

2. "He has gone to the grave with his people" - <u>wuri njə kə
    hwe dzimə kulə</u>.

It is common to say to a very sick person: "(If you go), greet
your father in the world of death: - <u>cika ta hya məɓa</u>.

Older people frequently refer to the ancestors casually. An
elder as he sits down tired and ready to rest may comment, "Oh
my great grandfather in the afterworld." Or when an older person
meets a person whose father has died previously, he may say, "May
the blessing of your grandfather in the afterworld help you with
your children." When one does something good the elders may say
<u>Lə barəka ra shi ranga kwahye</u> (May your ancestor bless you!).
The name of the ancestor is also used to swear to the truth, <u>Lə
shi ramyi kwahye</u>... (I swear with our ancestor...). If one is
lying, it is said that the ancestor will come and get him and take
him to the ancestor's place of abode.

The Kamwə are very conscious of the influence of the ancestors
in their lives. The ancestors have set the standard of behavior
and the values of the society. The ancestors can bring about misfortune if these are not upheld. However, if one is living according to tradition, the presence of the ancestors is very supportive
and comforting.

Practitioners

The Kamwə have several people whose responsibility it is to deal
with the unseen on behalf of the people. These include the specialists who deal with spirits, those who deal with medicine, those
who explain the cause of the difficulty and prescribe a solution,
and those who practice sorcery. The household head who is responsible for the welfare of the family and the chief who is responsible
for his village are also here considered practitioners. The seer
represents the supernatural and I have included him in this section

The Specialists

Spirit Man. The spirit man, mdi kə zəmə hyala, is believed to
have been given a gift and power by the spirits and God. He rids
people of troublesome evil spirits, and settles disputes by the
use of cocks. He gives out protective medicine against the vwə
spirits as well. He is a diviner-exorcist, getting rid of spirits
in a particular place rather than from within a person.

Diviners. There are two kinds of diviners in Kamwə society.
Mdi kə nədlera, the "crab man," works with crabs to tell the cause
of trouble and what to do for a cure. He is a diviner. The Kamwə
go to this specialist to identify a thief, for illness, for barrenness, to get instruction on moving the location of a home after
misfortune, to discover who or what caused a death in the family,
to find out if a marriage choice is the right one, etc. Small
sticks representing either things and people in one's life or
various causes of misfortune, are stood up in a pot in sand. The
diviner instructs the crab to do his work well. Then the crab is
placed on his back in the pot and the pot is covered with another
pot. The crab then turns over and walks around, knocking over
some sticks. Then the man examines the displaced sticks, inter-
prets them, and gives instruction to the client.

Another diviner who seeks out the cause and gives instruction
is mdi kənə kwahye. He works with a bag full of paraphernalia in
order to reveal the causes and the cure. He hangs the bag in the
hut and sits outside. He asks the bag questions and the answers
come from the bag. This is usually done at night.

Herbalists. The man who works with herbs, mdi kə lafwe, is the
medicine man. This is passed on like personal property to a son
and requires much knowledge and learning. One learns through
apprenticeship and his professional skill is a form of wealth.
There are two kinds of herbalists: a) mdi kəla wuyə kə mbə nkwa -
the person who digs medicines for curing purposes, an herbalist-
healer, and b) mdi kə gəpə nkwa - the person who works with poisons
to kill people, an herbalist-sorcerer. The herbalist-sorcerer may
place medicine near a person's house to kill him, or he may send

needles (tsaki) through the air that get the person at his house and kill him. He also may put poison in food or beer in order to kill. People are afraid of this kind of person and feel that they cannot trust him.

Diviner-Sorcerer. The sorcerer is called mdi kə yə nkwa wta, "the man who kills someone in a pot." This is a diviner-sorcerer to whom one goes at night to get retaliation for a death in the family. This specialist practices necromancy as he calls the spirit of the dead man to find out who killed him. He then brings the shadow of the killer into his pot and kills it with a knife. Subsequently he tells the brother how the killer will die, a certain kind of sickness, say, a fall from a tree, for example. Later when a man dies, as prescribed by the specialist, the brother goes to the funeral. At the suitable moment he takes off his shoe and, raising it high in the air, announces that the dead man was the murderer of his brother. This breaks up the funeral and the man is buried immediately. The slate is wiped clean at this point and there can be no further retaliation.

The Non-Specialists

Chief and Elders. The chief and the elders are responsible for community-level rituals in dealing with the unseen. In times of epidemic, drought, planting, harvest, and, in the past, warfare, the chief with the council of elders gives the orders and the chief of the tradesmen informs the people. The household head actually performs the required ritual at the required location, often at a crossing of paths. In the case of a barren woman who has seen an evil spirit, the chief of the tradesmen goes to where the paths cross or a mountain where she saw the spirit and makes sacrifice. In the past at wartime, the chief scattered medicine (guinea corn and herbs) over the army.

The Household Head. The elder in each household, zaya, is the ceremony leader for his group. He is responsible for prayer and ritual performance when there is sickness in the family, when there is barrenness, or whenever there is trouble and the specialist requires it. He is also responsible to see that his household observes the ritual observances set up by the chief and elders at the community level. He is the representative from his household to make community decisions and advise the chief. When a new house is going to be built and the ground is cleared, the household head puts a special piece of wood in the ground, has prayer to god, and dedicates the house. This is called fətə wci tə ya məlfyi, meaning the ritual placing of the wood where the house will be. Another prayer by the elders is required when the house is done and there is a big feast with beer drinking and well-wishing by the relatives and neighbors.

The Seer. There is a person in traditional society who can see things in the future. He is called <u>zakuli</u>, a seer. This ability is seen as a special gift of God. The seer farms like everybody also and receives no pay for his foretelling, but he speaks to the people on behalf of God.

Causes of Sickness

The Kamwə see sickness as having four possible causes, all related to the unseen. The diviner gives the information as to the specific cause and then gives instructions for getting well. Illness may be caused by:

1. *Evil Spirits* - in this case the person is told to go to the man with the special gift from the unseen to get rid of an evil spirit who is causing trouble. A specific sacrifice of appease-ment will need to be made at a specific place (often where the spirit was seen) in order for the person to get well. The only time an evil spirit is considered in a person is in the case of the mentally deranged or epileptic. It is then said, <u>hyala sa taghi</u>, "the evil spirits have taken over the head."

2. *Caused by Vwə Spirit* - in this case the person possessing the <u>vwə</u> spirit is described and the family of the sick person contacts and threatens him/her so that the soul of the sick per-son will be freed. Then he may get well.

3. *Poisoning (sorcery)* - in this case the only hope is to go to an herbalist with more powerful medicine for curing. It is difficult to save persons who are victims of poisoning.

4. *Disobeying Tradition* - failing to obey the ancestor teach-ing, <u>vasa</u>, requires a specific sacrifice prescribed by the diviner to be done at the grave of the ancestor.

If none of the above are the cause of the illness, the Kamwə say that only God knows the cause. In this way they can accept the illness.

Protective Measures

There are a number of protective measures that the Kamwə take in order to be safe from misfortune that might come their way. Charms are worn or placed in the field so that all will go well. Truth is discovered through trial by ordeal so that the guilty party is revealed. Faithful ritual performance keeps the spirit world happy so that the spirits will not cause trouble.

Charms

Spirit power is used for protection in the form of charms. <u>Laya</u> is a small leather case with special herbs which is hung around the neck or from a belt or around the arm. <u>Guri</u> is a rope covered with leather that is tied around the waist like a belt. Both are made by the herbalist and used to keep away evil spirits and keep one safe from harm from, e.g., knife wounds, poisoned arrows, or snake bites. In order to keep these charms effective the person wearing them may also be instructed by the herbalist to observe certain taboos, such as those against eating certain foods, or wearing the charm when having sexual intercourse.

Certain things in nature are considered to have magical power in themselves. Special leaves are tied to a stick and placed in a farm to keep people from stealing from the farm. This is called <u>shafa kwantərəza</u>. A similar protective device is called <u>gədla</u>. For this the herb is mixed with a thorn called <u>gədla</u> and put on a broken piece of pot on a forked stick in the farm. If anyone touches the farm, his hand will be spoiled by the protective magic.

There is no prayer or ceremony involved to assure that these magical acts get the desired result. It is taboo for pregnant women to cross a river without the protection of a charm. It is believed that this is very dangerous since evil spirits are apt to be living there. So when it is necessary for a pregnant woman to cross a river, she takes a blade of grass or something similar from the river, breaks it and places it by her ear or in her hand as a protective charm. She can then safely cross. At harvest time the guinea corn is pounded before it is put in the granary. The household head puts two or three corn heads (unpounded) in the granary. This is to make the crop most useful and sufficient. It is a charm of blessing.

Trial by Ordeal

When something bad has happened, ordeals provide an effective means of detecting the truth and determining the guilty party. The elders are important in calling for this kind of action or for giving their approval for the parties involved to go to a special area where disputes are settled. At Kamale the cockfight is the means of settlement. Near Uba the <u>Bunti pool</u> reveals the guilty party by requiring the disputors to run through the water after stating the truth before God and the specialist who deals with spirits. The people believe there is a spirit living there who prevents passage of the guilty party. The guilty party becomes paralyzed and can't get out of the water by himself. Different kinds of ordeals claim different powers.

For the <u>viti</u> ordeal the medicine man provides wooden prongs or broom grass and medicines. He then touches the neck of every adult one by one. The guilty party gets "hooked" and the elders determine the punishment. Another type of ordeal lies in the magic power of words themselves as they are recited to cause the truth to come out. This is used to detect who is practicing witchcraft or sorcery. All adults must say, "If I have done this bad thing, catch me." The punishment for this is to leave the society and move far away.

The <u>shafa</u> ordeal focuses on the power the <u>shafa</u> leaf has in itself as has previously been explained. The elders place the <u>shafa</u> on the ground and one by one each adult walks over it saying, "If I have done these bad things, kill my children."

The spirits are involved in revealing the truth through the cock fights at Kamale or through the accused being forced to drink a prepared herbal drink. As they do this, the person must say something like, "If I have done these things, let me suddenly die." or "be bitten by a snake." or "let my children die." etc. The specialist who deals with spirits, <u>mdi kə zəmə hyala</u>, is in charge of interpreting and explaining this ordeal to the people. Swearing an oath is essential for trial by ordeal.

Ritual Performance

Ritual performance, zəmə, is a significant way in which the Kamwə handle problems relating to such things as deviation from the norm, the unknown, reversals, barrenness, drought. All of these have been discussed in the last chapter as the ceremonial use of guinea corn was elaborated.

<u>Summary</u>

From the foregoing it should now be clear what certain anthropologists have meant by describing religion as the integrator (Keesing and Keesing, 1971:303) or governor (Wallace, 1966:4) of society. The theology (belief system of gods and spirits), religious organization (the specific paractitioners and the institutions within which they operate), theory of sickness and rituals of protection and cure hold together both the total worldview and the social structure itself. They both maintain the entity and integrity of the homogeneous ethnic unit, and provide the security for survival in the Kamwə world situation.

The visible world around the Kamwə is filled with invisible forces--some friendly and some fearful. Survival and social equilibrium are possible only by learning to call on the former to deal with the latter. **Figure 9 summarizes the belief in the** supernatural as seen and experienced by the Kamwə.

Belief in the Supernatural

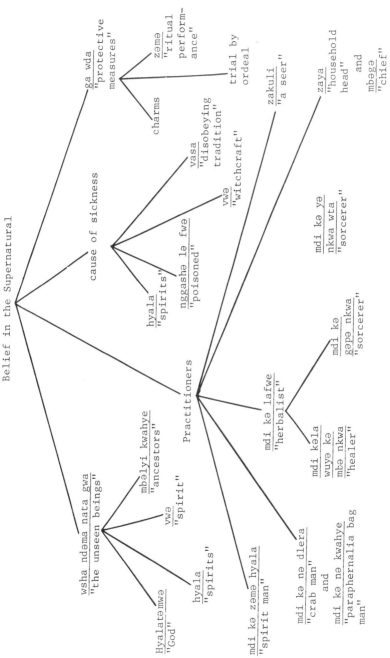

Figure 9. Belief in the Supernatural

6

The Kamwə Ideal Person

Since the Kamwə place so much importance on personal relationships, one of the domains that is prominent in the worldview is
the ideal person.   It is interesting to note that though the personal standards are high, the people have the beautiful characteristic of acceptance of each other in the real world.   For example,
when looking for a bride for a son, all of these qualities are
carefully considered.   But when one is chosen, she is accepted.
There is no attempt to make her over.   The Kamwə, like most face-
to-face type societies, are very perceptive of an individual's
personal character.   But this perceptiveness is used to build a
relationship rather than, as is often the case in western society,
for one to build himself up at another's expense.

In this chapter we will discuss the important personal qualities and how these are transmitted.

Important Personal Qualities

To understand Kamwə worldview it is important to recognize the
personal qualities that are valued.   I discovered these by asking
the questions: What does it mean to be a good citizen?   What
kind of a person do you look for as a marriage partner?   What are
the requirements for leadership?   From responses to these questions, a list of personal values became clear--and, thus, I
obtained a picture of the ideal person.   Characteristics of the
ideal person as seen by the Kamwə include: kindness and good
character, generosity, possession of riches, hard work, discipline,
showing honor and respect, good health, and living in harmony.

Kindness and Good Character

The Kamwə word for good character (məhələ) includes kindness.
To have good character one needs to be liked by those around him.
To be aware of others and to treat them with warmth and gentle-
ness is very important. The person needs to have many friends.
In choosing a wife, a man considers how the neighbors feel toward
the prospective bride. The man with no friends is called kəladawa.
He shows no regard for anyone and treats even his brother badly.
In no way could he be considered a man of good character by the
Kamwə. The man with bad character (ntimə məhələ) is cruel to
others and tells lies. Cruelty ('yagare) is defined as anything
that hurts your relationship with the other person. A jealous
person (shishi) could not be a person with good character either.
Figure 10 shows how the boundary of the concept of good character
and kindness becomes clear as the limits are defined by contrasting it with bad character.

shishi		'yagare
"jealousy"	məhələ	"cruelty"
	"good character and kindness"	
kəladawa		
"no friends"		

Figure 10. Good Character and Kindness

Generosity

Another very important characteristic is generosity. The
Kamwə refer to a generous person as one who is open handed, wasə
pela. He gives abundantly to everyone whether they are relatives
or strangers. At mealtime, anyone who is around is invited to
share in the meal. As a result, no one goes hungry. By giving
generously and ungrudgingly one knows that should he ever be in
need, others would give to him also.

The opposite of open-handedness is greediness, ('ini), stingi-
ness (cicitlə) or selfishness ('intəghi) (see Figure 11). The
stingy person doesn't want to spend his money or goods on even
his family. He wants everything for himself and puts great value

on his possessions. The greedy person not only keeps things he
gets for himself, but he also wants (covets) things other people
have. The familiar saying 'ini hwi kə mtə (greedy like death)
indicates how serious and fatal greed is regarded. The selfish
person thinks of himself first always and takes the best for himself. A person will get nowhere in life if he is not generous.

Figure 11.   Generosity

Possession of Riches

Another personal value for the Kamwə is riches. A person with
riches is called galipə. A rich person is one who is a part of a
family that has much guinea corn, many goats, many wives, many
children, and many friends. A family's wealth is seen in the size
of its farms, the size of its compound, the number of granaries
and animals. These factors are related, since the family constitutes the work force. The more people there are, the more grain is
needed for eating. All of this necessitates hard work and good
management on the part of the head of the family and his first
wife, plus the total cooperation of each of the other members of
the family. For example, the more people in the family, the more
huts there are that need to be built and kept in repair. Each
wife has both a cooking and a sleeping hut and each boy over six
to eight years of age has his own sleeping hut as well. Furthermore, the larger the gardens, the more manpower is needed for
farming. The more children there are, the more goats and goods
will be needed for "brideprice." A tremendous amount of organization, skill, and effort is required to gain riches. This means
that the head of a family, even though diligent, skillful, and
blessed of God, is unlikely to be wealthy before middle age or
old age.

The value of riches is that one can be more generous and have
many friends. If a person does not have, he cannot give away.
An individual's riches really belong to the family because he is
expected to help according to what he has. As a man takes several
wives, he is both extending his relationships and increasing his
obligation to give gifts and to assume other responsibilities.

he person with wealth pays a higher fee for the services of the
tradesmen and this helps level off the wealth. The need to be
generous and to put personal relationships first acts as a level-
ng agent so that all benefit from a man's riches.

A good example of this leveling action is the distribution of
he dowry. A bride brings great quantities of food (flour, salt,
beans, tiger nuts, guinea corn, goats, fish, etc.) and many calabashes and dishes to the groom's home. The necessary gifts are
given to the groom and his relatives. The bride still has great
quantities for herself--she might be considered the richest woman
in the village. However, people stop by expecting food from time
to time and she gives it to them. She also cooks food and goes
from house to house sharing. Takwale (1967) explains how she
keeps on giving presents, for if she does not give she will be
criticized as a greedy person. Nobody approves of greed. She
continues to give until all the food and wealth is finished and
he becomes like other women.

The poor man (<u>tiki</u>) has no money to buy things for his family
and has a difficult time arranging marriages for his children.
Sometimes the children of a poor man live with a more wealthy
brother and serve in his household. In this way the child earns
his keep and the brother pays the child's expenses. A poor man
seldom has more than one wife. Only if an only brother died would
he get a second wife (the widow who was left). A poor man is
either lazy or lacks health in the eyes of the Kamwə.

ird Work

As indicated above, hard work is greatly valued. When looking
for a mate for a son or daughter, the reputation that the person
has for hard work is important. To live comfortably, to get wealth,
and even to survive in a subsistence society requires hard work.
The lazy person (<u>mari</u>) is despised. A man or woman should be
hard working (<u>wghyana mələ tlənə</u>, "very hot in work"), and if he/
he is so, there will be food for the children and eventually
money for "brideprice." For illustrations of how this value is
taught through proverbs, see proverbs 1, 2, and 7, below.

scipline

Discipline ('yə) is taught early in life. It is very important
for one to learn as a child to carry responsibility and to work
and obey parents and elders. The relatives and neighbors all feel
free to discipline a child who needs it. Hitting (but not on the
head) and pinching are two methods of disciplining a child. If a
child runs away from punishment, he will get double when he is
caught. The undisciplined adult, (<u>kəlama 'yə</u>) never obeys anybody.

This is considered the result of not being properly disciplined
as a child. People tolerate the undisciplined adult, but do not
seek his friendship. See proverb 3, below, for an example of how
this value is taught.

Showing Honor or Respect

Honor or respect (həwəshe) is an important personal characteristic among the Kamwə. They say of a woman who fails to respect
her husband-- kutə nga za vəcə, ɓwagə nga malə ("when the husband
says one word, the wife says two")! The husband must respect his
wife by buying her clothes, providing salt and soup makings, being
the leader in farming, and listening and helping solve her and the
children's problems. Elders are to be respected and honored.
They, in turn, must respect others by being controlled and patient.
The greatest insult is for one's children to disgrace one in public by arguing, or refusing to do as they are told! In other
words, people are of highest importance and must be treated as
persons, not as machines. The person who has no regard for others
(wshəntə) is seriously handicapped. The disrespectful person
(ma həwə) doesn't listen to the elders, nor care for them. He
turns his back on them.

Good Health

Good health (gwagulangə) is also an important value. The person who has good health is said to be blessed by God or the spirits.
The person who is deformed is said to be so because of the spirits.
People pity him and he is referred to as being "spoiled," wuri kə
wdzə. A deformed body makes it much more difficult to find a
marriage partner. It is more serious to be a deformed male, since
a man is to be the leader of the home. To marry a deformed man,
a woman must consider whether she is able to take the lead in the
home even against society's dictates. The deformed woman, however, has some value as long as she can bear children. The deformed
do often learn to do useful things in Kamwə society. A blind man
can learn to make useful mats and rope in spite of his handicap.

Since all the family is involved in the production of food,
the health, as well as the size of the work force, is important.
For each member needs to have good health to do his full share.
Beauty is not so important as good health. A Kamwə proverb says,
ka zəmə nderə mbəlyi wə, "we can't eat the beauty of the wife."

Living in Harmony

Harmony (dabəghi) is another very important value. When the
peace and unity in a household is broken, a formal ceremony of
spitting guinea corn (tsahwi) is required. Before going to war

in the past, all problems between clan members had to be straight-
ened out so that there was harmony. No battle could be won if
there was disunity. The term daɓəghi refers to relationships
involved in living in the community, including those between a
person and his neighbor and a person and his leaders. When people
need help, this quality is evident in the ready response to those
needs. The Kamwə concept of peace and harmony is not merely
tranquility, calmness, and quiet, but it is the total welfare of
persons in community.

The importance of harmony is closely related to the group
awareness discussed in Chapter 2. The individual gets his identity from the group and that group must be unified. Harmony must
be reestablished when one moves from one group to another: from
child to adult, as a bride to husband's clan, as a widow back into
circulation after mourning. Ritual is required to see that this
is done. The enormity of sin is not that laws are broken, but
that it undermines and disrupts interpersonal harmony. When an
individual has been personally hurt (i.e., through acts of dis-
respect) ceremony is required to reestablish harmony. Harmony
is the wholeness of being and character both of individuals and
of community by which it is possible to cope with life and its
tensions.

How Values Are Transmitted

Values don't just happen, they are transmitted. The Kamwə,
like many peoples of the world, employ proverbs, singing, and the
influence of group life to teach their values to the young.

Proverbs

The Kamwə use proverbs to teach and reinforce the value of the
society. This is discovery-oriented teaching, since the person
hearing the proberb needs to make the application. Proverbs are
used mainly between those who know each other well when the one
using it is quite sure it will communicate the intended meaning.
Here are a few illustrations of much-used proverbs that teach
these values:

1. kwa yə wta.

    Literal translation: The goat is born with skin.

    Free translation: If the parent goat has a tough hide,
                           so will the little one.

Examples of Use: If parents are hard working, so will
                        the child be.

                        If parents are lazy, so will the
                        child be.

2. nga mdi kutə yemyi kwa wa wə.

   Literal translation: The water in the valley does not be-
                          long to one person.

   Free translation: Everyone can benefit by the river
                          valley.

   Examples of Use: Several people can compete for a girl
                          in marriage.

                          Everyone, by hard work, can achieve
                          because he has land and water avail-
                          able.

                          It is public--doesn't belong to one
                          person.

3. kəndə na kələ shəgwa kwa dləmbule kə hahalə wə.

   Literal translation: One who can't be raised in an old
                          chicken cage.

   Free translation: It is difficult to help the undis-
                          ciplined person who can't be confined
                          or controlled.

   Examples of Use: One can't help or live with a person
                          with bad character or who is undis-
                          ciplined.

4. dzəmə fwə ma-ranje tsa nə vava.

   Literal translation: A little monkey watches the mother
                          climb a tree.

   Free translation: The young learn what they need to
                          know from their parents by observa-
                          tion.

   Examples of Use: Children learn values from their
                          parents.

5. <u>kələntə cabwalə mə 'wa, lamə mə yemyi</u>.

   Literal translation: Don't take the nice-tasting cake that belongs in milk and put it in water.

   Free translation: Mix a thing of value with that of no value and you spoil it a bit.

   Example of Use: Don't tamper with something good that you already have.

6. <u>Kwa ya kankəlya 'i kwi-ra ra</u>.

   Literal translation: I want my mice in a crab hole (one that only has one entrance).

   Free translation: Don't fear something that you are sure of getting.

   Example of Use: Put your confidence in the right people.

7. <u>wdzi ta na we</u>.

   Literal translation: You don't have the bark of hemp to support you.

   Free translation: You are a very weak person (not physically fit).

   Examples of Use: You can't support yourself.

   You are not able to raise guinea corn.

   You lose at wrestling.

   You failed at arranging a marriage for yourself.

   You are lazy.

8. <u>balə kwantəkwa te balema na</u>.

   Literal translation: The chicken is not included in the slapping (his chin is not big enough).

   Free translation: Something important does not include you because you are not up to the requirements.

Example of Use: Women and children not allowed when
                       elders meet on important matters.

9. Ma wuri 'i mnə kə shik tə ka nə, kandə katsətəgwa we.

    Literal translation: If you spill oil, it can't be picked
                           up.

    Free translation: A person can't change what he's
                           already done.

    Example of Use: A lie told and scattered can't be
                           collected back.

10. Kandə wgyə ntəkə lyəgwa lə huntsə we.

    Literal translation: You can't separate excrement from
                           urine.

    Free translation: A man can't be separated from his
                           closest relatives.

    Example of Use: It's hard to go between family mem-
                           bers, i.e., husband and wife, father
                           and son, brothers.

11. Shikuri bathyə nda ka ɗantə tya.

    Literal translation: A little of a sticky leafed vege-
                           table spoils the whole thing.

    Free translation: A little of something out of place
                           spoils the whole thing.

    Exampes of Use: A bad person in a group can spoil
                           the whole group.

                           Don't let a small thing in your
                           character spoil your reputation.

Singing

Another way the Kamwə teach their personal values is by the
singing and dancing of the young unmarried girls. They informally
gather the news and make up songs about individuals using their
actual names in singing and dancing. They sing praise to one's
good behavior and also sing of one's bad character, one's stingy
or bad behavior. Singing about people in their dancing is referre
to as a cinyi lə na kwa mbwa. In this way, achievements and

behavior are made public, and the values of the society are reinforced and taught. It was the practice of Hebrew girls, after
victory in battle in Old Testament times, to sing praise (Judges
5).

Group Life

Underlying all of these personal values is the importance of
the group and of people's interdependence on each other. In a
face-to-face society like that of the Kamwə, the person who does
not operate where others can see him (interacting openly with
others) is suspect and feared by the society. He may be suspected
of stealing, greediness, laziness, possessing a vwə spirit, or
numerous other sins by the society. The loner is the worst kind
of person--a terrible person--and is referred to as a murderer,
one who poisons many people. If one eats alone he is considered
greedy. Many of the values discussed are attained only through
people. To have good character and kindness, one must be involved
with others who give one that status. To be a rich man, many
friends are needed. So one must share his wealth. To be respected,
one must show respect to others. To be generous, one must have
people around to give to. To be disciplined is for the benefit
of others and as the result of interacting with others.

The man who aspires toward all these personal values will be a
responsible person. He will fulfill his responsibility in providing food for his family, marriage for his children and help
for his neighbors and relatives. He will also meet his obligations to his various relatives. The individual can be nothing
without the group. To be accepted and in the favor of society
is essential.

The homogeneous group way of life provides the individual with
an arena for demonstrating his good character and sense of responsibility. Once again, the cohesion of the social unit depends
on individuals being responsible. Thus, the individual needs
the group and the group needs the individual. There is no notion
of an individual in isolation. He is always a person in context.
This is the Kamwə worldview. Figure 12 diagrams the important
qualities of the ideal person in the eyes of the Kamwə.

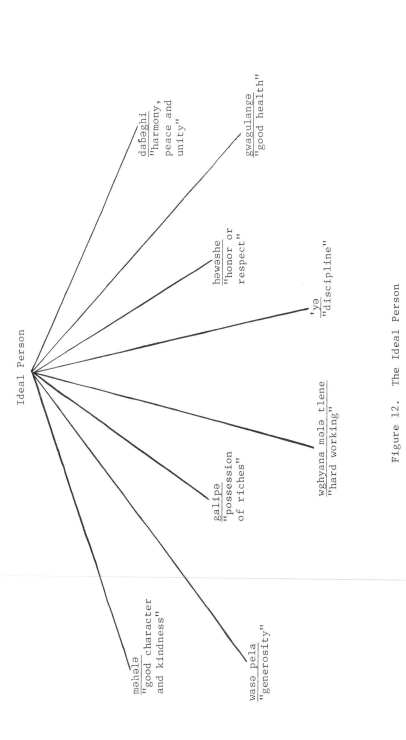

Ideal Person

mehele
"good character
and kindness"

wasa pela
"generosity"

galipe
"possession
of riches"

wghyana mele tlene
"hard working"

'yə
"discipline"

hewashe
"honor or
respect"

daƀaghi
"harmony,
peace and
unity"

gwagulange
"good health"

Figure 12. The Ideal Person

7

Worldview in the
Face of Social Change

The traditional Kamwə worldview has been described, and now
the current situation comes into focus. Tippett (1973b:135)
explains that there are no such compartmentalized entities as the
old way and the new, the traditional and the westernized. Rather
the entity of the living situation of today is an interpenetration
of the traditional and the westernized. Malinowski labeled this
the "new autonomous entity" (1938:xix). By examining the present
Kamwə situation this mixture of old and new will be made clear.

Social anthropologists who study West Africa have described
the behavioral change taking place under urbanization. These
social changes affect almost every aspect of life from the economic to the religious. For example, new roles have emerged,
especially for women, many new voluntary associations have come
into being, and housing adjustments have interfered with family
relations. These changes have been demonstrated by anthropologists like Little (1965 and 1971) and Marris (1962) and what they
have said may be taken as a rough generalization for all West
African urban life.

Some of the behavioral role changes are voluntary and made
possible by changing physical conditions like housing and market-
ing. Others are necessary adjustments to these and other forms
of acculturation. The Kamwə are no exception. They are experiencing the same kind of change. However, we should not assume
that the worldview of the people is also changing without an
examination of the case.

Something in the situation is stable--otherwise the social life
would disintegrate altogether. The authors of *Culture in Process*
(Beals, Spindler and Spindler, 1973:115) describe worldview change:
"...different forms of world view do not arise directly from the
environment, rather they develop slowly as a result of a continuing process of interaction between the cultural system and the
environment." The question we investigate in this chapter is
whether the worldview itself is changing. If so, to what extent.
Or are we simply facing a departure from old patterns to new ones
because of new external conditions but without major changes in
worldview. To what extent is the worldview of the Kamwə modified
by the pressures and opportunities of acculturation, and to what
extent does it resist them? Just what is changing and what is
stable? This quest calls for a description of the current Kamwə
situation.

In Relation to Mountain Orientation

Many of the Kamwə live on the plains now, but in some areas
the villages are still on the mountains. However, the men's side
of the compound is still the up-side toward the mountain nearby,
and the women's is the down-side. Only in the big town would you
find this disregarded. The clan burial grounds on the mountain
are still very much in use. However, in the big town the Christians have their own burial ground near the town on a raised area
so that the idea of height is retained. Kamwə who are Muslims
are buried according to the Muslim custom in or very near their
compound. Some older folks, even the Christians, prefer today
to be carried many miles to the clan burial grounds on the mountains to be buried.

Since colonial control was established the roads have been safe,
and there are no more tribal wars. It is no longer necessary for
the mountains to offer protection to the people. The mountain
does still act as a place where one can get building materials and
firewood, however. The people still feel that their roots are in
the mountains. The villagers on the plains know that they are
closely associated with a particular mountain. They still identify
with a mountain group and have more hostile attitudes toward the
descendents of the mountain clans with whom they used to be
involved in warfare. Some areas still have the saraka celebration to bring rain during which the people go up on the mountain
to dance. The language still reflects the mountain orientation
that was described in Chapter 3.

In Relation to Guinea Corn

Guinea corn is still very important to the Kamwə. It is eaten
by most Kamwə for the two big meals each day. However, some
people now grow rice also and, occasionally, eat rice for one of

those meals. The attitude toward rice is that it does not satisfy people. Many use it for a cash crop. Between meals the Kamwə eat a variety of food considered "food to fill the stomach." These include bean cakes, peanut sticks, cooked cassava, sweet potatoes, porridge, peanuts, and a cooked mixture of beans, guinea corn, and peanuts.

Today it is accepted by society for one to buy guinea corn. However, all the Kamwə (except those who become Muslim as children) still are expected to grow at least three large sacks of guinea corn. They may then buy the rest without hurting their reputations. Teachers and traders whose occupations take them off the land, often have to pay someone to grow their guinea corn for them on their farms. It is still the man's responsibility to provide the guinea corn for the family. However, today one doesn't have to wait for the society to decide to celebrate and sacrifice before planting or harvesting. The guinea corn taboos are dying out in the big town, but are still very evident in the villages.

Instead of storing guinea corn in granaries, the townspeople store it in sacks in a room with a cement floor. They stack the sacks on planks. The women can get their supply from the sack, but whenever they open a new sack they must tell the head of the house. In the early days, the head of the house portioned out the guinea corn to his wives once a week. He would give them equal amounts to cook for the entire compound plus a small amount to cook for the children, should they get hungry between meals.

In the early days, guinea corn beer, badle, and sweet drink, tya, were made mainly for special occasions: group work days, weddings, funerals, etc. Only in the dry season would the women have time to make these to sell in the market. Not often would anyone get drunk and the society strongly disapproved of intoxication. Today these drinks are still made locally by the women. However, because the women have more time available, they make these drinks any time of the year. They are sold in the market place on the two big market days every week.

However, there is now a new distilled drink called argi that has a very high alcoholic content. The women have learned how to make argi. Hitherto, women have never been allowed to drink beer, they just tasted it as it was being made. However, now a few women drink argi and become intoxicated. This distilled drink is available any day of the week in the big town. Elders are not supposed to drink it, because being drunk is not becoming to the position of an elder in society. However, many of the married men from twenty to fifty years old drink any time of the day and any day of the year. Getting drunk is much more prevalent today.

In the early days, the elders could call aside a younger person
who got drunk and explain the problems and his responsibilities to
his family and clan. The younger person would listen to the elders
and mend his ways. However, today the elders do not have that kind
of power because society offers other alternatives to security outside of the family unit. As was mentioned previously, beer (badle)
drinking is a means of honoring the elders, for it is regularly
drunk in order from the oldest down to the youngest. It is a
social event. Infrequency of availability and the low alcohol
content made drunkenness and addiction less of a problem than it
is today.

Ceremonial use of guinea corn has lessened because of the lack
of family unity today. The head of the house who was responsible
for religious things in the early days finds he can't really offer
a sacrifice and expect results if his family is divided. A son
may have gone off to the city to work or to school. Either separates him from his family in mind and spirit. Because the father
represents the family in talking to God or the spirits, the family must be united and in submission to him. It is dangerous and
useless to approach the spirits or God without proper family formality. These facts have affected both the household and the community ceremonial practices.

Today there are alternate solutions to the problems the Kamwə
faces: hospitals, courts, running off to the city, etc. However,
the community sacrifice, saraka, is still practiced in the town
when there is drought and quite often for the planting and harvesting cycle in the village areas. It is still sometimes prescribed by the diviners as part of a cure for illness also. Today
people are free not to participate in such ceremonies if they so
choose. Christians usually do not participate in them.

In Relation to the Supernatural

The Kamwə are still very conscious of the presence of the
unseen beings--God, good and evil spirits, and the vwə spirit.
However, there is little concern today with ancestor spirits,
especially among the young people. Some folks still swear by the
ancestor, but more swear by God--"In the name of God, if I've done
this thing, as the sun sets let my life disappear." The Kamwə see
God in a position of control and as the true judge. He wants
harmony for the people, but as long as there is peace, the people
don't bother much about God. It is still true, however, that as
a last resort man turns to God for help.

The diviners are still very important in solving the problems
the Kamwə face. However, today people go the western doctor as
well as to the diviner. Many people today still feel that the
unseen forces are the cause of sickness. Western medicine, however

does not solve the problem with spirits. Belief in the vwə spirit
is held by most Kamwə today. There is much family pressure to go
to the diviner rather than to get western medicine when one gets
sick.

Trial by ordeal as a means of determining the guilty party is
still used in the more remote areas. The custom is illegal today,
however. The government system provides courts, and a witness is
necessary to prove one guilty. So trial by ordeal is held secretly.
The church is against trial by ordeal or going to diviners as a
means of problem-solving. Christianity is a potentially effective
means of having peace of mind since God's power over the spirit
world is taught. However, many Christians find it very difficult
to claim this power and to stop going to the diviners and being
involved in trials by ordeal.

In Relation to the Ideal Person

Many of the characteristics of the ideal person still hold
true. One is expected to be kind, hard working, and disciplined.
However, schooling has turned the heads of many of the students
and they have a tendency to think they know better than the elders.
They feel they don't have to follow the advice of the elders.
They do, however, ordinarily continue to show honor and respect
by not talking back and offending them. Generosity is still a
very important trait. One must share food with anyone who comes
to his house at mealtime and a gift of food is often given guests
to take home. One is still expected to cooperate with his brothers.
Friends and relatives borrow clothes when they have a need for
them.

There are two standards for wealth today. According to the
traditional pattern, a large home with a large supply of guinea
corn and a large number of wives, children, chickens, goats, and
other animals shows wealth. This person is expected to help
people who need food by exchanging goods for guinea corn. The
new pattern of wealth is to own a shop with lots of goods, to be
able to loan money and to let people who are known buy on credit,
to have a fancy house with a cement floor and aluminum pan roof-
ing, and to have extra rooms for guests. Polygamy is still important, but it is not the only way to show prestige today. Some
elders feel that prestige is in the hands of the literate younger
shop owner who may even have money in a bank. People feel that
if one has money, one ought to show it in family size and/or a
fancy house.

Good health is still a very important value. In fact, it is
said that one of the big reasons the women are so attracted to
Christianity is because of the power that is available in Christ

over the spirits that make one sick and cause death.   The deformed
are still encouraged and cared for by the society.   Almost every
person in the society gets married.

To live in harmony with the group is still very important. Much
effort is put forth to keep peace and unity in the family and in
the neighborhood.   It is much more difficult for parents to instill
the traditional values in their children today because they are
away from home in school much of the time and they have alternatives to being solidly a part of the group.   These alternatives
are brought about by the provision of safety away from the group,
job opportunities by means of which one can support himself, and
standards for living set by the school system more than by the
family, etc.

In Relation to Group Awareness

Even though we are seeing a slowdown in the ceremonies practiced
by the Kamwə due to less unity in the family and a slow breakdown
of the traditional religion, the relationship of the individual to
the group is still very strong.   We will focus in on changes that
have taken place in regard to the family, the authority of the
elders, male-female relationships, and commoner-tradesman relationships.

Family relationships are still very important to most of the
Kamwə.   The terms of relationship discussed in chapter two are
used today with much the same meaning and obligation.   Brothers
are still responsible for the welfare of each other's children.   A
girl still leaves her clan at marriage and the husband's family is
responsible for her, since she joins his clan for the rest of her
life.   Should there be a divorce, she will, through the proper
"brideprice" arrangement, leave her first husband's clan to become
a part of her new husband's clan.   She does not ever return to her
clan of birth.

In the early days, the "brideprice" had to include live animals
in exchange for the daughter, but today cash is acceptable.   Goats
are a problem to care for when the children are in school because
they are not able to watch them and keep them out of gardens.   At
times the father himself must care for them.   Raising animals is
not so common and necessary in the economy today.   One is still
supposed to furnish a goat for the funeral of a relative of the
father's line.   But today the Christians can give money instead
of a goat on these occasions.

When school and vocation take a man out of the tribal area, he
usually still keeps in touch with the family and contributes finan-
cially to their welfare.   He knows that his family always will have
a place for him in the homeland.   When there is difficulty, the
family comes to the rescue.

e Authority of the Elders

The authority of the elders is eroding today due to the change
economy, and schooling. These make the youth literate, give
em new goals different from those of their fathers, and often
ke them outside of the Kamwə area. It has been said that the
achers are replacing the elders in Kamwə society. A young per-
n can go off to the city with or without his parent's permission
d support himself in his own way of life. Some work for wages
jobs that have recently become available, such as building,
rrying messages, road building, washing, farming, butchering,
d selling cooked food in the markets. It is possible for the
ung person to earn and save enough for his own "brideprice" so
doesn't necessarily have to go home or even get his parent's
proval for marriage or depend on the family network of responsi-
lity.

Many new leadership positions have come into the social life
th government rule and the influence of Christianity. It is
cessary to be literate for most of these jobs. Government leaders
clude county representatives, chiefs, civil servants, commissioners,
d counsulates. Church leaders include pastors, village evangelists
d teachers, church committee members, and choir masters.

The elders still feel it their duty to give advice to those
unger in their clan, but the youth do not feel as bound to listen
formerly, for they no longer depend on the elders for security.
spect is still shown to the elders in that one does not tell an
der he is wrong, but listens quietly. He may then ignore the
vice, however. The chief and elders in the early days were
sponsible for judging all the cases, setting the penalties, and
eping peace among the people. Today the law courts handle these
sponsibilities. The large family grouping under the leadership
the elders is still responsible to see that each family unit has
nd to farm. But today, father-son relationships are strained
cause of the many changes in society.

le-Female Relationships

The male-female and husband-wife relationships are also chang-
g. However, women still go about with women, and men with men.
is still the custom for men and boys to eat meals together while
men, girls, and younger children eat together. The head of the
use still is responsible for providing the guinea corn and meat.
men supply the vegetables and sometimes buy fish for the main
al. They continue to be responsible for firewood. A wife still
eds her husband's permission to go out to visit with other women
the evening. Since there are more homes with only one wife,
e husband may sometimes sit with the children while the wife goes
t. In a polygamous home, another wife watches the children.

Animal care is still divided between the man and his wife in
most Kamwə homes. However, sometimes because the husband is away
or when animals are being raised for money, the wife would care for
goats and sheep as well. Or the husband may raise chickens for
cash income. In the early days, women would sell their beer or
produce only in front of their homes, but today one sees them
actively selling goods in the market place. The husband still buys
clothes for the family, but the wife replaces the pots when they
wear out. Much more money is needed today for such things as school
fees, hospital fees, clothes, soap to wash clothes, a higher "bride
price" and hiring laborers to work on the farms so there will be
cash crops as well as food for the family. Fertilizer is used
today and a few Kamwə have plows and/or oxen that they hire out.

Most of the Kamwə women now have their guinea corn ground by
the mill. This saves them much time. They use the extra time for
collecting and selling firewood, making bean cakes, peanut sticks,
or other food or drink to sell, etc. Submission to the husband
used to be very important. However, today husbands and wives are
more responsive to each other.

Christianity, government, and the westernizing trend have all
caused women to want to be heard. As indicated above, the social
structure of the Kamwə society is such that the women traditionally
associate mostly with women. Since their responsibilities were
clearly defined, and they had a degree of economic independence,
it was possible for them to be involved in women's activities outside the home as well. However, it was necessary to get the husband's permission for such involvement. The church has found the
women very responsive to women's meetings. The women's organization provided opportunity for the women to do things together,
develop leadership ability, and share in community. Since all of
the women are "married into" the clan, they are anxious for close
fellowship. They meet regularly to sing, pray, and study together
They also go as a group to share their faith in the market.

Seeing that the church women's group was so successful, the
town women began to organize. They formed a very active women's
organization with their own leadership. Each section of the town
appoints a woman as chief and a woman as treasurer for the women's
group. Women who join must contribute to the finances at each
meeting. They also raise money by hiring out as a group to do farm
labor. Once a year, after harvest, each section has a big feast
for all the women. No men are allowed, except two male guards to
be sure all stays peaceful and to keep children and men out. However, today two women dressed in army uniforms guard the place of
the feast. There is dancing, singing and feasting. Some men come
and sit quietly as spectators in an area nearby. When the food is
served, the women serve the chief first, then the others including

the men outside. Sometimes there is drinking, too, and on occasion the women have made argi and some of them get drunk and spend the whole night out. A definite benefit from this organization is help in financing marriage celebrations in the homes of its members. Christian women did not belong to the town Women's Organization in the past, but now some are finding it a valuable contact with non-Christian women. The men are a bit skeptical about these women's groups as they see how powerful the women can be.

Commoner-Tradesman Relationship

Today the caste distinction between tradesmen and commoners is getting weaker. It seems that tradesmen who take on the eating habits and the "neat and clean" appearance of the commoner are allowed to eat with the commoner. Even today, though, there is little intermarriage between the two castes. The men and women of the tradesmen caste did the barbering in days gone by, but now the commoner is free to cut hair or fancy braid women's hair. The tradesmen used to be paid for their services with goods and guinea corn, but today money is more popular. Or it may be a combination of money and goods. The church has refused to use the tradesmen at funerals as undertakers, so the pastors are supervising and doing most of the undertaker work among Christians.

Because of the availability of goods from other areas in the market today, the commoner does not depend so much on the tradesmen. Today the women wear cloth clothes, so the blacksmith no longer makes women's clothes. The tradesmen still make the hoes, axes, pots, etc.; but leather baby-carriers, bows and arrows, shields, and spears are not used much any more. In fact, it is said that the tradesmen have a hard time getting money to pay their taxes.

In Relation to the Language

Many new terms are found in use in the language. New positions often are labeled with terms borrowed from the Hausa language, the one normally used for trade. Several of these originally came into Hausa from English. The following is a sample:

1.	makaranta - school	8.	pasto - pastor
2.	wakili - representative	9.	jibi - communion service
3.	Littafi Mai Tsarki - Bible	10.	komiti - committee
4.	Kansila - consulate	11.	bakati - bucket
5.	baiko - offering	12.	gomnati - government
6.	addu'a - prayer	13.	kwalaba - bottle
7.	ekklesiya - church (originally from Greek)	14.	agogo - clock
		15.	zumunta - meeting

Other new terms, or old terms with new meanings, include:

1. <u>ka zili Yesu</u> - Christians (followers of Christ)

2. <u>hyahyak</u> - to spend the night out drunk from drinking strong
    beer (taken from an old Kamwə word, <u>hyakə</u>, "to
    spend the night at someone's house")

3. <u>kadibili</u> - cloth clothes (taken from Fulani word <u>gudel</u>)

4. <u>pye səra</u> - foot washing ceremony for Christians (from
    Kamwə words "wash foot")

5. <u>ntivəntə</u> - forgiveness (now used between God and man — pre-
    viously used just for forgiveness between adults
    or an adult and a young person)

6. <u>ncə kə wsi lə Hyalatəmwə</u> - offering (hand a thing to God)

7. <u>argi</u> - distilled alcohol

8. <u>katsala</u> - an expert (previously in hunting, war, athletic
    events, but now also used for a good student,
    farmer)

Semantic change always reflects the social changes going on in the
society.

Today there are two camps tending to change the present patterns of usage in the language. One is the purist camp who want
to institute the traditional terms. The second is made up of young
men who come back from the cities. They are accustomed to Hausa
terminology and tend to use it mixed in with the Vəcəmwə. The
number of borrowed terms in use differs according to the particular
dialect area and how isolated the people of the area are. The subject of terminology and culture change among the Kamwə needs more
research.

Summary

The foregoing description has demonstrated two quite opposite
forces: 1) the existence of culture change, and 2) the stability
of values even when the cultural forms are new. We have seen how
the interdependent systems are slowly being adjusted to accommodate
modern developments. Wallace, in discussing the process of culture
change, notes that religion (belief and ritual) is a stabilizing
factor acting as a kind of governor. When there is change in the
religious system, the old provides the building blocks for the new.
"Old religions do not die; they live on in the new religions which
follow them" (1966:4). So it is with the presuppositions and

values--the worldview. They live on and are the building blocks
for maintaining equilibrium in a society. Christianity, the Hausa
language, the government, new facilities for economic ventures,
markets, the money economy, and migration to the towns are all
agents or instruments of change. Yet in spite of the considerable
change going on, many values are quite stable, though they manifest
themselves in new ways. The worldview lives on acting as a governor
of change.

In a later chapter we shall ask what this implies for church
planting in pagan areas, how fast the process of change ought to
be, and what new Christian forms may be innovated without destroy-
ing basic values of the indigenous worldview.

Before we go into a suggested strategy for presenting the Gospel within this worldview, however, we need to examine communication per se and its relationship to worldview.

PART III

Worldview
and Communication

8

Communication Defined

In order to have human communication there must be three elements: the production of a message by someone, the message itself, and the receipt of that message by someone. At times we communicate with ourselves, but usually there is an audience other than the producer of the message. Verbal communication is the kind most commonly considered as communication, but even a century ago anthropologists such as Garrick Mallery researching the American Indians (1880) and A. W. Howitt in his research on the Australian aboriginees (1904) were focusing on non-verbal communication. Recently, anthropologists like Hall (1959 and 1966) and La Barre (1964) and communicologists such as Berlo (1960) and Smith[1] are describing the defining non-verbal communication. Gestures, use of space and time, facial expressions, tactile experiences, postural habits are all culturally defined means of communication.

The Communication Process

Schramm describes how communication works (Mortensen, 1973: 28-31) as a source sending a message and the "destination" or receptor decoding the message (see Figure 13). The source chooses what signal he will use to get his message to its destination. Then the destination receives that signal and decodes it according to his own make-up. It is important for the receiver and sender to be in tune.

Donald K. Smith has worked out a typology that is largely non-verbal in a book on intercultural communication which is being prepared for publication.

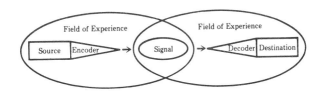

Figure 13.   Diagram of the Workings of Communication
             (Mortensen 1973:31)

The experience of both the source and the receptor affects the
quality of the communication. This field of experience refers to
a great variety of things, i.e., language, values, basic presuppositions, life-style,--the total accumulated experience. If the
circles have a larger area in common, communication is easier. If
the circles do not meet, then the communication intended by the
encoder is impossible. If the circles have only a small area in
common, it is difficult to get meanings from the source to the
receptor.

    In this document I have chosen to refer to the source (which
Barnett 1953 refers to as advocate) as the communicator, to what
Schramm terms the "destination" (which Barnett 1953 refers to as
acceptor or recipient) as the receptor and to the signal as the
message. The above model is a processual model and was chosen
because communication is a process. The communicator is different
at any point in time as is the receptor also. The message also is
different. In the concept of process, the parts are seen as ever-
changing, dynamic, on-going, continuous. Communication is moving,
not static, and has no beginning or end. In talking about and
diagramming communication we tend to arrest the motion like taking
a still picture with a camera. In looking at the resulting photo-
graphs it is necessary to remember that the reproduction is not
at all complete. For the interrelationships, the motion, the
dynamics were arrested when the picture was taken. It is important
to keep this in mind as the elements of communication are examined.

    The process of communication in which all men everywhere are
involved is well summarized by Schramm:

        You are constantly decoding signs from your environ-
        ment, interpreting these signs, and encoding some-

> thing as a result. We are little switchboard centers
> handling and rerouting the great endless current of
> communication. We can accurately think of communica-
> tion as passing through us--changed, to be sure, by
> our interpretations, our habits, our abilities and
> capabilities, but the input still being reflected in
> the output (Mortensen 1973:34).

All three elements in communication are important and at any
f these points there can be a breakdown of communication. So we
ill examine each one more carefully.

The Communicator

The communicator, as he determines to affect his receptor,
ncodes his message. Within himself. however, are several factors
hat make a difference in how well he communicates. His own ability
ith language and his communication skills make a difference in how
ell he gets his message to the receptor. Berlo says "...the words
e can command, and the way that we put them together affect (a) what
e think about, (b) how we think, and (c) whether we are thinking
t all" (1960:43).

The knowledge level of the communicator affects the communica-
ion also. He cannot communicate what he does not know or under-
tand himself. However, it is possible to be overspecialized and
o technical that the receptor cannot understand. When the com-
unicator feels that his knowledge is complete or infallible, there
s often little effective communication. But when he feels that
is knowledge is fragmentary and uncertain, genuine communication
an occur (Barnlund 1968:25). By recognizing that his facts and
eelings are limited, he becomes curious about the facts and feelings
f others.

The attitudes of the communicator are also influential in the
ommunication process. Not only his attitude toward his knowledge,
ut his attitude toward himself and the message affects the way he
ommunicates. He must have a positive attitude toward himself and
elieve in his message if he wants to effectively communicate, for
hese attitudes frequently come through in the message. His atti-
udes toward the receptor are important determinants of his effec-
iveness in communication also. Does he like the receptor? Does
e respect the receptor? Is the relationship between himself and
he receptor a vital one? A negative attitude toward the receptor
ampens the communication.

Another factor within the communicator that affects his communi-
ation is the position he holds in the sociocultural system. What
s his role? What kind of prestige does he represent? What func-
ions is he required to perform? What are his cultural beliefs and

values? How do they affect the way in which he communicates? In
cross-cultural communication situations this factor is especially
important and complex. The communicator represents one set of
values, beliefs, and behavior patterns which may be little known by
the receptor. He may see himself as representing the average middle class American, but he may be seen by the receptor as wealthy
beyond measure. He must realize that his place in the sociocultural
system is determined by the culture he is working in.

The place of the communicator in effective communication can be
compared with that of the donor culture in technical assistance and
international development programs. Foster (1973) explains the
great importance of being sensitive to the donor culture in order
to have effective directed change in the target culture. The basic
assumptions of the donor culture often include many assumptions not
felt by the target group in another culture. The assumptions of
Westerners, for example, often include: 1) the importance of a
position being determined by the number of people the incumbent
supervises, 2) the existence of unlimited good, and upward mobility
as the right way, 3) progress as the ideal, 4) the sacredness of
human life, 5) the ideal in agriculture being the highest possible
yield with the least possible manpower, 6) literacy as of top prior-
ity in developmental programs (Foster 1973:179-180). These are only
a few of the donor's assumptions that affect the perception of
problems and the strategies set forth for action in the target
culture. The communicator must be aware of these same problems
when he tries to communicate! His assumptions are those of his own
cultural perspective and his training often is designed for effectiveness within his own cultural framework. There are many possibilities for communication breakdown at the communicator's end of
the process.

The Message

The next element to be considered in the communication process
is the message itself. The message is the product that has been
created by the communicator for the purpose of eliciting a response
from the receptor. The code and content of the message itself is
important in determining the efficiency and effectiveness of communication. If the code that was chosen by the communicator is
foreign, the message takes a foreign hue. The code is any group
of symbols that can be structured in a way that is meaningful to
some person. It may be the language, music, art, dance, drama,
proverbs, the position of communicator and receptor. If the code
is one that is naturally used for communication, the receptor will
understand the message more readily. If the code chosen speaks to
two or more of the senses, the ability to remember the message is
heightened.

Nida, in his discussion of the communication of the message of Christianity, deals with the problems of adaptation of content:

> What is actually involved here is not the alter-
> ing of the essential content of the Biblical mes-
> sage, but the encasing of this message in a cultur-
> ally relevant verbal form...a fitting of the same
> content into such culturally meaningful forms as
> will be fit vehicles for communication of the
> message...What is done is to select significant
> features of the people's world view...and provide
> meaningful interpretations of the Christian content
> through the use of these indigenous symbolic forms
> (1960:180).

One of his illustrations was among the Toba people of Argentina who have sharing as a dominant theme. The message that was effective for them was not one of individual responsibility before God, but one of sharing--God sharing His Son, Christ sharing his life, and His Spirit, sharing of God's common gift as evidence of belonging to God, sharing with one another in this new fellowship of faith.

Whether the receptor feels positive or negative about the mes-sage being presented influences the way it is produced. If the feeling is negative, a carefully planned preamble may be necessary in order to gain a hearing. The receptor must be kept in mind as the message is being prepared. What code will he understand? What elements from that code will appeal to him and be easy to decode? What structuring of these elements would be most easily understood and remembered? What content of the message will be pertinent to his interest and needs? The message itself in both code and con-tent influences the communication.

The Receptor

The last of the three essential elements in the communication process to be discussed is the receptor. Berlo, in his discussion of effective communication, states, "...the receiver is the most important link in the communication process... One of the most important emphases of communication theory is a concern with... the receiver" (1960:52). Already I have expressed the importance of the receiver in choosing a code and the content of the message. The receptor's communication skills, his knowledge level, his attitudes toward himself, the message, and the communicator, and also his position in the sociocultural system are all important parts of the communication process. Misunderstanding or lack of ability to understand the message could be a result of trouble at any of these areas. For instance, he may see the communicator as his social superior and before the message is even given, his response is, "That's right." Or perhaps when pressed to do

something the response is "Certainly," because of the close friendship with the communicator even though the receptor knows he should
refuse. Or perhaps because he is old and has several wives when
the invitation to become a Christian is presented, he hears, "That's
not for me because I am a polygamist and God doesn't want me."

Interaction as Goal

The relationship between the communicator and receptor is one
of the key determinants of the effectiveness of the communication.
This leads to interaction, and interaction is crucial if there is
to be effective communication. Interaction involves interdependence, shared activity, shared experience, reciprocal role-taking,
the mutual expressing of empathy. When two people interact, they
put themselves "in each other's shoes." Each tries to perceive the
world as the other person sees it and tries to predict how the
other will respond. With interaction as a goal, one's ability to
affect and be affected by others increases.

Having briefly examined several key elements of communication,
I hasten to state that they are all interlocked and are interdependent. As has been stated, communication is a dynamic process,
and Figure 14 illustrates this process.

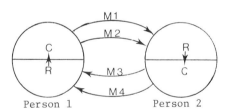

Figure 14. The Dynamic Communication Process

The receptor quickly becomes the communicator, making the communicator the receptor. Encoding and decoding are going on constantly
as these elements of communication are all intertwined.

9

Principles of Communication

Communication problems often arise because of a lack of understanding of the principles of communication. For this reason, I list some principles and will discuss them with hopes that we may gain a clearer understanding of the communication process.

The Central Role Played by Perception

Perception plays a central role in the communication process. One reacts as he has been trained in his culture, he finds what he has been trained to look for, he sees what he has been taught to expect and in a way that he's been trained to see it. He perceives reality, in short, in terms of his worldview. His language organizes his environment by placing arbitrary names on things and classifying things. These words affect what he thinks and how he thinks. Sapir expressed it this way:

> Human beings do not live in the objective world
> alone, nor alone in the world of social activity
> as ordinarily understood, but are very much at the
> mercy of the particular language which has become
> the medium of expression for their society...the
> 'real world' is to a large extent unconsciously
> built upon the language habits of the group. No
> two languages are ever sufficiently similar to
> be considered as representing the same social
> reality...Even comparatively simple acts of per-
> ception are very much more at the mercy of the
> social patterns called words than we might suppose...

> We see and hear and otherwise experience very
> largely as we do because the language habits of
> our community predispose certain choices of inter-
> pretation (1929:209-210).

I recall when I was first in Africa and learning the language. On
one of my regular visits in the town, one of the women asked if I
was pregnant. I was insulted, embarrassed, and must have looked
confused. She then explained that by leaving my one year old baby
at home, that indicated that I had no milk which most probably
meant another pregnancy. I did not yet have the insights of the
local perception in order to understand the message as originally
given.

A child gradually acquires a picture of the world he inhabits
and his place in it and how that world operates. This symbolic
world in his head as an adult is that about which he talks, for
which he fights and argues, and that which causes laughter and enjoyment. Berlo aptly says of perception:

> What we see is partly what is there. It is also
> partly who we are. Everything that we observe we
> observe through our own senses, our own experiences.
> We do, we must, observe the world from our own point
> of view, and we report it that way (1960:224).

Continuing experiences affect a person's perception of himself and
the world about him. No human being ever sees all, but only that
which is in accordance with his past experiences and present needs.
Each person's culture training and experiences cause him to perceive some things and ignore others.

Gestalt psychology, which emphasizes the whole as being more
than the sum total of its parts, reinforces the fact that we see
a thing only in part, but we perceive it whole. The gaps are filled
in in the gestalt from experience. The gestaltists have developed
the concept of "closure" which accounts for the psychological strain-
ing toward closing the gestalt. Barnett explains the "closure"
concept as:

> ...the presentation of a part of a configuration
> field of tensions and stresses which seeks equili-
> brium through supplementation by the missing part.
> When this missing part is realized, the gestalt is
> closed; and the subject thereupon experiences a
> relaxation of the tensions that were occasioned by
> the incompleted process (1953:434).

So, in communication what we see or hear is only part and closure
is brought about by one's imagination and formed by one's experience

iderstanding how one's perception affects the message as it is
:constructed by the receptor from the symbols, makes a big dif-
:rence in the communication. Better yet, to strive to understand
)w the receptor perceives himself and the world about him lays a
)lid foundation for effective communication.

Meanings Not in Words

Meanings are in people, not in words. Communication often
:eaks down because the communicator believes that the meaning is
ı the words, rather than in the people who use them. Meanings of
ırds depend on the experience of the user/receptor. People assign
ımilar meanings only to the extent that they have similar exper-
ɛnces. The word "hospital" triggers quite a different meaning to
ıe person who has only visited casual friends there, the person
ıo has been a patient regularly because of an incurable disease,
ıe person who has never been inside the building, the person who
)rks there, and the one who has watched a loved one slowly die
ıere. The experiences of the receptor are the reservoir out of
ıich a meaning is extracted and attached to a given stimulus. No
vo persons attach exactly the same meaning to the stimulus. Since
xperiences constantly change the reservoir, meanings change, too,
)r every individual. New experiences in life raise needs and
ɛsires that cause a person to search for new meanings from time to
ime. These provide fertile areas for communication stimulus.

Kraft (1976a) defines a "new meaning" as "some idea or concept
hat has not previously existed in the mind of a given person."
ɛ notes that the component parts of that particular idea were
lready in the mind but not in the combination in which they exist
fter the stimulus has resulted in new meaning. Barnett has
ɛscribed this process well in his recombination theory:

> In defining an innovation as something that is
> qualitatively new, emphasis is placed upon reor-
> ganization rather than upon quantitative variation
> as the criterion of a novelty. Innovation does not
> result from the addition or substraction of parts.
> It takes place only when there is a recombination
> of them (1953:9).
>
> Fundamental to this point of view is the assump-
> tion that any innovation is made up of preexist-
> ing components...An innovation is, therefore, a
> creation only in the sense that it is a new
> combination, never in the sense that it is some-
> thing emerging from nothing (1953:181).

So, as Kraft explains, new meanings ordinarily result from the
receptor responding to stimuli in such a way that he reworks material already in his mind into new concepts. In the communication
process the message is the communicator's expression of information
and new information for the receptor must relate to something
already in his mind in such a way that it stimulates reorganization
of that material. If it does not relate in this way, the new information does not result in new meanings. It is simply stored or
forgotten. The stimulus for such reorganization or recombination
is the receptor's discovery of the actual or potential relevance
of the new meaning to his life. The meanings of what is said is
found in the minds of people, not in words.

The Importance of the Precise Context

   The precise context strongly influences the meaning in communication. The isolated word has minimal meaning. Words need
context in order to have specific meaning. Sentences provide such
a context. But isolated sentences can easily be misunderstood.
They need a situation in order to be most clear. The same sentence
used in a missionary letter to the sending Board and in a missionary letter to the individual supporters could have very different
meanings. The total context would include the kind of material
one is writing or hearing as well as the individuals involved in
the communication, the time of writing, etc.

   Tippett, in dealing with Fijian material culture, recognized
the importance of the context:

>   In general terms an artifact is an ax, a bow, a
>   bowl, a canoe, a sacred object, and thus would
>   have roughly the same meaning to all in the group;
>   but at the same time a particular ax or sacred
>   object might have vastly different meaning and
>   function to different persons in the same group...
>   (1968:27).

Different homogeneous units have different criteria for evaluating
a spear. The men, the women, the carpenter, the fisherman, the
craftsman, the warrior, and the hunter all look for different
qualities depending on the function they see for it, the context.
The spear in Fiji was a device for getting food, a means of showing
wealth, an opportunity to show one's skill, useful for the dance,
etc. It is never something that stands alone, but it belongs to a
context. It is **crucial** for the communicator to understand the
importance of the precise context in the transfer of meaning.

Malinowski, in his fieldwork in the Trobriand Islands, realized w very important the precise context is to the actual meaning of word or sentence. He saw translation not as simply inserting an glish word for a native one, but as describing wide fields of stom, of social psychology and of tribal organization and life at correspond to one term or another. The meaning of a single rd is "only intelligible when it is placed within its <u>context</u> <u>situation</u>...the conception of context must be substantially dened, if it is to furnish us with its full utility" (1927:306).

Barr emphasizes understanding the total context in order to derstand the meanings of biblical language. He discusses the lation of thoughts and language, recognizing that there are nguistic limitations to thoughts. Recognizing that the Hebrew nd holds a total picture of the living being (the soul with the dy as its visible manifestation) while the Greek sees two dis- nct entities in the body and soul gives a better understanding r the Greek New Testament expression of Hebrew thought. To gain derstanding of the Old Testament, he says it is not relevant to cus on its contrast with the Greek thinkers, but to see how the eas differ from the total context of that period--the Canaanites, e Arabs, the Babylonians. He sees theologions as often overlook- g the total context and focusing on detail to the point of mis- nstruing the meaning, e.g., Hebrew being quite extraordinary 961:8-20).

Meaning is derived from the interaction between information d context. Kraft (1977) defines the importance of context as at part of meaning that is the function of the culture-specific ture of an event. In order to understand the events in the ble, the context must be thoroughly analyzed and taken as seriously the information presented concerning the event. If the import- ce of the context is relatively higher, the meaning is more lture-specific, e.g., women praying in public without headcover- g (I Cor. 11:10). If the importance of context is relatively wer, then meaning is more closely related to human commonality, g., do not steal (Ex. 20:15). He notes that Scriptures that seem us to come closest to a clear statement of a portion of the supra- ltural will of God for man's conduct (e.g., the commandments of sus - Matt. 22:37-40; the listing of the fruits of the Spirit - l. 5:22-23; the Sermon on the Mount) are phrased at a level of straction that largely extricates them from specific application the original cultures in which they were uttered. These are en given specific application in the cultural context of the ader. When the cultural context of the reader (i.e., the Kamwɔ) close to that of the original author's situation, the meaning apt to be closer also. When the context is further removed, e meaning will be also. Precise context strongly influences aning in communication.

The Relation of Communication to the Social System

Communication affects the social system and the social system affects communication. All communication takes place in a social context or frame of reference. Who is interacting with whom? Why are they interacting? In what manner are they interacting? What is the role and behavior relationship between them? Who is the authority? What is the situation for this social interaction? These questions must be considered for effective communication to take place. Knowledge of the social system of the receptor helps one predict what the receptor believes (his worldview), what he knows, and how he will behave in a given situation. This knowledge sharpens communication considerably.

In the Kamwǝ situation, explaining something to the son of a chief or to a blacksmith of the village should be two different experiences. The responses will reflect different social backgrounds, different expectations from the group they represent, a different degree of importance for the society as a whole, a different degree of openness or resistence to what is being said.

The lines of communication are a part of the social context, also. The question must be asked, in this society do the women spread the news, the old men, or is it the young people? Each individual is a part of several social groups (Baker 1934:32-33). His behavior, beliefs, values, and attitudes all represent those of the groups of which he is a part. Some of the Kamwǝ social groups are the family, the elders, the school children, the women's organization, the youth choir. Knowing where a person fits in society aids communication. It is also important to know where I, the outsider, fit in the society. For as the receptor listens to me, he has assigned me to a role within his society that affects the way he hears what is being said.

The social system regulates what can be discussed, where, and by whom. Certain subjects are discussed at mealtime and others are not. Certain subjects are talked about by the men as they relax together at the end of the day. Other topics are appropriate for talking around the fire as a family and sometimes with neighbors or guests. The society determines what can't be said as well e.g., complimenting the parents on the beauty of a child. This would be calling the child's presence and desirableness to the attention of the evil spirits. They believe that harm would surely befall him if such a thing was said.

The social system can exist only if the lines of communication are held open. Social systems depend on communication for their very existence. Communication provides a means of showing respect to those to whom it is due. For people to work together and live together communication is essential. To show or develop influence in the community there must be communication. To make friends requires communication. It is an integral part of the social system in all parts of the world.

The Importance of Being Specific to Receptor Needs

Communication that is specific to the needs of the receptor is likely to be perceived as important by the receptor. In communication the receptor always has a choice of "tuning out" and paying no attention to the message at all. For this reason the special needs of the receptor must be considered in the way the message is presented. Cohen talks about the order in communication and notes "if a communicator first arouses the subject's needs, the information will be accepted more readily than if the arousal of need follows the presentation of the information" (Sereno and Mortensen 1970:286).

The needs of the receptor need to be understood as he perceives them, i.e., in terms of his context or frame of reference. Often the communicator sees the needs from quite a different perspective. We must, therefore, learn to meaningfully interact with the receptor in terms of the latter's categories (worldview) in order to be able to empathize with that person. For example, many a western cross-cultural worker sees the people he serves as needing the convenience of water piped into their homes. This is often, however, a need that they do not feel, at least to the extent that they are willing to give up their socializing around the village well to get it. Supplying this need has often disrupted important social patterns, on the one hand, while ignoring needs that the people feel deeply, on the other hand.

The more specific to the receptors' felt needs the communication is, the more effective it is likely to be. Speaking to needs not felt, or even in generalities concerning felt needs, puts too great a burden on the receptor, since it requires him to go to great lengths to make the specific applications. When the communicator knows his receptors' felt needs and is specific to them, a clearer picture is received--one that is much more apt to affect the thinking and behavior of the receptor.

Feedback Exerting Control

Reactions serving as feedback exert control over future messages. "Feedback" is the term used to describe the return messages sent by the receptor back to the communicator while the latter is speaking. Feedback may consist of facial expressions, verbal communications, gestures, expressions of emotion. It is an indication that the communicator can use to determine whether his message was clear and got through. It can be a guide to the future actions of the communicator--he can change his message, restate it in a different way, illustrate it, etc., as he sees necessary according to the feedback. However, as I have stated above, it is not just a one-way process. For in order for there to be ongoing communication, the communicator and receptor roles are constantly changing from person to person and both are mutually interdependent for feedback (see Figure 14, above). To be alert to feedback is essential for effective communication as it indicates what is being heard on the part of the other person and enables the communicator to adjust his presentation of the message.

Feedback symbols vary from one language to another, so it is necessary to learn the ones of the language in which one is communicating. The intended meaning of feedback clues, as of all communicational symbols, is agreed upon by the language community. The cross-cultural worker needs, therefore, to learn to understand and to provide the kind of feedback clues intelligible to those with whom he communicates.

On The Value of Verbal Symbols

Verbal symbols are of limited value as they obscure as well as reveal meaning. Verbal symbols serve as a tool for labeling and manipulating our conceptions. They are used to represent what we perceive to exist in the real world. Symbols mean what they mean because a group of people agree that they ought to signify that meaning and use them for that purpose. The meaning of a symbol is, however, more than this assigned "dictionary" meaning. Any given symbol triggers a variety of responses in the minds of the hearer. For example, the word "wedding" has quite different meanings for the bride, the groom, the pastor, the parents of the bride, the janitor of the church, the organist, the counselor, the florist the older unmarried sister of the bride.

Concerning the limitation of symbols, Nida says:

> On the one hand, they reveal truth, for they help
> us to identify, explore, and interchange concep-
> tions; but they also obscure, for they have the
> pernicious tendency to be slippery, never meaning
> just one thing but several things, not standing
> for a definite object but symbolizing a conception
> (1960:69).

Symbols are meant to facilitate the flow of meaning from the mind of the communicator to the mind of the receptor. They do reveal, but they also obscure meaning.

The Importance of Discovery

Communication that carefully guides the receptor in discovery is usually internalized and affects behavior. This principle suggests that when the receptor has the impression that the new information has come to him by way of discovery, it is more a part of him than when he is simply told it by an outsider. Kraft (1973b and c and 1977) elaborates on this principle. This discovery can take place only as the receptor identifies with the communicator. The communicator seeks to lead the receptor to the discovery of the content and value of his message by his own involvement and example. He is not presenting the receptor with a carefully sealed package to act as an alternative to what he already has. He is sharing himself and his experience. As the receptor gets involved, then, in reciprocal identification he begins to discover for himself the relevance of the message for himself. Nida emphasizes the importance of the role of both the communicator's and the receptor's personal involvement:

> No effective communication can possibly take
> place unless the participants stand in relevant,
> understandable relations to one another. The
> source must have a valid role within the context
> or his words will be relatively meaningless"
> (1960:178).

In order to understand better just what identification is, I will discuss inner identification as Nida presents it. Inner identification is taking seriously the value system (worldview) of the other person: it is being aware of his ideas, understanding his viewpoints, and being genuinely sympathetic with his struggle for self-expression. Nida lists four levels of communication based on the degree of identification:

1. *level one* - the message has no significant effect on the
    receptor's behavior. The message is self-validating and
    the communicator is largely irrelevant.

2. *level two* - the communicator identifies with the message
    and he himself acts on it, with the receptor altering his
    immediate behavior, but no permanent change takes place.

3. *level three* - the message concerns the receptor's whole
    value system and the communicator must identify with the
    receptor <u>and</u> the message in order to affect the behavior
    of the receptor.

4. *level four* - (the deepest level of communication) - the
    message has been communicated so effectively that the
    receptor feels the same type of communicative urge as that
    experienced by the communicator. The receptor identifies
    with the communicator (1960:164-166). This involves dis-
    covery and results in behavior change.

Much of the learning in non-western societies is discovery
learning. In the Kamwə society as in many other societies, when a
child does something unacceptable, a relevant proverb is quoted.
The child then has to think and discover the meaning of this proverb
for his situation. Learning is more than just assimilating quantities of information. The learner learns how to learn as he takes
information that is of value to him and applies it to his life.
Jesus' method of teaching strongly reflects the discovery principle.
He seemed hesitant to simply verbalize who He was. He, rather,
lived a life that exemplified who He was and allowed those around
Him to discover for themselves. Deep life-changing communication
takes place when discovery learning is involved.

Restructuring and Adaptation

Adaptation of the message as it is restructured by the receptor
can be effective communication. At times, the receptor in his
restructuring of the message will come up with something quite new.
Such restructuring may result in effective communication even though
what is "heard" is not exactly what the communicator had in mind.
Belshaw, in his study of the synthesis between economics and anthropology, cites an illustration of an occasion in which a missionary
considered his communication effective even though the restructured
message was quite altered from that intended by the communicator:

> We at length came upon the chief...Yes, he would
> sell us a site, and at once trotted us round a
> triangular block, right between the boat landings.
> But he was not going to take barter for land; it
> must be pigs and some tobacco, the coin of his
> realm. We deferred the purchase to a later visit.
> On the shore we faced each other again to say fare-
> well. He looked at me, and I looked at him. In
> that brief glance we summed each other up. "Here,"
> said he to himself, "is the man I want. Now I'll
> have a boat, pigs, tobacco, axes, knives, calico,
> desirable things of all kinds. True, he's a mission-
> ary; but that doesn't concern me. Best of all, I'll
> be the biggest chief on the coast, and have pro-
> tection from the bushmen. Moreover, he seems a
> pleasant fellow, and shows one respect. Can't go
> far wrong in taking him. Am sure he's soft and

> easily managed." And I said to myslef, "I like
> the chief. He's a pleasant old fellow--though not
> so old either. Can't see much of his eyes, but he
> has a passable face, and a fairly good smile; seems
> genial, and unobstrusive, and does not say much.
> Should get on well with such an ally. Feel sure
> he's soft and easily managed."...The object of our
> search had been gained (1954:52).

The receptor plays an active part in the final result of commuication. Shineberg, in her detailed historic account of the sandalwood trade in the Southwest Pacific, emphasizes the importance of the receptor who is very much involved in the outcome and plays an active role in the communication:

> Europeans of education deplored the fact that through
> the trade, an inferior version of their civilization
> was introduced to the islanders of this region; that
> the least worthy individuals and only certain material
> components of western culture were presented to them.
> I have argued that this is an entirely European-
> oriented view which implies a purely passive role in
> the contact situation by the Melanesians themselves.
> The evidence seems clearly to show, on the contrary,
> that the islanders played a very lively part in their
> relations with the Europeans and that they endeavored
> to turn the coming of the white men to their best
> possible advantage by acquiring the desired goods,
> by using their vessels as a means of travel and, where
> possible, by obtaining their assistance to pay out
> their enemies (1967:215-216).

Missionaries have often been criticized for imposing on their converts, but in reality the converts (receptors) have appropriated that which they have been concerned with and often their motivation is different from that of the communicator. Somewhere in the communication of Christianity to the Bataks, the church heard the message and adopted it to fit her situation. The Christians approved of certain Batak musical forms for social use but not for use in the religious worship (Tippett 1963). This again shows how the receptor is the decision maker and his discovery of the message given often includes results that are effective but unanticipated by the communicator. "Effective" communication must, therefore, be defined as more than the simple restructuring of the message in such a way that the concepts in the mind of the communicator are transferred clearly to the minds of the receptor. Adaptation and resulting behavior are a part of the effectiveness of communication.

10

Understanding Worldview
as a Point of Reference
for Communication

Communication is a complex process. We have already highlighted
some of the basic elements and principles of communication. We will
now look at its relationship to Kamwə worldview. When attempting
to communicate Christ and His message to the Kamwə one must recognize at least three worldviews as points of reference for the communication: 1) Kamwə worldview, 2) the communicator's worldview
(we'll assume a western one at this point), and 3) the worldviews
seen in the Scriptures. The difference between worldviews is one
of the greatest barriers to intercultural communication. We have
come to understand Christian meanings in terms of our basic assumptions, concepts, and values (which we assume to be true without
proof). We seek to communicate these Christian meanings, then, to
members of the receptor culture who will only be able to understand
them in terms of their basic assumptions, concepts, and values
(which they assume to be true, without proof). But the Christian
meanings themselves can only be discovered by exegetically disen-
tangling them from the basic assumptions, concepts, and values of
those in Scripture with whom God was interacting.

American Worldview Defined

The Kamwə worldview has been discussed in the earlier chapters.
To better understand the American worldview[1], let us take a look at

---

[1] The author is aware that there are many exceptions to these general-
izations. The greatest of these occur in the various identifiable
subcultural groupings such as Blacks, Chicanos, Amish, Hutterites,
etc.

merican values as seen by Arensberg and Niehoff (1974:207-231). They are attempting to describe a national "core" in the American middle class Anglo culture that has its origins in Western European culture.

1. Achievement is valued more than inheritance in determining an individual's position.

2. People tend to rely on voluntary associations rather than on strong kinship ties.

3. Achievement and success are measured primarily by the quantity of material goods one possesses.

4. Polarized thinking tends to put the world of values into absolutes, i.e., moral-amoral; right-wrong; legal-illegal; success-failure.

5. Two-fold judgments tend to force Americans into positions of exclusiveness.

6. Americans tend to moralize and judge others on the basis of their code of conduct.

7. Work and play are considered to be two different worlds.

8. "Time is money."

9. Effort is good in itself.

10. Americans have activist, pragmatic values rather than con-templative or mystical ones.

11. Americans have a faith in "progress" and a constant view toward the future being bigger and better.

12. There is an **accent on youthfulness** with adults attempting to hold back middle and old age.

13. A conquering attitude toward nature exists.

14. All people should have equal opportunities for achievement (if they accept the basic beliefs and behavior of the social majority).

15. A high value on individuality exists.

16. American humanitarianism is highly organized and impersonal.

From this brief outline of American worldview we turn to worldview
as it is a part of Scripture and the message itself.

Worldviews Compared

   To illustrate the significance of worldview for communication
purposes we will consider an Old Testament command and the use
of music from the perspective of three different worldviews, i.e.,
that of the Kamwə, of the American, and of the Scriptures.

Worldview in Relation to Authority

   God gave Moses a commandment for His people: "Honor your
father and your mother, that your days may be prolonged in the land
which the Lord your God gives you" (Exodus 20:12, NASB). All throu
ancient Hebrew history in their nomadic period and through the mon-
archy and even in their post-exilic literature we find that the mos
important components of the social structure were the family group
and the tribe. Consequently, the relationship between parents and
children was of fundamental importance. In order to carry on the
heritage there must be children. Children were a sign of God's
blessing and provision (Ps. 127:3, 128). The people saw God as
involved in whether or not a woman had children (Gen. 30:2). In
those days the child normally had to grow up to his father's pro-
fession whether it be that of farmer, cattleman, craftsman, priest,
or judge. Wolff gives a clear picture of the training of a child
in ancient Israel:

> The craftsman's cunning, to which a man is introduced
> by his father, cannot be distinguished from a man's
> dealings with things in the town and in the country,
> with animals, and above all with other men and with
> himself. The young person is to learn to live with good
> weather and bad, with the changing times and seasons,
> with the laws and with experiences of suffering, with
> life's unsolved riddle, and with his God. Most of the
> subjects of education of this kind are to be found in
> the collections of proverbs. Others are preserved
> in stories and in the Psalms. Here we are shown that
> a considerable part of education came through the
> accounts that fathers gave their children of their own
> experiences and the things that befell them (Ps. 44:1ff;
> 78:3ff; Judges 6:13) (1974:179).

Aging was a process of acquiring desirable qualities: experience,
understanding, wisdom. The father was the authority figure in the
Hebrew family (Exodus 12:3, Mal. 1:6). It was important to treat
parents well. In fact, the death penalty was fitting for anyone

ho struck or cursed his father or mother (Exodus 21:15, 17). A
erson's behavior toward his parents was to be one of respect
Lev. 19:32) and heeding their advice (Prov. 23:22, 24, 25), and
ne which brought joy to them (Prov. 10:1). To mistreat parents
ould bring disaster (Prov. 30:17). Honoring father and mother
as essential for long life according to the Hebrew worldview.

Jesus in His teaching repeated this commandment and reaffirmed
ne necessity of obeying it (Matt. 19:19; Lk. 18:20). Paul in his
nstruction on relationships to the early church at Ephesus reminded
nem of this commandment given by God (Eph. 6:2).

The Kamwə worldview also emphasizes the importance of honoring
ather and mother. The family unit is the most significant social
nd economic unit. Traditionally it was the most significant poli-
ical, educational, and religious unit as well. Children are a
ign of God's blessing as well as an indication of one's wealth.
especting the elders, listening to their advice, and depending
n their wisdom and experience gives them the position they deserve
nd pleases God according to the Kamwə tradition. To displease the
lders and be cursed by one of them means that misfortune and per-
aps death will surely follow. The meaning of the commandment of
od to honor your parents would be understood in a way quite simi-
ar to the way it was understood in Old Testament times because
f the similarity of Kamwə and Hebrew worldview with regard to the
amily and respecting the elders.

The American worldview as defined above emphasizes the indivi-
ual and places great value on being young. The elders are not
ne center of the social unit and when retirement age is reached,
 person's value to society is often very minimal. Because of
ressure for acquiring material goods and being self-sufficient,
ne elders in society are often neglected and overlooked. The
ommandment of God to honor father and mother is often interpreted
 mean that children provide for the care of their parents when
ney are old (mainly focusing on their physical needs rather than
 social or psychological ones). It also means be kind to them
nen you are with them, don't abuse them, tolerate them. But in
astern society, it is not the old, but the young who have the
nswers to life's problems. As a result of this striking contrast
 worldview, the meaning of the biblical concept is hard for us
 grasp and requires much teaching to be understood. However, the
amwə will very easily understand the biblical meaning if they are
t confused by the American cross-cultural teacher. This is an
ea where western theologians can learn from the Kamwə under-
anding.

Figure 15 illustrates the way in which worldview can hinder
ommunication. The Kamwə with the guidance of the Holy Spirit can

understand parts of the Scriptures that are given to a people with
a worldview similar to theirs in a clear and meaningful way (A).
When biblical knowledge is taken and processed through American
thought patterns and then communicated, however, the meaning is
apt to be distorted with the American worldview acting as an
obstruction to the message getting through to the receptor (B).
The missionary should be a catalyst to facilitate direct understandings (Path A) rather than an obstructor of such understanding
(Path B).

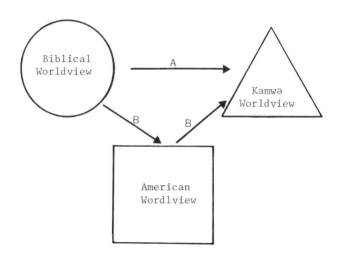

Figure 15.   Worldviews and Their Effect on Communication

In discussing the relationshop of conversion to Christianity
and culture, Kraft (1963) illustrates and diagrams the tendency
of the early church (Acts 15) and more recent missionary effort
to require conversion to another culture in order to be acceptable
to God. His plea is to recognize that any culture is an acceptable vehicle for God's interaction with man. Any worldview is
likewise an acceptable framework for God's communication.

Worldview and Music

We may illustrate this matter from a study of the role of music
in the three cultures in focus here. In Old Testament times, musi
was an important part of home festivals: farewell celebrations

Gen. 31:27), greeting someone special (Judges 11:34, I Sam. 10:5), easts (Amos 6:5). It was used by high and important families as n accompaniment to their prophecy. Music was a part of weddings Jer. 7:34), funerals (Jer. 48:35, 36) and royal feasts (II Sam. 9:35). It was used in celebrating victory (Judges 5) and for he temple dedication (Ezra 3:10), and to crown the king (I Kings :39, 40). It was used to call people together for worship (Num. 0:1-10), to give war signals (II Sam. 2:28), to announce feasts Ps. 81:3) and to give warnings (Jer. 6:1). Dancing, singing, and nstrumental music all went together on many of these occasions. inging was often done antiphonally (Ps. 13:20). Music was used or therapy for Saul when he was bothered by an evil spirit (I Sam. 5:14-23; 18:10). Music expressed joy and sadness and excitement. ainer (n.d.) describes music being used for tragic scenes, i.e., orture and executions. In Daniel's day, when everyone was to bow o the golden image, there was musical accompaniment for this group tion (Daniel 3:5, 7, 10, 15). Flutes, harps, trumpets, and cymals were some of the popular instruments of the day. Often the casion for music was a group activity, but flutes were used as musement when walking or traveling.

Music was provided in the temple for all worship and festivals. whole lineage was devoted to it and were supported by the people or this functional role. Throughout the Bible "men who furnished e orchestras and choruses for worship stood next to the kings and iests in prestige" (Madeleine and Miller 1954:466). Specific mes of musicians are listed along with other leaders in Neh. :17 and Neh. 12:46. Harper's Bible Dictionary (Madeleine and ller 1954:466) notes that musicians were sometimes spared the ath penalty suffered by their brothers. It also mentions the ct that the early Hebrew traveling players (II Kings 3:15) were so metal workers and diviners who went from one community to other, playing and repairing as they went.

To the Hebrew, music and dance were a means of expression used r religious occasions or for non-religious occasions. The flute s the main instrument that was played alone. So for most music ere was a group experience and dancing, singing, and instruments re used to celebrate, worship, and communicate. Music was a ans of expressing unity as a group.

The Kamwɔ are also a musical and rhythmic people. They often me forth with spontaneous songs as a means of expression of elings. Songs are sung when grinding grain or hoeing or doing oup work in building or farming. For special occasions, e.g., r greeting a visitor or bidding someone farwell, it is proper to ng and dance to the accompaniment of the drum and sometimes also ringed instruments and flutes. Whenever there is a festive casion, there is singing and dancing. Such occasions include

market day, naming ceremonies, weddings, and funerals. When the
moon is full, the community often gathers to dance and sing to the
beat of the drum. The drum is used to accompany wrestling matches
and group games, indicating mounting excitement. When there is
drought, the people dance on the mountain to attract God's attention. The young girls traditionally made up songs about people's
behavior, and this functioned as a means of social control. When
someone was kind and generous they'd sing about him, or when someone slept with another man's wife they would sing about him. However, Christian songs to the traditional Kamwə tunes have become
so popular they they are replacing the social control songs. As
previously explained, the musicians come from the tradesmen caste
and are a professional group who play stringed instruments, flutes
and drums. They are paid for their services in food, clothing, or
cash nowadays. These musicians are sometimes hired to sing praise
songs in honor of special people. They make up the ballads as
they sing them. For these occasions, it is a performance and the
group does not participate in the singing. Women and girls,
especially, sing often, but men and boys also sing on special
occasions (except at funerals). Singing and dancing is a very
natural way for the Kamwə to express their joy and sorrow. Music
symbolizes for them a natural way of participating in a group,
oneness with a social group, expression of deep feelings, sharing
and confirming one another.

Music to the American is more of a specialized field. It is
not so much participation as enjoying those who are professionals
or who have special talent. Most of the musicians have chosen to
be such and received training. What one learns in training is a
skill for performing music created and written by others. Today,
with the use of guitars and folk singing, creativity and self-
expression through music are increasing. Group singing does unite
people for the moment but does not ordinarily have a lasting effec
Dancing does not often go along with the singing and, again, is
more a particular skill developed or learned strictly for purposes
of recreation or, in the case of professionals, to earn a living.
Traditionally, singing, piano and organ have been used regularly
for Christian worship. The use of other instruments is quite
restricted, and drums are almost never used. The dance has not
been used traditionally as a means of religious expression. In
general, music is used for relaxation, for group identification
(the kind of music one enjoys is a badge), for expression (as song
composed by specialists are learned and produced), for mood setting, and for religious worship. Music by the professionals is
to be appreciated and enjoyed by the non-professionals.

It becomes obvious that each of the three cultures here examined has basic presuppositions concerning the function of music,
the appropriate use of music (if music is used at all), who can

produce the music, when it can be produced, and the kinds of music needed. All of these must be considered when the church wishes to use music in a cross-cultural situation. The music must fit the values, needs, and basic assumptions of the local community if it is to communicate clearly.

We have illustrated the variance in worldviews with a command from Scripture and the use of music. An awareness of the specific worldviews involved lays the groundwork for clear communication. Since the communication process involves stimulating meanings rather than transmitting them, understanding the worldviews is crucial. In the next chapter we will focus on some specific communication results.

11

The Results of
Understanding Worldviews

The worldview of the communicator, that of the receptor, and
worldviews in which the message itself has come must be considered
as points of reference for effective Christian communication.
Since it is not possible to directly transfer or transmit meanings
in the communication process, understanding the variance in worldviews and building on that understanding will help insure that the
meaning stimulated is the intended meaning. We have already discussed the importance of the communicator, the receptor, and the
message itself in the communication process. Now we will consider
the results of understanding worldview in relation to the receptor,
the communicator, the message, communication forms, worship forms,
church structure, and leadership roles.

Worldview and the Receptor

I have chosen the matter of worldview as the main focus of this
document because it is often neglected. Because of this neglect,
the message often becomes distorted and the Christianity which
comes as a result does not fit the culture and has limited appeal
to the people as a whole. As already explained, when the receptor
restructures or decodes the message from that encoded by the communicator, he does so from within his own worldview. His experiences, values, conceptual framework, and basic presuppositions
are all at work as he restructures the message. Whether he continues to listen, or responds favorably, or changes his behavior
depends a lot on his own worldview. By consciously focusing on
the receptor's worldview and seeing him in his sociocultural context, the communicator can encode the message in such a way that
it can be clearly and easily understood.

In order to teach Jesus' command, "Love your neighbor as your-self" (Matt. 22:39), much receptor-worldview-information needs to be considered. Questions like these must be investigated: What kind of commitment is involved in expressing love in this culture? What existing relationships involve love already? What are the important ingredients in expressing love--exchange of material goods, spending time together, being available when needed, shar-ing the workload? Who is considered a neighbor in this society?

The values of the receptor culture must be built upon in order to have effective communication. Today, throughout Africa, many groups of people are in search of their "ethos," their unique being, their essence. The people are becoming disillusioned as they real-ize that the ways and values of outsiders will not fully serve them. Recognizing this, many are in a search to discover the essence of their traditional cultural forms. As the cross-cultural worker recognizes this struggle within the worldview, he can present his message in a way that will be acceptable or appealing to the receptor. To know that one can remain a Kamwə and still be a Christian is important. Foster, in discussing technological change, recognizes the importance of the values of the people:

> ...the technical specialist...who knows his host country
> and the local symbols of primary importance, can both
> avoid mistakes and capitalize on opportunities that
> would otherwise be missed...a specialist familiar with
> local nationalistic symbols may see ways to arouse
> enthusiasm for a community project by organizing it
> around a traditional fiesta, or by using puppets who,
> in language, costume, and wit, epitomize the group's
> self-image. When a specialist knows what people are
> proud of and understands why, he sees innumerable ways
> for using this knowledge to help them through the
> process of change (1973:75).

The worldview of the receptor culture should influence the way in which Christianity is presented. When western (Christian) schools were established to reach out to the Hausa (Muslim) society, they were unsuccessful because of the Hausa worldview. The Hausas believed in and operated Koranic schools and they saw no need for what they saw as inferior western schools that taught an inferior western ideology. However, today they are more open to western schooling because they see the job opportunities open to the westernized segment of their country.

The worldview of the receptor culture should influence the choice of the words and concepts employed in communicating the gospel. Nida illustrates this from Scripture itself in the use of the phrases "kingdom of heaven" and "kingdom of God" among the Jews. There was a reluctance among the Jews to use the personal

name for God. Sometime prior to the time of Jesus, the use of
Jehovah had become taboo, and it was no longer uttered by the
people. As a result, linguistic substitutes were used--"the
Almighty," "the Holy One," "Heaven."

> It is not strange, therefore, that the Gospel of
> Matthew, which was directed to the Jewish constitu-
> ency, should use a substitute type of phrase, and
> it is equally understandable that Luke, who was
> intent upon explaining the true character of
> Christianity to people of Greco-Roman backgrounds,
> should use the phrase "kingdom of God" if he were to
> be understood (Nida 1960:38).

He also explains that in the early church both phrases were used
almost interchangeably depending on the participants in the communication.

Worldview and the Communicator

As discussed above, the communicator needs to be aware of his
own worldview in order to control interference from it when communicating with a person who has a different worldview. It is
possible to use all the right words and grammar to express a concept, but fail in communication because the basic presuppositions
are wrong. The communicator's worldview affects how he understands
Scripture. Western interpretations of the Word often hold that
denominational groups of Christians are acceptable. But to per-
petuate African tribal groups within Christianity is often considered unacceptable for we say "the Bible says that we are one in
Christ" (John 17:21, Eph. 4:4).

Tippett cites (in an undated paper) another problem that arose
as a result of misunderstanding based on the communicator's worldview.

> The early New Zealand nativistic Hauhau movement
> used the Bible to its own neo-pagan ends, justi-
> fying it on the score that if Anglican, Wesleyan
> and Roman Catholic interpretations were justified,
> so was a Maori one. They accepted the Bible as
> the word of God and norm for faith and practice,
> but the missionary advocate's denominational com-
> prehension out of foreign religious controversy
> led the converts into heretical syncretism based
> on Maori mythology (see also 1971:59-73).

If the missionary could have shown by his words and actions that
he felt a oneness with the other denominational groups, a oneness
in God as all are seeking to serve Him, the nativistic Hauhau

movement might have been able to cooperate at a certain level and to see themselves as ministering to a segment of the population that was not attracted to the other denominations. The focus needs to be on the commonalities in belief and practice, rather than on specific doctrinal differences and denominational distinctives.

The worldview of the communicator should be understood as a jumping off place. One should recognize it and use it carefully, all the time broadening one's perspective and focusing on where the receptor is in his own worldview. As one makes an effort to understand another person's worldview, he becomes established in the learner role. Feedback can give a lot of information if the communicator is tuned in and learning. A conscious attempt on the part of the communicator to share the receptor's point of view develops a healthy respect for the receptor and paves the way for meaningful interaction.

Worldview and the Message Focus

The worldview that underlies the form of the biblical presentation of the message, and its relation to the receptor's worldview influence the way in which the material is immediately understood by the receptors and the amount of explanation that is needed to make it understandable. For instance, the story of Ruth and how the elders in her in-laws' family arranged for a second marriage after her husband's death would need no lengthy explanation to the Kamwə. They have similar customs and the relatives have an obligation even as the Hebrews did to "raise up the name of the deceased on his inheritance" (Ruth 4:5). Much more explanation of what was going on is needed for those with a western worldview. But just because the communicator from the West needs explanation does not mean the non-westerner does.

Where Greco-Roman worldview assumptions underlie the form in which the message is presented, the non-westerner has difficulty. An example of a teaching that shows this philosophical orientation is Galations 2:20 (NASB), "I have been crucified with Christ; and it is no longer I who live, but Christ lives in me; and the life which I now live in the flesh I live by faith in the Son of God, who loved me, and delivered Himself up for me." Crucifixion speaks of an unknown means of punishment and the Kamwə would find this figurative use of it difficult to follow. The idea of the Christian no longer living but Christ in him might be hard to grasp when presented in that Greek-oriented form. The only spirit that actually lives in a person from the Kamwə point of view, is the vwə spirit which is in certain people not by choice, but at birth and throughout life. However, if the individual does not use it for evil, it can be used for good. The Western philosopher can say, "I no longer live...I now live...," but for those with an African orientation to daily living, it is not easily understood.

In order to understand the meaning of Scripture, one needs to understand the worldview of the people with whom God was working. For through the ages God has worked through culture to bring human beings to Himself.

Worldview and Communication Forms

The values and basic presuppositions of the receptor culture need to be considered in choosing relevant communication forms. Willoughby long ago recognized the importance of the local forms of expression in his work with the Bantu:

> Prayers are dramatized as well as spoken. To a primitive people, action is as natural as speech, and gives vent to overcharged emotions as nothing else can do. Dancing and singing go together, "Songs of war and other sad occasions," said a Mosuto to me, "are the only ones not sung with the feet." Like living chiefs, discarnate spirits are often greeted with the clapping of hands and that shrill ululating cry that African women know so well how to utter. People of the old Kongo kingdom chant the virtues of the spirits, to the accompaniment of drum, harp, and trumpet, always concluding their praise with the clapping of hands--an indispensable "Amen" (1928:369).

If Christianity is to meet the needs of the African and to provide a faith that allows him to feel "at home" it must include local communication forms. I have observed the effectiveness of Christian songs (with the local tunes) carrying the message of Christ to Kamwə areas where they had never heard of Christ before. The songs were originally composed for use in church, but because they were such a natural expression of the Christian faith, and because of the role of music in the culture, the Christians sang them on the road, in their homes, when working, and at informal get-togethers. Non-Christians began to learn them, too, and one day when the evangelist got to a remote village for the first time he discovered that the Christian songs as they were "sung with the feet" had come long before and the door was opened to explain who Christ is.

The local communication system should be examined and used as much as possible for the communication of the Gospel. Having most of the Christian activities in the church building (based on western worldview and lifestyle) may not be the best for a face-to-face society. The church is to be people. It may be, therefor that men's meetings should be held in front of the house of the most respected man where men regularly gather after the day's work on the farm, rather than in a foreign, impersonal "church" buildin

The role of dialoging and monologing within the society should
ʲe investigated. Who monologues and on what occasions? What are
ʰe qualifications of the one who monologues? When is dialogue
ʳsed and who participates? Among the Kamwə the chief, the elders,
ʰe prophet, the diviner, and the storyteller all use monologues
ffectively for stating the facts. However, after the facts are
ʲtated, there is ordinarily opportunity for dialogue. This inter-
ʳction, though, must follow the culturally patterned structuring
ʲf social relationships. This means that certain people do not
ʳctively participate on certain occasions (such as children or
ʷomen at a public meeting where the elders and/or the chief are
ʲresent). This pattern could usefully be followed. The church
ʲeader could state the dogmatic facts of Scripture in monologue
ʲashion and then open the meeting to dialogue as a means of lead-
ʰng the people toward an understanding of the significance of the
ʲacts. However, the old men are the wisdom of Kamwə society and
ʰeir presence must be noticed to give them the respect that is
ʲue. When a young man with a gospel message uses the monologue
ʲpproach without acknowledging the presence and importance of the
ʲlders he is insulting them.

Tippett sees dialogue as an instrument for bringing together
ʲarties who either misunderstood each other or were alienated. He
ʲees dialogue as a possibility between persons, or between the
ʲastor and his congregation, or between religion and culture,
ʲetween the world and the Church, or cross-culturally between faiths.

> ...if I speak and do not listen that is <u>monologue</u>,
> but if I am prepared to share in the experiences of
> the other party I may engage in dialogue...because
> I can learn from him in the sharing. Thus from my
> own missionary experience...my understanding of the
> Old Testament has been deeply enriched from dialogue
> with the Fijian people, and my appreciation of the
> meaning of sacrifice has been deepened by dialogue
> with the Indian Christian poet Tilak. In the area
> of forms of worship there is much that Christian
> missionaries might have learned had they approached
> their converts in dialogue at this point, and the
> young churches we have planted are much poorer
> because of our monologality (1973a:38).

ʲn many parts of the world the bulk of learning takes place through
ʲialoguing. If that is the basic local form for communication, the
ʰurch needs to consider limiting the monologue approach. Is the
ʲell-nigh exclusive dependence of western Christianity on monologue
ʲreaching Scriptural?

Understanding worldview provides a firm basis for using relevant communication forms. Teaching through the use of proverbs and story-telling times, emphasizing the involvement of the group, and scheduling fellowship and evangelism times according to the patterns of the receptor culture are all possibilities for communicating more effectively. The use of such means receives eloquent endorsement in the Scriptures.

Worldview and Worship

Worship needs to reflect the people's worldview in form, content, place, and time. Jesus, in talking with the Samaritan woman, took the focus off of where the worship took place and focused on how--"in spirit and truth" (John 4:20-24). This has to be worked out within the cultural framework. Westermann, on the basis of his missionary work in Africa, discusses Christianity as it is transmitted into African life, adapting African forms and using them for its own purposes:

> Old African life was rich in forms which brought
> colour and variety even into the tiniest village
> ...There are innumerable fine African customs on
> the occasions of birth, marriage, illness and death;
> in connexion with the education of children and their
> entry into the community of the adults; in seed-time
> and harvest, and the building of the house. Most of
> these could be preserved in a Christianized form and
> would contribute to the deeper penetration of Chris-
> tianity into the soil of Africa, thus saving the
> Christian from being cast adrift from the past of
> his own people. Both School and Church should make
> it their task to encourage and foster the old folk-
> songs, folk-dances, drum festivals, dramatic func-
> tions and other games, and thus preserve for every-
> day life something of its former colour and movement
> (1934:112).

In order for Christianity to be other than a foreign religion, African ideology and values must influence the forms of worship. The music and art used in worship should come out of the local culture if it is to be a natural and true expression of the worshipper to his God. If the people are accustomed to actively participating in showing their love of God and service to Him, the Church should provide opportunity for such group participation. African independent churches, for example, often ritualize the offering so that everyone takes his offering to the altar rather than being served by ushers. Seating arrangement in church should reflect the relationships between people as seen in the worldview. The formality or informality of worship should be related to people's values and presuppositions.

For the content of worship to be meaningful, it must be based n where the worshippers are in their Christian experience, their aily needs that God wants to meet, and Scripture as it relates o where they are. Tippett has made a study of the hymn selection nd the Scripture selection in the churches in the Solomon Islands. cripture choice among the Methodists strongly reflect the foreign issionary emphasis with didactic passages being the most important 1967:299). In church services and daily worship, the Bible is ore a norm for living than an aid to devotion. The hymns were ranslated by the missionary and, Tippett feels, emphasize the issionary's rather than the receptor's spiritual experiences. ippett observes that hymn collections are formative in developing he character of an emerging Christian community.

The size of the worshipping group and the place and time for orship, furthermore, will be most satisfying if they are based n an understanding of the people's ideology. The size of the roup to which one can relate in a meaningful way varies from ulture to culture. The location of the church building needs to e decided on the basis of how the people see themselves, their eighbors, and the Supernatural. In the area in which I served, he missionary chose a location for a church between two villages hinking that both would be involved. But in reality, these two illages did not have a good relationship, and the people never ot around to finishing the building. Later a church was built n the center of one of the villages along the main artery for eople going to neighboring markets. There it was successful.

Questions like the following must be answered in order to plan or relevant worship: When do the people feel a need for help rom the Supernatural? Are there reminders for worship already in he homes? When and why does the Christian need the help of the ocal diviner? When and how does family teaching take place? How o the people express joy and sorrow? How much is the group nvolved and what group is involved in times of sickness and pain? hat time of the day is it natural to gather? How is group unity xpressed? What kind of symbolism is used in pre-Christian con- acts with the supernatural?

Worldview and Church Structure

The values and presuppositions of the local people should be he basis for the structure of the church. Throughout the Bible e see God working with man using the social structure that the eople understood. Early in the Old Testament, the household eaders carried the responsibility for family altars and sacri- ices. Later the priests (a family being set aside for the priestly ole) were the ones to offer the people's sacrifices to God. They lso were responsible for the word of God. For a while, then, God

allowed a king to exercise spiritual leadership over the people.
God filled him with His Spirit and he was expected to study the
law of God and live by it. Prophets were used by God also to make
His word known to the people. They were called by God to speak,
live, and dramatize His word so the people could hear and act
accordingly. God used culturally meaningful expressions to which
the people could comfortably respond: dramas, miracles to show His
power, anointing with oil, washing to purify, ascribed status and
sacrificing in obedience to God's request. These were all customs
the people already had in their conceptual framework.

In the New Testament there is more emphasis placed on the
believer as being acceptable to God through Christ, having a priest
function (I Peter 2:5), and being responsible for service to God
and man. Leadership and church structure developed according to
the needs of the church. The disciples who were trained by Christ
were the founders. When a problem arose over the neglect of Greek-
speaking widows, the believers under the guidance of the Holy
Spirit chose seven men to take care of this problem (Acts 6). These
men were formally prayed for with the disciples laying their hands
on them in blessing. As the Church spread, there were not enough
apostles for each local church. The churches were placed under
the rule of elders and overseers who were appointed by God, anointed
by the apostles and recognized by the church as called of God so
that they might be able to accomplish the task they had been given.
Other leaders included prophets, who were Spirit-filled proclaimers
of the Word of God, and teachers who encouraged and helped build
the church. Paul and Barnabas were chosen by God to be sent out
by the church; and fasting, praying, and laying on of hands were
a part of accepting this special task.

In summary, leadership in the Bible follows existing cultural
models and is according to needs felt by the people in the situation. Ladd comes to the conclusion that one can't be dogmatic in
the understanding of the organization of the Pauline churches.
He says there was likely no normative pattern of church government
and that "the organizational structure of the church is no essential element in the theology of the church" (1974:534).

However, there are some very obvious constants in Scripture that
relate to leadership in any church and they are: 1) A faithful
waiting on God and a readiness to hear and obey His Spirit is
essential. 2) All the members of the church are God's elect and
are to be led by His Spirit. All the members have their special
call and personal ministry as a part of the Body of Christ. 3) This
Body of Christ, then, corporately through the empowering of the
Spirit, constitutes an organic ministry that renders service to
God. 4) Authority and leadership in the church must be God-given.
And human beings are His tools in commissioning those God-appointed
ones. 5) Pastors exist for the church, not the church for the pastor

) The Church exists for God. 7) The clergy and the laity are the
ame people and most of the biblical teaching deals directly with
he whole people of God in their relationship to Him and to each
ther. However, God does intend for the church to have leaders.

In examining the leadership patterns in Scripture, it becomes
lear that the church of the West is suffering from too sharp a
istinction between clergy and laity. The formality of religion
as sought to separate the sacred from the secular. Stott suggests
hat the laity today wants a building looking like a church, a
lergyman dressed suitably, services of the kind he's been used to,
nd to be left alone himself (1968:30)! In the early church the
aity was very much involved in ministry. Ephesians 4:11-18 refers
efinitely to the involvement of the laity. However, this separa-
ion has come gradually through the history of the church. In the
econd Century the institutionalization of the catechumenate took
lace; in the Third Century a ban on lay preaching occurred. From
he Fourth Century the pastorate was given certain state privileges,
mmunities, and titles. In the Fifth Century the clergy began to
ear special clothes. By the Eighth Century the laity no longer
nderstood Latin and the clergy began having their own language,
ulture, and liturgy. Lay preachers were an important feature of
ietism and of several Ninteenth Century revivalistic movements.
ut on the whole, Protestantism did not change the separation of
lergy and laity as much as it should have. Today the laity in
he churches in the West tend to hand over nearly all of the
bligations and privileges that are theirs by divine right as
hristians to the paid clergy to do all of God's work. How different this is from the call of God to the clergy to "service" the
aity (Stott 1968)--helping the people of God so that the laity
an do God's work.

Summary

Thus we can see how worldview can and should affect the church
structure and the leadership patterns within the Church. God has
ot approved of any single system as exclusively right. It is,
herefore, important to meet people where they are and to use
structures with which they are familiar and comfortable. Using
heir ideology as a basis results in a system they can understand
nd manage so that daily energy can be used for serving God and
hristian growth rather than simply in making a foreign system
ork.

As we have seen, understanding worldviews is basic to having
lear communication. Whether the worldview is that of the communicator, the receptor, or the Scriptures, an awareness and alert-
ess to it makes it possible to communicate Christ in a more meaningful way. If communication forms, worship, and church structure

reflect the values and presuppositions of the people, these people
will feel that God accepts them, loves, them, and wants to work
in and through them.

PART IV

Application and Conclusions

12

Historical Analysis
of the Kamwə Church

It is necessary that we now take a close look at the church that has been planted among the Kamwə. The Christianity that we will be investigating is that which was planted by the Chruch of the Brethren Mission.[1] In order to gain an understanding of the Kamwə church we must attempt to construct a picture of things as they really were and of events as they really happened. The way in which I will attempt this is to employ the method labeled by ethnohistorians as the culture continuum type (Dark 1957:233, 268). In this scheme an even balance is sought between the synchronic and diachronic aspects of culture. The synthesis is both spatial and temporal.

I will deal with three synchronic layers in a diachronic analysis in our attempt to understand Christianity among the Kamwə. Synchronic studies will be done for the mid 1950's, the mid 1960's, and the mid 1970's (Figure 16). I have chosen these periods because they represent points in time when I was present on the field and in the process of collecting data. These three synchronic studies will give insights into the development and growth of the church.

The Roman Catholic Mission has been working in the Kamwə area in Nigeria and the Lutheran Brethren in the Cameroons--each in areas not primarily focused on by the CBM.

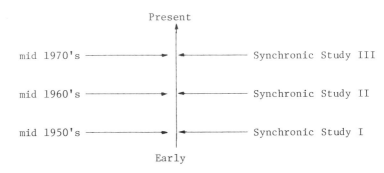

Figure 16.   Spatial and Temporal Synthesis

Synchronic Study I

The Christian work in focus here was first introduced to the Kamwə in Nigeria when several lepers returned from the leprosarium run by the Church of the Brethren Mission in Garkida about 80 miles away. Kraft (1976b) has described and analyzed this earl period of Christianity. The lepers had left the Kamwə area previously as very sick men with little hope for living. The discovery and use of sulpha drugs, however, resulted (in the early 1950's) in their release—either cured or to be treated as outpatients at a clinic near their homes. While at the leprosarium, these Kamwə men heard the gospel and had much time to discuss it and evaluate it in Bible study groups. Some of them accepted Christ and became ardent followers as He put new meaning into their lives. They sang Christian songs to the local indigenous tunes of that area. They got regular instruction in what Christianity was all about in this long period of social dislocation and freedom from pressure. They attended semi-formal schools set up to teach reading, writing, and Christianity. Some had purchased and learned to read portions of the Scriptures in the Hausa language.

The Kamwə never expected to see these people again because they were so sick when they left the area. When they returned in the early 1950's, people were amazed and listened to their story. Besides seeing that these lepers had experienced physical healing, they heard them share their new-found faith in God through Christ. The first advocates of Christianity were adult Kamwə men who had spent time in God's Word. They recognized that Christianity would be good for the Kamwə. They drew parallels between the Christian way and the traditional Kamwə rules against murder, stealing, adultery, jealousy, and cruelty. These sins were punished by the most dreaded of all the evil spirits--the smallpox spirit. The Christians emphasized cleanliness and the people responded favorably to this, too. They taught that God (Hylatəmwə) was supreme and powerful over the spirits the people feared. They composed Christian songs about their faith, using the indigenous tunes.

As the Christians told their story of their experiences with God, others became interested in becoming followers of Christ. As a result, they set up semi-formal schools like the ones they had attended in Garkida. At first the classes were held in the daytime and mostly children attended. But when parents showed an interest in the new ideas to which the children were being exposed, they requested an evening school. Evening schools were added with more focus on the adult population. In this way the Kamwə people were made aware of Christianity as a new option, were allowed to discuss it, ponder it, and attempt to decide how they felt about it. They were not pressured for conversion. At this point, some of these teachers were paid a small salary from funds available to a church in a neighboring tribe. But they still farmed and lived in a style comparable to that of the villagers.

At the request of the Christians in the area, missionaries were sent to live and work among the Kamwə in 1957. By the end of that year there were six official preaching points with semi-formal schools (called Christian Religious Instruction Schools). The next year the Christians were formally organized into two churches with the membership at 242 (102 members at Mbororo and 140 at Kwaka, Grimley 1966:151). At this point in time the rules and regulations of the church were a prominent part of the preaching in the neighboring Church of the Brethren area. Since the Kamwə Church was a part of the same church structure (Lardin Gabas) the rules and regulations could not be ignored. Kraft lists these rules and regulations as including proscription against: 1) retaining household images, 2) visiting diviners, 3) practicing polygamy, 4) drinking native beer, 5) showing reverence to ancestors, 6) gambling, 7) working or going to market on Sunday, 8) participating in indigenous funeral observances (1976b:440). Until this point in time the Kamwə were not aware that conversion to Christianity involved so much conflict with the indigenous customs. As the people began to recognize the heavy list of rules and regulations many felt that Christianity was too much of a risk and was really not meant for them.

Primary schools were started in the area by the mission at about this same time. Children who were beginning to be exposed to and attracted by western influence were often responsive to Christianity as well. Christianity was especially attractive to

the women because of the power of Christ over the evil spirits.
They were concerned about the safety and health of their children.
Since their worldview explained such problems as caused by the
spirit world, Christianity presented answers to this immediate
and real need.   Though many men were attracted to Christianity,
their worldview was in sharp contrast with these Christian rules
and regulations: status was closely tied in with polygamy, beer
drinking was a socializing experience confirming the hierarchical
arrangement in the society, the household head was responsible for
relationships with the supernatural (i.e., household sacrifices
and getting the help of diviners when called for) as well as
relationships with his clan which most certainly involved participating in funeral observances.   As a result, not many elders
really became church members.   The men active in church were
usually young men.

Synchronic Study II

By 1965 the Kamwə church membership was 3,337.   As the church
grew, the two organized congregations (with missionary assistance),
initiated and supervised sixty-five preaching points (each with
its semi-formal Christian Religious Instruction school).   It was
felt that the baptized members in four clusters of these preaching
points should now be formally organized into four new churches.
A cell-like division was, therefore, effected, resulting in a total
of six organized churches in place of and covering the same territory as the original two (Figure 17).

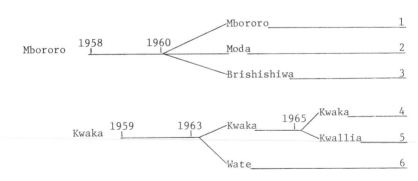

Figure 17.   Cell-like Division of Kamwə Church

A pastor was appointed to each of the six churches. These six pastors met together monthly to supervise and strategize for the work in the Kamwə area. Each preaching point (with its CRI school), then had an evangelist-teacher living in the village who met monthly with the pastor in charge of his area. Most of the pastors had Bible School training. The evangelist-teachers had at least four grades of school, and some had a Bible School short course. By this time, financing had become more local and very few evangelists were paid by mission funds.

There was still one missionary family living and working among the Kamwə. However, the western influence was limited by the fact that no missionary had stayed more than a few years in the area. The missionaries had encouraged the local preachers to do the preaching. The missionary who arrived in 1966 and worked in the area until 1973 felt very keenly that the Kamwə should be making their own decisions and supporting their own work. By 1968, he organized an Advisory Committee. It made decisions concerning the dispersing of church and mission funds for the work, and solved the problems that arose with the leaders. At first this committee was made up totally of Bible-school trained leaders. Later, however, Christian lay leaders came to serve on this committee as well. The need for laymen on this committee became obvious when the matters the committee dealt with came to include pastors' salaries, and churches needed to be asked to raise and sometimes increase the salary. In 1968, the part of pastors' salaries paid by mission funds was cut off and the pastors had to be supported completely by their own congregations. By 1969, a fee was collected from church members for obtaining funds for the Advisory Committee to distribute for God's work among the Kamwə.

A Wycliffe Bible translator arrived in 1967 to begin a translation of the Kamwə New Testament. The Hausa Bible was being used by the leaders (usually translated orally when read publicly) but the people as a whole had a very limited knowledge of Hausa and especially so when teaching Christianity's deep life-transforming concepts. However, the Bible School training had been in Hausa and the church had come to use many Hausa terms, i.e., <u>adu'a</u> "prayer," <u>taruwa</u> "meeting," <u>ekklesiya</u> "church,"[2] <u>tuba</u> "repentance," <u>wa'azi</u> "preaching."

---

[2]The inadvisability of borrowing this word from Greek becomes more obvious when used among non-native Hausa speakers. In a non-native context it loses even the slim basis that native Hausa speakers have for determining its meaning.

Nigeria became an independent nation in 1960 and gradually
through the 60's the local church was given more and more authority.
In 1968, the mission primary schools were taken over by the government. However, since religion is one of the subjects taught in the
school, the local church leader teaches Christianity in the School.
The organization of the church is not indigenous, but the Christian songs used in the church and informally out of church are
indigenous. Often village church groups meet, seated on the ground,
under a tree near the CRI School. The witness of Christians is
indigenous. They all live at home with their people and daily
come in contact with non-Christians. Unfortunately, however, the
approach for converts has been on an individual basis.

The Women's Organization, "a voluntary association" (Weber[3]
1947: and Little 1970), was organized in the mid 1960's and became
very strong and important for the growth of the church. The
women meet weekly for singing, Bible study, and prayer. They raise
funds for the work of the church and they give testimony as a group
in the market place. All the women of the area get together for a
three-day celebration once a year, and this is the highlight of
their program.

The church faced administrative problems in this period. The
mission rule was that only ordained elders could administer the
Communion and baptize new converts. There were only two elders
for the sixty-five preaching points, so each church could have
Communion and baptismal services only about twice a year. Also,
with the church growing so fast, there was a shortage of leaders
for the most effective and essential follow-up work after conversion. There also were leadership problems in getting some of the
graduates of the Bible School to return to their home areas after
they finished their training. If they came from the mountains,
they wanted to live and work on the plains so they could get and
use oxen and plow for farming. This was a means of showing the
prestige of training and their new status in the society. There
were continual problems for the individual Christian as his family
put pressure on him to do such things as donate a chicken for a
family sacrifice, take a second wife, and participate in traditional celebrations. The trained pastors of the area churches
dealt with these problems and advised the people.

---

[3]Weber defines <u>verein</u> (voluntary association) as "a corporate
group originating in a voluntary agreement and in which the
established order claims authority over the members only by vir-
tue of a personal art of adherence" (1947:151).

Synchronic Study III

By 1975 the Kamwə church membership had reached 7,500. These
embers are organized into ten churches with responsibility for
pproximately 65 additional preaching points, each with its CRI
chool. The church continues to grow. From July 1976 to January
977, John Guli reports that 1,500 new converts have been baptized
personal correspondence). There are now eight ordained elders
eading the work. There is no foreign missionary working in the
rea and the church is mostly self-supporting (with the exception
f about $400 per year of outside funds for the literacy program).
he Ekklesiyar Yan'uwa a Nijeriya (Church of the Brethren in
igeria, previously called Lardin Gabas) of which the Kamwə churches
re a part (statistically just over one third) became independent
rom the mission in 1972-1973. They soon moved to set up a more
ocalized church structure by dividing into sub-districts accord-
ng to the three large tribal groups represented. At this time,
he Kamwə church became the Eastern District. One person was made
verseer of each district and responsible for the total work of
he church in that area. The Advisory Committee for the Kamwə
s still functioning and provides an important place for laymen
o share in the church leadership.

In 1972 a literacy campaign was launched and an emphasis on
iteracy has continued until today. The Church has taken the
esponsibility of teaching adults and children who do not go to a
ore formal school to read. The Gospel of Mark in the Kamwə
anguage came off the press in 1972 and the entire New Testament
n 1975. Other written materials in Kamwə include: Vecə
tyeengi (folktales, with old orthography), 1970; Tətəkə Jangga 1
first primer, new orthography), 1974; Tətəkə Jangga 2 (second
rimer, new orthography), 1975; a small covenant and baptismal
ook; God's Answer and The Christian Life, two small Scripture
ift Mission books for catechism use. In the 1970's there are
few more government schools in the Kamwə area, but as yet,
niversal primary education has not been put into practice.[4] The
overnment schools only include that section of the population
hat is within the established age range for school, so there will
robably continue to be a need for a literacy program.

---

he government has pledged to implement universal primary education as quickly as possible and steps are being made in that
direction.

In order to give training to more of the leaders in the church, in 1971 the Bible-school trained men were organized so that each trained a group of village evangelists to work as a team holding three-day meetings in the various villages for teaching the Bible and Christian living. More recently, two-month Bible Schools have been set up to train the lay leaders, and this program includes an advancement plan.

Times of celebration for the church, such as the dedication of the New Testament on January 1, 1976, include much indigenous expression of joy and excitement. The people come in village groups, many of them from many miles away, singing, drumming, and dancing. The rich Kamwə traditions are enjoyed by the Christians. There is opportunity for speeches and drama on these occasions, too.

The Church has also begun to come before God as a group to pray when there are problems such as drought. The chief and elders traditionally set aside a day of no work, with feasting, and sacrificing along with dancing on the mountain in order to bring rain. The Christians have not participated in this but now have set up their own service as a functional substitute.

In 1974 the leadership of the Kamwə church decided that poly-gamists who believed in Christ could now be baptized and become church members. This was a reversal of previous mission policy and makes it possible now for household heads and important vill-age leaders to be Christians. However, the church leadership positions still are geared to being literate and monogamous.

The Women's Organization is still very strong and attractive to the women who become Christians. They are an active group and carry much of the support of the church.

Summary

The indigeneity of the Kamwə Church had its beginning when the church was planted. Christianity was credible since it was brough by adult Kamwə men and it was similar at many points to the tra-ditions. The first teachers/preachers were laymen and their faith was expressed in indigenous songs. Most of the western worship, doctrinal, and organizational forms, characteristic of the other churches in this area, were, however, adopted by the Kamwə. In the mid 1960's, the Kamwə took more responsibility for decision-making and the supporting of their own work. This was facilitated by the fact that no missionary stayed long in the area. The women's organization became strong and fit well into the women's community as defined by the traditional social structure. Today the church is more on its own than ever with no missionary on the scene, a

Kamwə translation of the New Testament, an Advisory Committee to
allocate funds for the work, and largely local financial support.
Indigenous solutions to current problems have been developed in
such areas as the plan to have each trained leader train a team
of lay leaders, in adjusting the church rules so that they are
more culturally relevant, in the development of Christian prayer
services for rain in time of drought and in the harvest praise
and dedication of offering service. These latter are functional
substitutes for traditional group activities. They, plus yearly
Christmas and New Year's celebrations (the latter commemorating
the dedication of the Kamwə NT), demonstrate that the Church is
on the move and each year brings more of an indigenous flavor to
its development.

13

Introduction to Strategy

We have seen how the receptor reconstructs the message according to his worldview, how the communicator is affected by his own worldview in presenting the message, and how the Gospel message itself is embedded biblically in still different worldviews. The task of the cross-cultural missionary is not to destroy the worldview of the receptor, but to bring Christ into it. In order to do this he must understand the religion and worldview of the receptor and perceive the various needs to which the Gospel must speak in order to be understood readily and clearly. Tippett notes the importance of the receptor's value system for church growth:

> First, with respect to the initial acceptance or rejection of Christianity, the value system determines the natural disposition of a people to Christianity, as hostile, congenial, or syncretistic... Second, it should give him deeper sympathy with those to whom he goes, and indicate stepping stones along which he can lead his converts to higher ideals and motives that will be both meaningful and acceptable to them as outworkings of the step of faith taken at conversion. Knowledge of the convert's old value system is thus important at the level of follow-up after conversion (1971:156-157).

When working cross-culturally we cannot speak of our approach as if it were something ready-made that we simply deliver as a mailman delivers a letter. For it must be presented in terms that speak to the real anxieties and questions of a people in their cultural milieu. Garcia highlights the fact that the Christian message affirms and works with the receptor's culture to identify and emphasize those truths that our Lord may wish to make explicit in that situation.

> ...this Good News will come to its recipients as something that will affirm their own character as persons; they will discover that to be a Christian does not mean ceasing to be what one is. They will discover that Christianity can energize their culture and free them from their fears and cultural oppression (1973:27).

In emphasizing the value of the receptor culture, however, we must heed Tippett's warning that:

> In the non-Christian religions there are certain elements which may be described as stepping stones to the Gospel. At the same time there are other elements in diametric hostility to it. So the evangelist needs to remember these two facts and approach people of other religions with courtesy and sympathy, using the stepping stones to make his contacts, trying to understand what the other religion is saying, but at the same time guarding with care the basic gospel message he seeks to transmit (1973b:87).

The Gospel message itself must not be changed, though the dress it wears, the manner of approach, and the emphasis must all be relevant to the receptor's worldview if the true Gospel is to be communicated.

Kamwə Worldview

Before we suggest strategy based on worldview-oriented communication, let us review briefly the necessary backdrop to any study of the Kamwə worldview--the man-group relationship. The Kamwə person is seen with solid roots--only valid as a vital part of the clan group that defines his relation to all other people and to his environment. His family membership defines his behavior in relation to other Kamwə clans, to the non-Kamwə, and to those within his own clan. Being a Kamwə separates people within the clan according to caste, sex and age into symbiotic groups. Even though today these divisions are becoming a little less clear in practice (especially by the "schooled" youth), they are evident still in the Kamwə worldview.

In summary, the components or domains of Kamwə worldview, as has already been discussed in this book are briefly listed below.

Mountain Orientation

The mountain orientation of the Kamwə speaks of origins, security the supernatural, necessary provisions. The language still reflects the mountain in speaking of location, direction and movement.

Guinea Corn Complex

Guinea corn is more than the staple food of the Kamwə. It is seen as God-given, holy, used for ceremony and sacrifice purposes, and closely tied in with the individual's worth indicating the close relationship between the supernatural and the human.

Active Supernatural Forces

The Kamwə are aware of unseen forces at work in everyday life. These forces in the spirit world are responsible for problems of ill health, poor relationships between people, some social control, and natural disasters (i.e., drought), as well as for the riches and blessings man receives. So there is much activity with the spirit world in the form of sacrifice and prayer to keep a good balance so that life will run smoothly. Mediators and other practitioners guide the people in dealing with the unseen.

Personal Values

Personal values that represent the worldview and act as both regulators and maps for behavior include kindness and good character,generosity, good health, hard work and discipline, riches, peace and unity, honor and respect for the prescribed people. The ideal person has a corporate awareness that applies in reality to both the individual and the group. In reciprocal relationships within the group, the service role is corporate as well as individual.

The Need for the Kamwə Church to Consider the Worldview

To Insure Individual Growth in Christ Who Speaks in Kamwə Personal Relationships

It is important that the Kamwə Christian still feels like a Kamwə. His Christianity should be such that he feels at home in it. The individual is still a vital part of his own society. It is dangerous to be seeking after security in a foreign system where the measuring stick also is foreign so that one never really gets to where he wants to be. It is the obligation of the Kamwə Church to put Christ clearly in focus so that the individual growth that is necessary and expected is growth in Christ.

To Establish the Congregation (Koinonia) with Indigenous Corporate Unity

The group is all-important in Kamwə worldview. When one becomes Christian he still has the basic need <u>to belong</u>. Besides remaining within the local family group, it is important that the Church itself be a meaningful group. The individual before God is seen only dimly from the Kamwə perspective, but the corporate group before God is clear and functional. Reciprocal relationships and the service role must be considered for this new group. When the individual joins the group, a change in status and role expectation is involved and the Church needs to face this responsibility and to capture the indigenous idea of man's existence depending vitally on the participation in the group. God's Word is clear on establishing a group (I Cor. 1:9-10, II Cor. 8:3-5, I Jn. 1:7, Eph. 5:18-24). This group is multi-individual in its makeup and multi-interactional in its nature and function.

To Bring about Directed Change that is Meaningfully Acceptable

The missionary, the local Christian leaders, and the zealous Christian witness are all change agents in a changing society that is more in touch with the outside world than ever before. Arensberg and Niehoff setting forth the basic cultural factors that need to be understood to successfully direct change include felt needs, local environment, motivation, social structure, religion, participation of recipients, and timing of introduction. They state that, "Technicians have given too much emphasis to the technical aspect of their jobs and not enough to the human aspect" (1964: 9). The same kind of thing could be said about much Christian work. For any change to be meaningfully acceptable, it is essential that it be closely in tune with the worldview of the receptors.

To Make Christianity Flexible and Satisfying in a Relevant Indigenous Way

The Kamwə Church needs to consider seriously this worldview in order that Christianity be made an attractive option for all the people. The Gospel, until recently, has been appealing to the segment of society that is westernizing. In order for the Gospel to speak to a broader segment of society, it will be necessary to remove the western dress.

I would not want to suggest that we return to pre-Christian days for our vision of what the Kamwə Church should be, but rather seriously look at present Kamwə worldview in both the rural and the town area. Because of the variety and amount of westernization in the various areas, the Church needs flexibility in order

to be relevant and satisfying to all. In the town, perhaps, the
present style of service may need little alteration. But is this
format doing the job in the small village? Questions like these
need to be asked of all areas: What does Christianity have to
offer the Kamwǝ? What are the areas where Christians are struggling
Can the Church help meet these needs? What are the obstacles that
keep men from accepting Christ? What does the Bible say about
these issues?

To Develop Indigenous Faith and Practice

Christianity has entered the Kamwǝ area as a foreign system of
faith. Sometimes acceptance of Christ puts a superficial veneer
on one's life, but the Gospel is meant to have a deep life-changing
effect on man. For this to happen within a person or a group,
there must be a searching of the Scriptures under the guidance of
the Holy Spirit. As one's faith grows, the behavior and practice
of that faith is an outworking of the inner experience. This provides excitement and motivation for further growth of the faith.
As human beings, either as individuals or as corporate groups,
place themselves before God, God will take them within their cultural framework and do great things with and through them. This
allows God to work without the western limitations.

To Further Spread the Gospel in the Cultural Framework

The Church needs to seriously consider the Kamwǝ worldview as
it seeks to further the spread of the Gospel. Questions like
these should be asked: What are the interests of the non-Christian? What does the Bible say to these? How can the presence
and concern of Christ for the non-Christian be expressed and felt
through the Church? What are the natural ways to approach these
people? Where are the natural ties of communication for reaching
out on Christ's behalf? Concern for the relation of Christianity
to the indigenous worldview is a vital part of the mission of the
Church because the mission is to the world where they are.

To Capture the Family Responsibility Idea for a Sanctified Chris-
tian Ministry and Duty

The idea of belonging to a family and fulfilling obligations
within that group as well as depending on the group is a positive
value in Kamwǝ society. When an individual sins, the whole family
is affected (as in Ex. 20:4, 5), when there is blessing of God on
an individual, his whole family shares in it. When there is sickness and need, there are relatives who are responsible to help.
Even in the case of death, the extended family group provides for
those surviving (as in Ruth 3 and 4). In both youth and old age
the family takes care of all the needs. The various service roles

and the receiver-of-assistance roles are all intertwined. This
whole family responsibility idea, which is very similar to the
Hebrew system, needs to be taught as Christian from Scripture
and used in relation to Christian ministry and duties.

   Wolff used Deut. 26:5-10 to illustrate the fact that in the
different epochs of Israel's history the fate of the individual
in Israel was largely the fate of his people:

> The acknowledgment made by the former...when he
> delivered up his first fruits in the sanctuary is
> indicative: here the change over from 'I' to 'we'
> and back again to 'I' is typical of the fact that
> the history of the individual coincides with the
> history of God's people, in the changes experienced,
> in the troubles endured, and in the benefits enjoyed:
> A wandering Aramean was my ancestor; and he went
> down into Egypt...The Egyptians treated us harshly
> and afflicted us...Then we cried to Yahweh the God
> of our fathers...and Yahweh brought us out of Egypt
> ...He brought us into this place and gave us this
> land...And behold, now I bring the first of the
> fruit of the ground, which thou, O Yahweh, hast
> given me (1974:216).

Wolff sees man's destiny throughout the Old Testament as fourfold:
1) to live in the world (created a living being Gen. 2:7; Joseph
sent by God to preserve life Gen. 45:5; 50:20; need to choose life
Deut. 30:15-20; how to avoid death Prov. 13:14, 15:24, etc.),
2) to love his fellow-man (need to deal rightly and love man
Lev. 19:17f, Ex. 23:4f, Deut. 15:12-18, etc.), 3) to rule over
creation (over animals Gen. 1:26, 28; to cultivate the vine Gen.
9:20f; to be steward over the world Ps. 8), and 4) to praise God
(Ps. 8 and 145) (1974:223-229). These all focus in on man's service roles as well as his need of assistance from God to carry
them out. The family responsibility idea which is indigenous to
the Kamwə must be captured and sanctified in understanding the
meaning of being in God's family. If the new Christian sees his
following Christ as joining a family with responsiblities and
benefits, his Christianity will be tremendously meaningful.

Specific Suggested Strategy Based on the Kamwə Worldview

   We now come to the point where we need to lay down specific
strategy for the benefit of missionaries and national leaders
working among the Kamwə. We have listed above such needs as individual needs, the need for the group, the need for meaning, the
need for indigenous cultural forms, the need for indigenous faith
and practice, the need for outreach, and the need for a service

ministry. In the light of these needs we will now enumerate eight
specific strategy suggestions: 1) follow the homogeneous unit
principle, 2) present an integrating Gospel, 3) follow more indigenous leadership patterns, 4) use more Kamwə terms in the Church,
5) use indigenous communication forms, 6) use meaningful ritual,
7) use innovations based on current developments, and 8) develop
indigenous theology. I recognize that the missionary (or national
leader even) is not free to choose or require that these strategies be followed. I would hope that these specific suggestions
would provide stimulus for discussion and consideration by the
leadership of the church. My goal throughout this volume has been
to seek relevant ways to communicate Christ to the Kamwə. If the
indigenous leaders choose to use some of these ideas or find this
a motivation to create their own strategies to further the Kingdom of God among the Kamwə, I will be satisfied.

14

Strategy:
The Place of Indigenous Culture

The indigenous culture is the arena and also the pool of resources for a meaningful Christianity for the Kamwə. Adegbola suggests that the missionaries have only tried to transplant the Christianity and problems of western Europe of the 16th Century onwards:

> Can it be true that...Christians from primal
> societies, as in Africa, were not given all the
> possibilities and all the material that would
> have enabled them to make an appropriate selec-
> tion, and were therefore forced to seek to re-
> discover in their traditional religious rites
> some vital elements of the religious experience--
> such as the sense of total devotion, of being cut
> to the heart..., of deep symbolism, or of parti-
> cipation of the whole person in worship? Were
> they offered all the wealth of the tradition of
> the first millenium of the Church extending from
> end to end of the "oikueme," or were they pre-
> sented only with a dry, moralizing type of
> Christianity? (Taylor 1976:75-76).

Recognizing that there may be deficiencies in today's Kamwə Christianity we focus the strategy suggested in this chapter on the indigenous culture.

In striving for a more meaningful and lasting Christian exper-
ience we build, in this chapter, our strategy on the homogeneous unit principle, presenting the integrating Gospel, and indigenous leadership patterns.

Strategy Built on the Homogeneous Unit Principle

McGavran developed the homogeneous unit principle in the context of church growth. He defines a homogeneous unit as "a section of society in which all the members have some characteristics in common" (1970:85). Members of a homogeneous unit think of themselves as enjoying a common bond of unity and at the same time feeling different from others. In his analysis of growing churches he has noted that "men like to become Christians without crossing racial, linguistic, or class barriers" (ibid:198). He sees the many different races, cultures, and classes as a great "mosaic." They create a great dynamic that must be harnessed to effectively fulfill the mission of the church as set forth by Christ Himself (Matt. 28:19, 20).

The homogeneous units that exist among the Kamwə need to be considered in planning for the future. As has been explained in Chapter 2, the Kamwə feel that the individual can be nothing without the group. The most important group to which the individual belongs is the family unit. The Church must be careful not to extract the individual from the family unit, but to reinforce the family structure in these days of change. One way this could be done would be by having family camps which would focus on Bible study, emphasizing God's intent for the Christian family. Camp is a good time for discussion of problems and applying the Word to where the Kamwə really are. The Church could also easily sponsor community activities which would involve the whole family. The family structure could also be reinforced by giving offerings as a group.

Jesus emphasized the importance of belonging and acceptance in a group in his ministry. After healing the demon-possessed man, Jesus sends him home to tell his people what great things the Lord has done for him (Mark 5:19). When Jesus met and talked with the Samaritan woman, He sent her to get her people so that they might all hear His message (John 4). The parable of the lost son, as told by Jesus, stresses the joy in the unity of the family (Luke 15:11-32). The group emphasis is also evident as we read of the early church: Lydia and her household (Acts 16:15), the Roman centurian and his household (Acts 16:30-34), Cornelius and his family and friends (Acts 10:24-48).

The clan is another significant homogeneous unit in Kamwə society. Since historically each Kamwə mountain group was a related clan that represented a cohesive unit that often stood against the next Kamwə mountain group, care must be taken in the planting of churches. The villages that cooperate the best are those that have a common heritage. These are accustomed to working together and some already have leadership for the group. To demand that two villages that do not have a common heritage work together, share leadership, etc. is to know that much time and energy will have to be used to make it functional. And it may never work. It is better to use the existing Kamwə divisions for establishing churches.

Another homogeneous unit existing in Kamwə society is the caste division. The church has largely ignored this and on occasion offended the tradesmen by rejecting their services. At present, if the tradesman becomes like the commoner in diet and behavior, he is accepted by the Christians. However, still there is not much intermarriage. The Chruch has offended the tradesmen by refusing to hire them as undertakers and musicians at Christian funerals. The Church has pretty much ignored the skilled musician, hiring him perhaps for weddings only. It seems that this situation should be studied by the Gunduma (District) Executive Committee (previously called the Advisory Committee) and some changes be made. Perhaps the Church could sponsor activities that would require their services and hire them, or at least give them opportunity to donate their skills for Christ's work. The commoners do not want to touch a corpse, so at present the pastors are functioning as undertakers as well. This is seen as competition by the tradesmen. The traditional symbiotic relationship between the castes should be recognized and accepted as it now exists in Kamwə society. I have previously mentioned in Chapter 7 the recent changes in their role.

The homogeneous unit principle speaks to the importance of the group of elders in the society, too. Since they are the wisdom and backbone of the society, the Church must deal with them as a group and be careful not to slight them. The section on leadership strategy at the end of this chapter deals with this issue. By recognizing the importance of the elders and setting an example by showing them the respect they deserve, the Church can help bridge the gap that is becoming evident between them and the 'schooled" youth. The elders could be used as resource people in the teaching of the youth and the young person can be reminded by the Church of the rich heritage that is theirs in the elders.

Other homogeneous units that must be considered are the male community and the female community. The women's organization has already proved successful as it meets the needs of the women specifically. However, a men's group has not yet been established to meet the specific needs of the men. Such a group might focus on such things as Christian involvement in community affairs, farming techniques, group ownership of a plow and oxen so that all might benefit, and discovering meaningful things as they study God's Word together.

Recognizing the existing homogeneous units in these changing times is a way the Church can be in touch with the individual's needs. A continual emphasis on reciprocal responsibilities based on relationships, especially kin obligations, will help the Christian to be seen as a responsible person in the community and will help communicate a Christ who cares.

One further consideration related to the homogeneous unit. Wagner notes the importance of the Church group composition in relation to church growth:

> For optimum conditions of growth, the group com-
> position of the congregation needs to be compatable
> with the felt needs of the unchurched people in the
> community for social companionship. Unchurched
> people presumably know nothing of 'oneness in Christ,'
> as Christians do, and thus lack the spiritual moti-
> vation that Christians might have for developing
> close associations with people of other homogeneous
> units. For this reason heterogeneous churches which
> are adding new memebers from their community are
> atypical (1977:27).

This says that the group composition of the congregation affects what people are attracted to that Church. Heterogeneous churches often fail to attract the unchurched. In a town situation such as Michika, where there are traditional people and also more intellectually-oriented people, there may be a need for two church groups. This need may be met by having two services with one speaking to each of the homogeneous groups specifically. Or it may be more effective for each to have its own place of worship and be a distinctive group so the more traditional leaders have opportunity to lead.

Strategy Built on Presenting an Integrating Gospel

Having examined the homogeneous units that exist within the Kamwə worldview, now we will look at the need for Christianity to be presented in such a way that the whole person can be reached and used in Christ's service.

Traditional religions in Africa permeate all parts of life. Mbiti expresses it this way:

> Wherever the African is, there is his religion:
> he carries it to the fields where he is sowing
> seeds or harvesting a new crop; he takes it with
> him to the beer party or to attend a funeral cere-
> mony; and if he is educated, he takes religion with
> him to the examination room at school or in the

> university; if he is a politician he takes it to
> the house of parliament. Although many African
> languages [Kamwə included] do not have a word
> for religion as such, it nevertheless accompanies
> the individual from long before his birth to long
> after his physical death (1969:2).

Since the Kamwə already feel very close to and dependent on
supernatural beings, it is very important that the organized
Church not divide up life in such a way that one may be "Christian
on Sunday" with the rest of life not so important as long as one
is in church on Sundays. In western thinking, there is compart-
mentalization in all of life (i.e., politics, religion, social
structure, economics, etc.). In the Kamwə worldview people are
seen as interacting continually with supernatural and human
beings.

The world of the Kamwə is still a whole. Every daily act is
colored by his conceptions of the supernatural forces, ever present and ever threatening. If Christianity is to speak meaningfully, the emphasis must be on the daily walk with God. For this
reason the Old Testament picture of God loving and desiring to
lead His chosen people who resist and are sidetracked in their
daily activities would be very meaningful. God's patience and
long range goal for humans is made clear in his dealings with the
Hebrew nation. Proverbs 3:5, 6 speaks to the need for all people
to acknowledge God and follow His direction. Some New Testament
passages that speak of the presence and power of God for the
whole person include Phil. 4:13, Eph. 3:16, and I John 3:23, 24.

This daily walk with Christ can be encouraged and assisted if
the activities of the Church are based on the felt needs of the
people. This study of worldview shows how the individual/family
experiences the need for help outside of himself in times of sickness. The Church leader or dedicated Church layman trained in
helping out and praying over the sick needs to be available and
involved when the Christian faces sickness. Prayer for God's
power, guidance, and assistance as well as advice on what to do
next is needed at this time. Then when one is well again is
another natural time for praising God and sharing earthly goods
with Him. There will be times when the whole church community
needs to be involved in supporting a sick person in prayer as well
as praise for healing.

In order to help the Kamwə be constantly aware of his relationship to God and to practice his faith daily, functional substitute will have to be found for old forms, lest cultural voids
develop (e.g., those created by no longer needing to appease the
spirits). Tippett explains how Christian worship in Melanesia

had to supply forms that were culturally appreciated while also
fulfilling equivalent social functions to certain pre-Christian
forms. The Anglicans used a simple liturgical unit that served
as a natural step from animist food-production and fishing ritual
to its Christian counterpart.

> Leader: Let us pray for God's blessing on the fruits of
>   the earth and the labours of men.
>
> Congregation: The eyes of all wait upon Thee, O Lord!
>   And Thou givest them their food in its proper time.
>
> Leader: Bless, we pray Thee, O Lord, all those who work in
>   the gardens or fish in the sea, that we may safely
>   gather in the crops of the earth and the food of
>   the waters; and grant to all planters and traders,
>   and to all who sail in the ships and work on planta-
>   tions, that they may receive a fair reward of their
>   work, and may praise Thee by living according to Thy
>   will; through Jesus Christ our Lord. Amen (1967:
>   269-270).

This Christian liturgy serves as a <u>functional substitute</u> for pre-
Christian incantations and charms that called on some ghostly
aid to make labor expended in the fields and at sea effective.
It is a substitute because it satisfies a felt need, but it also
provides for involvement in worship on the part of the individual
and group.

Although the Kamwə Church now uses very little liturgy, perhaps
it should consider liturgy for meeting specific needs in the life
of the people. The use of liturgy helps supply a connection with
God in times of deep need, provides for participation on the part
of the lay person, affirms oneness in Christ, provides expression
in a form that can be easily memorized, and helps integrate the
Gospel into one's total life. Liturgy suitable for worship services could include prayers for entrance and dismissal from
church, confessions, ten commandments with congregational response
and offertory prayer. Liturgy for other occasions might include
naming ceremony, house dedication, the bride's leaving her natal
clan, wedding, installing leaders in the church, funeral, planting, harvesting, and Christian celebrations such as Christmas.
In preparing the liturgy it must be kept in mind that at present
a large percentage of the Kamwə are illiterate. But a leader
could read the more difficult part and the congregation the
response if necessary. If the material were kept simple (for the
benefit of newly literate people) it might provide stimulus for
learning to read also.

The Kamwə Church must be sensitive to the natural times when the people gather for special occasions of celebration or calling on the Supernatural for help. These include childbirth, naming ceremony, marriage, house dedication, funerals, planting, harvesting, etc. If for some reason the Church cannot be involved in a given local festival, it is important they they have a functional substitute that meets the same needs for the Christians. These special occasions will also help affirm oneness in Christ. Loewen (1967) discusses the loss of festive life with the coming of Christianity and deals with the implications of this and the need for functional substitutes.

According to Kamwə tradition, every person has a place in the whole with appropriate responsibilities and duties. As a child grows up he gradually takes his place, integrating into the responsibilities of society. By the time he is old, he is wise and able to lead and make decisions for the group. The picture given by Paul in Eph. 4 and Romans 12:4-8 of Christ as the head and Christians as the body emphasizes the individual working parts that are necessary. Every Christian has some function in the body, and by discovering his gifts from God can and should find his place of service in the Church. It is important that the new Christian becomes integrated into the body of Christ and knows his place and responsibility in both society and fellowship. This status defined will help him give service to the whole.

Biblical Christianity ought to be characterized by being integrated and interdependent as the various members of the body of Christ are important to each other and to the work of the Kingdom. Care must be taken to move from integrated and interdependent Kamwə culture into Christianity (see Figure 18, Path A). It is much more difficult and cumbersome to guide the Kamwə to Christ via individualized and compartmentalized western culture (see Figure 18, Path B).

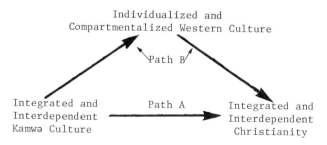

Figure 18. The Way to Integrated Christianity

Strategy Built on Indigenous Leadership Patterns

Reyburn deals with leadership in the Church and African ideology. He sees the importance of developing the right kind of leadership for the African Church. The well-trained leadership (by
western definitions) limits the possible number of leaders because
of the cost. Such leadership, however, often does not effectively
transform the society due to the distance between the leader and
the congregation. He sees the need for a lesser emphasis on
academic training for pastors and a more enlightened and rooted
congregation.

> The Gospel is a living testimony which must seek
> its roots in the lives of those who profess it, in
> their living, in their social structure, in their
> ideals and hopes. The roots of Christianity cannot
> go down far in any society without confronting in a
> truly startling fashion human traditions. If Chris-
> tianity finds its roots, it does so because it chal-
> lenges and questions every aspect of the soil in which
> it seeks its rooting. This in no way implies that
> Christianity is merely a sociological institution,
> but it does imply very strongly that a Christian lives
> and witnesses to his conversion in terms of a society
> and cultural form. This is the medium of his com-
> munication. This is the area of his Christian respon-
> sibility (1957:165).

> The present climaxing rise of nationalism and inde-
> pendence does not at all guarantee that the Cameroun
> churches will become independent and strong churches.
> What it does mean is that the church must move to
> the level of its own sociological reality. When it
> can see (as individuals) that what it has preached
> for so long can and must be applied in living witness
> to African values and social structures it will find
> the frontier along which it must battle for its true
> existence...it must be said that the church of the
> Cameroun [or the Kamwə] cannot begin to set down its
> Christian roots until it plants them in its own human
> soil. It may take many years before these roots can
> produce the fruits of a vital Christianity. However,
> without such a foundation there is little hope for an
> African church, a transformation of African society,
> and a living witness of Christianity in Africa (1957:
> 168-169).

For the Church to be rooted in Africa instead of in a foreign ideology, the indigenous base must be within the social framework of the people and leadership is an important issue.

Due to the fact that the Kamwə church is growing so rapidly, leadership continues to be a major concern. Up until the present, the standards for leadership have been on the basis of Western norms and most of the leaders are men between the ages of 20 and 40. The indigenous leaders in the society have been overlooked by the church. Now that polygamists are accepted into church membership, these local leaders come into focus. The fact that they have already proved themselves as able to lead, and that they already have followers, should make it worthwhile to use this ability and talent in the church structure when they become Christians.[1] Their status is both ascribed because of their age and achieved because of their experience and individual effort (Linton 1936). The wisdom of Kamwə society is found in the elders. It is important for the equilibrium of the society as a whole that these indigenous leaders continue in their present status and role.

---

[1] God seems to work with societies according to the existing patterns with which the people are comfortable. In the Old Testament polygamy was the accepted marriage pattern and we know that many of the great leaders whom God used were polygamists: David, Solomon, Jacob. The law even gave instructions for the polygamist situation regulating rather than condemning polygamy: "If a man takes a second wife, he must continue to give his first wife the same amount of food and clothing and the same rights she had before" (Ex. 21:10 TEV). At one point God told David that He gave him his many wives (II Sam. 12:8).

The New Testament is silent about polygamy. Only three passages, variously interpreted by scholars are thought by some to apply: I Tim. 3:2, 12 and Titus 1:6. The most culturally appropriate interpretation of these passages is that they proscribe "digamy," the remarriage of a man after his wife has died (The Expositor's Greek Testament, Vincent's Word Studies in the New Testament, Scott's Pastoral Epistles, and others). These are descriptions of what it means for the church leaders to be "above reproach." In Greek society where polygamy never existed (Westermarch 1922:40-50), being married to one wife and having children that one managed well along with a well managed household were required if a leader was to be "above reproach." Nowhere in Scripture does God recommend divorce. Being above reproach in Kamwə society would most certainly include managing well a household with many wives and children. See Kraft (1973a) for more detail.

Although the "schooled" youth do not directly take their cues
for behavior from the respected elders today, the elders still
have considerable influence in the amount and kind of change
allowed.

In order to use the indigenous leaders in the Church, the
requirements for such positions will need to be changed. At present, literacy is required and most of these older men are illiterate. A system that recognizes their strengths and abilities and
provides training bypassing the literacy requirement may be necessary, especially if they are not interested in becoming literate.
It is important that they not be viewed as second-rate leaders!
A special training program that supplied each of these men with
a reader (perhaps a younger person), like a "scribe" in Bible
days, could be organized and offered if these natural indigenous
leaders are to be used as leaders in Christ's work. This reader
would spend time regularly working with the leader. However, the
older man should make the selection as to who will be his helper,
what specifically in the Bible he will study, and thus be given
the role of decision-maker at an early stage in the training.[2]
This training could be done most effectively, I would think, in
his own village and by studying and leading at the same time.
Helps for organizing such a training program will be found in
"theological education by extension" materials (Winter 1969, and
Mulholland 1976).

The indigenous leader is measured by his congregation, not in
terms of his theological training or his ability to focus on the
abstract, but because of his capacity to meet the culturally conceived needs of the people in worship and spiritual as well as
physical matters. His ability to lead them in their own thought
forms and be relevant to their daily lives is essential. Other
places of leadership in which the indigenous leaders should be
used are as prayer leaders, serving the communion, and serving
on the local decision-making committee of the church. They need
to be able to participate wholeheartedly within the Church
structure.

The Church structure among the Kamwə reveals several levels
(see Figure 19). All of these levels could include the indigenous leaders. In fact, all of these levels _must_ include the indigenous leader.

---

[2]If a younger man is used he should understand that he is "a man
under authority"--he is not to be an authoritarian decision-
maker.

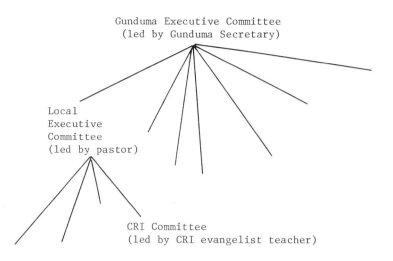

Figure 19. Leadership Structure of the Kamwə Church

There should be flexibility enough in the leadership structure for some groups to have Bible-School-trained men, others semi-literate leadership, and others strong elders who may be illiter-ate-- according to the make-up of the local Church. "Any growing church should supply its own leadership, commensurate with its social and academic levels at any given point in time" (Tippett 1967:335).

15

Strategy:

Focus on Communication

We have seen the importance of the indigenous culture, in general, in planning strategy for the Church. Having considered the homogeneous units, the integrating Gospel, and indigenous leadership patterns, we now turn our focus to communication itself. In this chapter we will discuss the use of Kamwə terms to express Christianity, specific communication forms in the society, the use of meaningful ritual, and the use of innovations based on current developments.

Nirmal, in his investigation of Indian festivals, sees feasts and festivals as an important aspect of any religion. He sees a two-fold purpose for these expressions: to keep religion alive and to affirm some religious or theological truth connected with them (1976:79). To him the main emphasis of the Christian faith has been on the "salvation or redemption in history" principle which makes Christianity unique. He sees the celebration of Indian festivals as the framework to proclaiming Christ and His message.

> Is not our God the Lord both of history and nature?
> We certainly affirm God's lordship over nature theo-
> logically in our doctrine of creation. But we have
> not translated this theological affirmation at a
> practical level--the level of worship, the level of
> religion. I believe that by adapting some of the
> Indian festivals we will be able to express our theo-
> logy of nature at the level of 'religion' and enrich
> Christian worship in India (ibid.:82).

e urges Christian imagination and experimentation in worship
ervices. "The question of 'what' is the question of 'theology,'
ut the question of 'how' is the question of 'symbolism.' Finding
uitable symbols is not always an easy task" (ibid.:83). We will
ttempt strategy for more meaningful worship with the focus on
ommunication in this chapter.

Strategy Built on Use of Kamwǝ Terms to Express Christianity

In an attempt to make a foreign message a functioning part of
he indigenous scene, the terms used are an important part of the
ommunication. Malinowski discusses the problem of meaning. He
llustrates how crucial it is to have words in their proper
ative cultural setting in order to understand the meaning.

> Instead of translating, of inserting simply an
> English word for a native one, we are faced by a
> long and not altogether simple process of describ-
> ing wide fields of custom, of social psychology
> and of tribal organization which correspond to one
> term or another. We see that linguistic analysis
> inevitably leads us into the study of all the sub-
> jects covered by Ethnographic field-work (Ogden
> and Richards 1927:301-302).

Nida sees the urgency of using native terms for expressing
Christian truths in Bible translating:

> A translator may know the meanings of the Greek
> and Hebrew with amazing clarity and yet fail to
> translate accurately because he does not understand
> the pagan religious vocabulary. The translator
> should know the pagan religions thoroughly. This
> may seem strange at first, for so much emphasis
> has been placed on Bible teaching on the mission
> field. This emphasis is correct, but the native
> words which must be used in teaching Biblical truth
> also have meanings in the pagan religious system
> (1947:204).

t is important that the people use local terms as much as possible
n talking about their faith, in the worship services, and in
heir reaching out to the non-Christian. God wants His message
o feel natural and speak intimately and personally to the Kamwǝ
eart. The more foreign terms used, the more Christianity is
going to seem like a foreign religion.

Christians often get the impression that there is something
holy and special about the Greek words themselves in the Bible.

If this should be true it is not because it was holy or special
when it was first used to refer to the Church. Ecclesia, which is
now translated "Church," in the First Century, simply meant the
lawful assembly of a Greek city state, comprising those with full
citizenship rights and excluding foreigners and slaves. Even in
Acts 19, the word is used secularly three times referring to the
assembly fixed by law. The word was taken over and used by trans-
lators of the Septuagint for the Greek-speaking Hebrews of the
Dispersion. Jesus used the term only on two occasions in our
recorded Scriptures, Matt. 16:18 and 18:17. But in Acts, it is in
common use. In I Corinthians ecclesia is used to refer to the
local church (1:2), the Church Universal (10:32) and a household
Church (16:19) (Tippett 1958:12-14). So we see a secular term
being captured for God and given new meaning.

This is what must be done more in the Kamwə Church. As the
Church seeks after expressions in the native language to describe
the borrowed terms, spiritual growth is bound to take place.
Tippett notes that in history semantic growth and spiritual growth
go hand in hand:

> Historic periods of spiritual growth have always
> been likewise periods of semantic growth. We see
> this in the words of Jesus, of Paul, of Augustine,
> of Coverdale and Tyndale, of Luther and Calvin, of
> Wesley, and of Hunt and Hazelwood in Fiji. Further-
> more periods of real religious strength growing in
> experience are reflected in semantic growth in the
> indigenous vocabulary, by the discovery and develop-
> ment of terminology with strong apostolic affinities
> (1958:59).

The Kamwə Church is still using many Hausa terms. Many of these
would be easily translateable into Kamwə. An illustration here is
the name for the women's organization, Zumunta Mata Ekklesiya,
which is a combination of Hausa and Greek. The non-Christian
women's organization has a Kamwə name Tsini gwa rə mbəgə myə,
"the gathering of women with their chief." The Hausa word for
offering, baiko, was used for many years but now a phrase meaning
"hand a thing to God," ncə kə wsi lə Hyalatəmwə, is used. Other
terms which could be investigated in order to find a Kamwə term
would be: addu'a "prayer," pasto "pastor," komiti, "committee,"
malami, "teacher." Much more research and study needs to be done
in this area. These terms may be understood by the "insiders," but
what do they communicate to the non-Christian? Since the purpose
of the Church is to communicate Christ to the world, terms which
the Kamwə regularly use should be used as much as possible.

The kind of development that takes place in Christian theology is closely related to the kind of vocabulary items that are used. **Borrowed words and concepts used in theology can result in totally** indigenous concepts being attached to those words with syncretism the most likely result. If the terms and concepts are largely indigenous with conceptual transformation through Christian teaching and use, the result will likely be indigenous theology. When foreign words are used they have their base in another culture. As a result, the meaning they take on in the receptor culture is often quite different from that which was intended. The denotative meaning can be taught, but the connotative meaning is often radically different. It may sound like another local word and that would cloud the meaning, or it may just be labeled as part of "that foreign religion," or it may be completely meaningless. Archaic Kamwə terms are as bad or worse than borrowed words. They are empty in meaning because they are dead.

As much as possible one should try to use the current religious vocabulary with its denotative and connotative meanings and begin to add new meaning or to reinterpret it from a Christian perspective (Nida 1947:11-30). An example here is the Kamwə word for God, Hyalatəmwə. The meaning as it was used in pre-Christian times was the Creator, an unseen being who lives far away in the sky, the true judge, one who is always there if you cannot get anything else to work in solving your problems. When this word was taken over by Christianity, more teaching on the nature of God and his relationship to man was required. But the Kamwə term shortened the teaching considerably even if the meaning had to be expanded. The term used for Lord is Tlamda. Its meaning is "the one in charge of the house, "master," "owner," "household head." In Kamwə society he makes decisions on behalf of his household, he provides for each member's needs, and they, in turn, respect him and seek his advice. So a Christian meaning has been added to a common, everyday term--it has been captured for Christ. The terms have been redefined and expanded--this is linguistic transformation.

There will be times when a completely new term will be needed. Such occasions include: names of persons and places, terms for socio-religious rites not practiced in the local culture (i.e., circumcision, concubines, etc.), government positions, law terms, war terms, unfamiliar occupations. When foreign words are used (i.e., names), they should be made to follow the phonological system of the language (i.e., Matthew becomes Matta in Kamwə). Sometimes two native terms can be combined to make a new term that will communicate (i.e., concubine being translated "lesser wife").

As the Church innovates, Kamwə terms should be used as much as possible. Since tsahwi is the family ceremony for thanking God, confession, and seeking His assistance in the traditional religion, why couldn't it be used for family worship in Christianity?

Now that the Kamwə have the printed Word of God, there will be more of a tendency to think and worship in Kamwə. Until now, all the leaders have been trained with the Hausa Bible and often in the Hausa language. Now is also an ideal time to begin studying the Word and seeking God's guidance in theologizing in the indigenous language. The doctrinal potential of the language needs to be discovered and exploited. The Christian leaders must seek native expression for God's truths and Christian concepts as they study the Word. The vocabulary must be expanded to be adequate for the Christian experience of the Church. Tippett sees this as "a continuity of the forces and factors that operated in the Apostolic Church" (1958:57), suggesting that:

> We have here a method of God's work with man. So
> much there is to glorify Him, which lies dormant in
> life, awaiting discovery, awaiting the right mind
> to discover it and give it to mankind. Nothing
> brings home this truth better than the study of
> biblical and ecclesiastical ethnolinguistics...
> (ibid:56-57).

The job of the Church is not to import foreign words to convey ideas that may be foreign, but to discover indigenous concepts to serve as the instrument for their expression. Besides capturing the language for Christianity, it is neccessary to capture the indigenous communication forms also.

Strategy Built on Indigenous Communication Forms

The communication forms used influence the message itself. Berndt distinguishes between the form and content, recognizing the importance of the forms used:

> As the water is the "content" which takes the "form"
> of the glass into which it is poured, so the content
> of the Gospel can take any number of shapes and forms.
> These can be the forms of architecture, sculpture,
> painting, poetry, drama, rhetoric, music, and the
> dance. It would be a dull Gospel if it came to us
> shapeless. In fact, it cannot. Conversely, there are
> no limits to the many facets in which the beauty of the
> Gospel can be brought out; this can be helped through
> the endless color and variety of the many arts in any
> number of combinations (1961:155).

Strategy: Focus on Communication

God has made it possible for man, His chosen creature, to worship
the Creator in many wonderfully different ways. In order for this
expression to be meaningful and to speak out to the non-Christian
Kamwə, the communication forms must be indigenous.

It is important before we go any further to recognize that a
good majority of the Kamwə (80 to 85 percent) are not functionally
literate. Many of these have not had the opportunity to become
literate, but many have no desire to become literate. I realized
again, when doing my recent research, that even some who had had
literacy classes found it an impractical skill and did not read
when they actually could. Perhaps the satisfaction gained did not
compare with the energy and determination required to read. Weber
describes the illiterate as a very skillful person with tremendous
ability to see--pictures, actions, significant happenings in
nature and human life, and with ability to "paint" in words a picture of the meaning. Character **description** from the illiterate
is done by storytelling.

> The Western missionary who had come to teach became
> the pupil. The longer he who had come as a literate
> among illiterates lives with these 'letter-blind'
> people, the more he realized that he himself was
> blind among those who could see; that he was a stunted
> poor intellectual with only one means of communication
> (through pallid abstract ideas) among imaginative
> artists who thought and spoke in colorful, glowing
> pictures, actions and symbols.

> If we were to pass on to illiterates the message of
> the Bible we must first liberate this message from
> the abstract ideas of our catechisms and doctrines.
> We must learn, and use, the illerate's method of
> communication. We must proclaim picturesquely and
> dramatically rather than intellectually and verbally
> (1957:18).[1]

What are these indigenous communication forms that need to be
captured for Christ and His work? I have chosen several to be
discussed as possible vehicles for God to use.

---

[1] This is true, of course, only as long as the fact is not allowed
to mean that literacy is not an essential goal for the Church or
an excuse for neglecting Bible translation or training a literate
leadership. This approach is important for the original genera-
tion of old people converting from paganism but subsequent gen-
erations may require literacy for survival.

Singing

As I have already mentioned, the Kamwə Christian songs are set
to indigenous tunes and the people love to sing. These Christian
songs are learned even by non-Christians and carried to areas
where no evangelist has yet gone. These songs are used when
people are walking as a group and when people are working. Rhythmic singing is common while the people do such things as mixing
mud for building, pounding grain, and hoeing in their farms. Individual Christians create the songs and lead as they are sung in
the worship service. New songs are being added and old ones
dropped all the time, so the songs meet the needs of the day. To
this point the songs have not been collected and put into perman-
ent written form. There might be value in recording them so that
the old songs could be revived at a later date or so that each
song leader would have a larger selection from which to choose.
However, since most churches have more than one song leader, the
prospect of running out of songs really isn't a problem. Since
some of the present song leaders are illiterate, a dependence on
written songs would make them feel inferior. It is important,
for the time being, that songbooks not be used for the congregational singing because of the high rate of illiteracy. I think
that the songs are learned more quickly in oral form. They are
more immediately usable outside of church by those who have
learned them if they are not dependent on songbooks. Writing the
songs might also inhibit the creativity of those who produce them.

Eventually, though, it might be important to record Kamwə hymns
in hymn books. Wiant writes about the success of the Chinese
hymnbook which included indigenous Chinese hymns:

> In spite of the fact that Christianity had been
> introduced into China in three previous periods
> it had not survived, mainly because it had not
> become rooted and grounded in the genius of the
> Chinese themselves or found any expression that
> was native to her culture patterns...

> The committee which had final authority in the choice
> of hymns gave careful consideration to the principle
> of Christianizing the ideals, festivals, ceremonies
> and functions which have dominated Chinese life over
> many centuries of her existence. By this process it
> was hoped that such hymns would be integrated into
> the very fabric of the life of the people. This
> ideal was successfully achieved (1946:430).

The book was bought by non-Churched folks who desired the high
moments and experiences of life interpreted in accordance with
Christian ideals and with Chinese patterns of life. These occasions

luded: celebration of first birthday of a child, celebrating
sixteenth birthday, memorial to ancestors, grave-sweeping cere-
y, wedding ceremony, funeral ceremony, home dedication, special
stivals, etc. Hoeing songs and boating songs were also written
replace secular work songs.

Klem tells of an experiment with the Yoruba of Nigeria in which
book of Hebrews was set to their folk music in order to com-
icate in a form the people understand and can respond to easily.
points to the fact that both the Gospels and the Old Testament
w that such use of poetry and music to enhance the communica-
n of God's Word are very Biblical. The results of this experi-
t showed that the use of traditional music to present the Bible
s not detract from what is heard or learned, that retention of
message is improved, and that the non-reading masses readily
ntify with the indigenous image presented. The response to
s method of those who can read is also very positive (1977:160).

In our own illiterate beginnings we have a beautiful illustra-
n of God's gift of poetry and song. The Venerable Bede writes
Caedmon, a stableman who was contacted by God in a dream and
ld to sing to the glory of God. He, untrained and illiterate,
le up beautiful songs (and verses) of praise to God. When he
s then given instruction in the events of sacred history, he
rned it into melodious verse: the Creation, the whole story
Genesis, Israel's departure from Egypt, their entry into the
d of promise, the Incarnation, Resurrection, coming of the
ly Spirit, the teachings of the Apostles, etc. "All...agreed
t Caedmon's gift had been given him by our Lord..." (680:245-
3).

By way of suggestion to the Kamwə Church, it would be good to
sider getting some indigenous Christian songs for use on
ecific occasions (as the Chinese did) when the people need to
lebrate, pray, or work. It would be worth experimenting with
tting portions of Scripture to indigenous music. This may be a
d tool for Scripture memory work. Certainly the Kamwə Church
to be commended for her use of indigenous music and encouraged
continue using it for furthering the Gospel.

uma

The kind of drama that is natural for the Kamwə makes great
e of role-playing situations. To dramatize Scripture is to know
e passage thoroughly, to know the situation in its context and
en become a specific character in order to communicate the mes-
ge. The drama is usually performed outdoors in natural surround-
gs. The spontaneous script and the local color makes the message
forgettable. The Bible really comes alive as the dramatists
ke it a real life experience free from the bondage of time and space.

Nida refers to John V. Taylor's description of a moving drama of the Fall of Man by three players at Buloba College in Uganda:

> Adam and Eve, dressed like peasants in bark-cloth
> were seen cultivating in the shade of a great tree.
> Adam became weary, and throwing himself down slept
> while Eve continued digging with slow, tired move-
> ments. Then, far away one small drum began to throb,
> menacing and horribly insistent; and to the rhythm
> of it a girl, swathed in a scarlet cloth, with a long,
> green train dragging behind her over the dry grass,
> danced out the Temptation. It was an extraordinary
> dance of undulation and slithering movement, with
> her two hands keeping up a ceaseless flickering at
> the level of her eyes. And opposite her Eve also
> danced her reluctant, frightened, slow surrender to
> fascination and desire. Louder and louder grew the
> throbbing of the drum, more intense the serpent's
> hatred, until Eve, who was already fondling the
> fruit that hung from the tree, suddenly tugged it
> from the branch and sank her teeth into it. At that
> instant the drum was silenced, and the snake slid
> quickly away into the surrounding darkness (1954:
> 196-197).

The Kamwə could do a lot more with drama in order to communicate the Christian message. Scenes from the Old Testament or the New Testament can be brought to life through the indigenous drama forms under the guidance of the Holy Spirit.

Dance

The dance is a combination of music, art, and drama. It was used in the Old Testament by the Hebrews and their neighbors. Berndt lists four possible reasons why the Hebrews danced: 1) honorific, 2) exhibitionary, 3) utilitarian (imitative magic), and 4) spontaneity (expression of joy)(1961:17, 18). He sees the dance as expressing the unity of body and soul and man's one-ness with nature. He quotes Weman in an African Christian's description of the fight within himself:

> We feel joy because we have flaming fire within
> us, and it comes out through our mouths. Some-
> times it is so strong that we are bound to dance.
> This fire, which has been in us since our creation,
> can be lighted in different ways. Sometimes it is
> lighted by the devil. When Satan is in charge of
> lighting, the fire comes out with sinful words and
> sinful deeds. When the fire is lighted by God, it
> comes out with praises to him for what he has done.

Therefore the flaming quality depends on the one
who lighted the fire. I think Satan is trying
his very best to win our praises.

As Christians, it is our duty to prevent Satan from
lighting that fire. In order to prevent him, we
ought to light the fire by the power of God. If
we do not do it, Satan will light it, because the
fire needs flaming. We must plead for God's power
in lighting the fire (1960:186).

Berndt continues:

However much missionaries may try, they cannot throw
out the African dance without wounding an entire
culture...This does not mean that the old cohesive
factor of the dance must be discarded and that the
new cohesive factor call "Christianity" must be
substituted. Rather, how much stronger the force
of Christianity could be if it were combined in
dance forms!

At first, they are shy of performing...But once they
are under way, they are transformed; broad grins
appear on every face, eyes begin to sparkle, arms
and legs begin to move, bodies sway gently and freely,
and hands start to clap the free rhythms. Now they
can be themselves (1961:140-141).

The Kamwə are a rhythmic people and dance is one of the most
popular indigenous communication forms. Many of the dances have
all ages of women (arranged according to height) dancing in a
circle and all ages of men in another circle. The dance is not a
spectator sport but one in which everybody participates. To my
knowledge, the Church uses the dance expression mainly to welcome
dignataries and for special celebrations (e.g., the dedication of
the Kamwə New Testament). I feel that the Church should reeval-
uate the dance and its use as an indigenous form of communication
which could be used more by God. Perhaps the dance should be a
vital part of the Church's ministry for by singing the Christian
songs with the dance, the message is presented in a form that
speaks to the mind and the emotions. This was the case when people
danced before the Lord as David did.

Oral Arts

Oral language arts are close to the heart of the Kamwə. They
take great pride in verbal skills. The ability to speak well is
one of the prerequisites for leadership. Proverbs and storytelling are used to teach, for they are a summarization of the great

oral teachings. In order to understand the proverbs one must
spend time sitting and listening to the stories of the elders,
for frequently the proverb is the summary of a lesson taught by
a whole story. The entire context from which they came must be
understood, since the meaning of proverbs is tied to their contexts. The Church needs to possess these oral skills for Christ.
Proverbs used in preaching would help drive the message to the
heart quickly and help in its retention also. Bible storytelling
could be used in the informal setting of the evening campfire.
The use of both of these communication forms would strengthen the
Church and challenge the Christian as well as create a Christianity
more attractive to the non-Christian.

Riddling is another oral art among the Kamwə as it was among
the Hebrews (e.g., Samson's riddle of the lion and honey). The
riddles have fixed answers and the listener is not expected to
be creative in his answer--it is more a matter of discovering the
answer rather than of inventing a novel answer. Riddling is used
more for enjoyment than for competition. Kraft, in his analysis
of the Hausa riddling system, makes the observation, "When one
gets to be a "Knower" of the riddles, both the question and the
answer parts, he passes, as if from one grade of school to another,
from the status of 'outsider' to that of 'insider'" (1975:19).
Finnegan recognizes that insight into the nature of people's
behavior is regularly expressed in riddles. This insight is communicated via images, visual and acoustic (1970:442-443).

Smith (1950) lists some riddles from Africa which refer to God:

1. "The small hole is full of God's creation."
    Answer: "Grain" (6).

2. "I brought a thing from God that cannot be taken off like
    an ornament."
    Answer: "Ears" (6).

3. "Which is God's tree that no one can climb?"
    Answer: "The reed" (234).

4. "What is the coloured blanket that God unfolds during
    the rain and folds up again afterwards?"
    Answer: "The rainbow" (234).

Could it be that the Kamwə Church might capture the art of riddling
for God's use? This vehicle has real possibilities, especially
for teaching biblical information. It may be a useful way to
teach children in the home devotion environment.

Klem, in his study of the use of oral communication of the
Scriptures, notes:

> This kind of identification through the use of
> traditional art is so highly prized by African
> groups that skillful use of proverbs and metaphor
> can count more than a detailed discussion of the
> facts of a court case. Such use of oral skills
> is regarded as valid evidence and a logical form
> of argument. It would seem that careful use of
> these figures and proverbs by an outsider would
> create a most favorable climate for his message
> to be heard with interest. To be without them is
> to be hopelessly marked as a foreigner who has no
> interest in the culture of the land (1977:98).

The oral arts provide a system for preserving traditions, reward-
ing group loyalty, expressing communal pride, spreading the news,
gaining social approval and enjoying a good time with friends--
all wrapped up in one (Finnegan 1970).

In the Apocrypha (Ecclesiasticus 44-50) there are several
long chapters recording the singing of praise to the heroes of
Israel. The hymn, "Now Praise We Great and Famous Men", which
we use, comes from this passage. Praises were sung of David as
referred to in I Sam. 21:11 and by David for Saul after he died
II Sam. 1:19-27.

The Kamwə also use praise songs in which they employ great oral
skills. These praises are sung to the founders of the clan, the
relatives who have gone to be with the ancestors, and people still
living. Often a praise-singer is hired to perform for a group.
Klem writes of the Yoruba custom of praise singing:

> A person may sing part of [a praise song] privately
> to give him strength and courage to face a crisis
> situation. From a psychological point of view it
> seems very well suited for helping a person to build
> a positve self-image. On public occasions it helps
> to build the individual's ego, displays his wealth
> and reminds the entire community of its historic
> roots. This strengthens the identity of the group
> and supports ethnic solidarity (1977:104-105).

Could praise singing perhaps be used on special occasions to honor
God, the ancestors, and the Christian, to give strength and support to church members, to strengthen the church family and cohesion within the body of Christ?

It is important that flexibility be maintained, since it is
characteristic of African oral art. The objective is never to
tell a story with the exact same wording and that may be why it
is always interesting to hear the same story but with the individual

oral art of the storyteller as a vital part of it. The artist
creatively rearranges and restates in picturesque imagery the
essential parts of the story so that each performance is a fresh
creation.

The Church must carefully use suitable indigenous communication
forms as she seeks to meet people's needs in the name of Christ.
Arising then out of communication forms we will deal next with
ritual.

Strategy Built on Using Meaningful Ritual

In order to plan strategy for the church it is necessary to
consider the meaning of ritual in the Kamwə worldview. Geertz
sees ritual as composed of sacred symbols functioning "to synthe-
size a people's ethos--the tone, character, and quality of their
life, its morals and aesthetic style and mood--and their world-
view--the picture they have of the way things in sheer actuality
are, their most comprehensive ideas of order" (1966:3). The world
as lived and the world as imagined are fused through ritual into
one. He emphasizes the fact that ritual provides the models of
reality (in the cultural worldview) and the models for reality
(in the social norms). So it is ritual that helps one feel comfortable when there is change of status on the horizon, crisis
(such as ill health), or a situation that is too big and important
for man to handle without help from the supernatural.

Monica Wilson sees rituals as providing a form for acting out
conflicting emotions and ambivalent desires. She sees rituals
as expressing: 1) transition or the change in status, 2) dependence, 3) reconciliation, 4) mutual sympathy and comfort, and
5) a social order with a hierarchy of rights and obligations
(1971:63-66). She sees ordinary people craving for the endorsement of important occasions by some power beyond themselves.

> The occasions of ritual are constant as we have seen:
> birth, maturity, marriage, death, public crisis or
> rejoicing. The individual, torn by feeling, needs
> help. He needs to be taught what to feel and how to
> express it...To refuse to celebrate any ritual at a
> crisis is in a sense a denial of dependence upon one's
> fellows; it is a withdrawal into oneself, an assertion
> that one chooses to be alone in grief or joy (ibid:126).

The Kamwə tradition is full of ritual--both personal and communal. Ritual prescribed by a society gives the individual confidence in himself when there is a change in status. It also
gives him stimulation to conduct himself with courage in his new
status. Personal rites of passage have to do with the stages of

life an individual passes through--childbirth, naming, initiation,
engagement, marriage, childbearing, old age, death. Communal
rituals include rain-making, planting, first fruits, housewarm-
ing, threshing. As we have seen in our discussion of Kamwə worldview the kind of ritual, the formula for the ritual, the performer
of the ritual, the place of the ritual, the prescriber of what
specific ritual is suitable are all outlined by the society.
Guinea corn is an important part of the ritual life of the people.

Tippett warns against leaving voids when one becomes a Christian: "Magic was involved in the very stuff of life and should
Christianity take the place of animism, these social services of
animism should not be left as voids in the daily life" (1967:12).
What is the Kamwə Church doing about ritual? She needs to study
the traditional ritual and cooperate where she can and innovate
Christian ritual to enrich the old forms or in substitution for
the old forms. But Christian ritual must be based on cultural
forms with which the people are already familiar. Among the
Kamwə, guinea corn should be used as often as possible. It speaks
of harmony and homogeneity, as well as of God's concern for their
welfare. If the church does not employ indigenous ritual, the
Christians will adopt foreign ritual that is not so meaningful and
quickly establishes Christianity as a foreign system.

Monica Wilson points to a major problem in the development of
new rituals:

> Rituals cannot be invented. Their impact is partly
> due to their antiquity or even timelessness. New
> symbols may well up from the subconscious and 'catch
> on,' in the way in which a new poem or song catches
> on because it expresses what the hearers feel; but
> equally, the new symbol or rite may <u>not</u> catch on.
> It is felt to be meaningless or irrelevant (1971:129).

Nida notes that Jesus insisted on inner motive--not external
behavior. Insofar as the Old Testament consisted of purely ceremonial and ritual ordinances, he abolished them by His actions.
However, He did not say that symbolism was wrong.

> Though Jesus repudiated the false claims of a per-
> verted ceremonial structure, he did not either in
> word or deed, violate any of the moral laws of the
> Old Testament revelation. Nor did he in any way
> suggest that symbolic behavior is wrong, for he
> himself instructed the symbolic meal of the new
> covenant. Nevertheless, he insisted that this rite
> was a commemorative event, not a magic medium for
> imparting mysterious power (1960:31).

The danger as I see it is that Christians be locked into foreign rituals that fail to meet their needs. If Christianity does
not satisfy, then there will remain a felt need to follow old
ritual patterns in order to be able to face everyday living. A
people who are used to experiencing reality through ritual may
find life quite empty when dogma and foreign ritual replace that
meaningful ritual. It would be far better to encourage indigenous ritual patterns and reinterpret them to express Christian
meanings. Recognizing that ritual to be meaningful must well up
from within, I merely want to suggest some possibilities to help
break down any barriers or blocks that may exist so that the
Holy Spirit can then lead and cause that creation of Kamwə Christian ritual from within.

First let us examine the format for becoming a Christian:
"covenant" class (six months), baptism class (six months), then
church membership. Perhaps it would be more effective if the
initiation format that the people are familiar with were followed
and the initiatory stages (separation, transition, incorporation)
described by Van Gennep (1960) were made more clear. The whole
body of Christ needs to recognize the separation. During the
separation time the leaders should give intensive training that
would include memorizing of Scripture and learning how to live
for Christ. At this time, the convert should be made especially
aware of the fact that the power of evil spirits over a person is
a thing of the past and that they are now ready to move out in the
power of Christ. Perhaps this transition period should take place
in one or two weeks with the group away from home (the church
already is used to camps and conferences and they have been successful in the past). At the end of this period, then, would be
the incorporation at which there would be <u>much celebration</u> and
feasting and rejoicing in the Lord. These new members of the
body would, in this way, be made to feel they are a vital part
of the ongoing work of Christ.

Turner (1964) has analyzed the transition ("liminal") period
in detail and the instruction period for baptism could benefit
by a better understanding of what is happening. Baptismal candi-
dates are transitional beings who are "betwixt and between" all the
fixed points in the space-time of structural classification. They
symbolically are "undifferentiated raw material" and they have
nothing. It would be good to find a Kamwə term, if possible to
refer to this state in a person's change of status. The chief
probably goes through this before becoming a chief and the bride
goes through this when she ceremonially leaves her own family and
goes with nothing to the groom's house to be a nobody and undergo
instruction from his family for several months before the wedding
actually incorporates her into his family as a wife. Some Kamwə
clans have youth initiation rites in which the liminal period is
very important.

This transition period is characterized by "undoing, dissolution, decomposition: and these are accompanied by "processes of growth, transformation, and the reformation of old elements in new patterns" (Turner 1964:341). This is the period for "growing" a Christian as the worldview of the Kamwə would express it. It is not just a time for acquiring knowledge. It must be seen as a change of being, stemming from a transformation of worldview. Turner sees three processes at work in the liminal stage:

> The first is the reduction of culture into recognized components or factors; the second is their recombination in fantastic or monstrous patterns and shapes; and the third is their recombination in ways that make sense with regard to the new state and status that the neophytes will enter (1964:345).

It seems to me that some of the rich symbolism that is used to signify transition in the society should be used in connection with the baptismal class. If possible we should find some way of marking these members who are leaving an old life in animism and being prepared for a new life in Christ. Until now, the church has relied on western style classes to communicate mere information about Christian belief and practice. There has been no emphasis on "acting out" or actually practicing Christian behavior. According to the Kamwə worldview, ritual is needed at a time like this to make the teachings relevant to where they really are. The importance of ritual to the Kamwə at such times can hardly be overestimated.

Incorporation into the body of Christ is marked by an imported, unelaborate washing ritual, baptism. Such a ritual, though not indigenous, could certainly be made more meaningful if it were elaborated upon in indigenous ways. Perhaps special food should be cooked and dancing and singing, natural Kamwə ways of expressing joy, take place. Drama could add meaning to the occasion as well. Mbiti, who recognizes that the power of music in the communication of the Christian message needs to be harnessed, suggests the use of drums to dramatize the meaning of dying and rising with Christ (1971:119). After baptism, more focus should be placed on giving Christan responsibility to these "new creatures in Christ" in order to recognize their new status. In the West, we seem to be fearful about giving much responsibility to a new Christian, but it is important that the society recognize and act out the new position of those who have been incorporated in Christ.

The problem is not so much what ritual does for people as what it says to them, how intelligible it is to the participants. The "Christian" funeral as practiced among the Kamwə follows a very western format where Christians gather for Bible reading, singing,

and prayer and within a few hours from death the burial and funeral
is all over. Many have expressed dissatisfaction with this ritual.
The pastors, because they have been forced to replace the undertakers; the old folks, because the group of the dead person is not
given due respect in such a short service; the tradesmen, because
they have been cut out of their role as musicians for the dancing
and as undertakers; and relatives of the deceased, because they
have not had a chance to work out their grief.

The Christian ritual relating to death must be restudied with
the Kamwǝ worldview in mind. Suggestions for meaningful ritual
must come from the indigenous ritual and then new Christian meaning can be taught as ritual is captivated for Christ. The length
of traditional funerals is related to the importance of the
deceased to the society. The close relatives are marked by the
way a vine is tied at their waist, and special dances by prescribed
groups honor the deceased. Food is brought in by specific relatives and cooked and served to several different groups: wtsǝgǝ -
"children of daughters who have married into another clan,"
makwǝlyi - "the wife's people"; ngwalyime - "all daughters married
or unmarried"; kata - "clan members"; lighi - "tradesmen." A
funeral is a time when people share and together work out their
grief and readjust to life without the deceased. The mourners
symbolize their grief by performing a libation ceremony. The close
relatives have their heads shaved at the time of burial and then
not again until the period of mourning is over (seven months to a
year). The Christian church needs to consider more carefully the
emotional, spiritual, and physical needs of her members at the
time of death and to incorporate meaningful indigenous symbolism
into Christian funerals.

Attention must likewise be given to the symbolism involved
in the most important Christian ritual of consolidation, the communion service. The focus is on an already established group and
on strengthening its feeling of belongingness. The love feast
is celebrated by everyone preparing his own food and bringing it
to church to share in a fellowship meal. After this meal, foot-
washing is practiced (in keeping with Church of the Brethren
tradition), followed by the "bread and the cup." In the latter,
guinea corn mush is used for the bread, and enduma juice (which
must be specially bottled and preserved, since it is not usually
drunk) or koolaid or fizzies for the drink. It is served by
passing it through the congregation. A shortage of ordained min-
isters to administer the communion has meant that this ritual of
consolidation takes place only one to three times a year and only
when the ordained minister can be present. Communion is a ritual
that takes place only in the church itself. My questions would
be: How could the communication of meaning be improved by adding
or altering the ritual to incorporate meaningful indigenous ritual.
Could the communion ritual be more flexible with respect to when

it is used and where? Could the communion ritual be used to give
Christians strength in times of need when they are apt to go to
the diviner for help? Could an indigenous drink be used?

Mbiti explains the connotative meaning of beer drinking in some
parts of Africa. "Beer is the symbol of friendship, communion,
one-ness, and acceptability; and it is used by many African societies in ceremonies, festivals and covenant-making" (1969:138).
The New Testament communion service conveyed these meanings to
those who participated in it. If there is a local drink which
has these connotations, shouldn't it be considered for the communion service?

There are other Kamwə indigenous rituals that could provide
the basis for creating meaningful Christian rituals. One would be
the family ceremonial center, ɗa məlyə. A family devotional experience patterned indigenously as to time, place and participants
could be established. This would include the head of the household committing the members of his household to God as well as
a time for focusing on the family heritage and meaning for today
as related to years gone by.

Another area where indigenous rituals can give clues for meaning is in offerings to God in the church. The when, how, why and
what must all be related to the Kamwə worldview in order to be
meaningful. Many of the independent churches in Africa have the
members in the congregation bring their offering to the front of
the church, expressing the joy of giving by singing and dancing
as they do so. Perhaps offerings should not be taken every week,
but when the village people are apt to have cash. If offerings
are taken only at special times it might be that the amount needs
to be broadcast as it is when gifts are given at weddings or baby-
naming ceremonies. It may also be better to follow Old Testament
patterns by encouraging people to give something other than cash,
for God accepts handwork, grain, goats, calabashes, etc. He asks
us to give from what we have to show our love and appreciation to
Him.

Indigenous planting and harvesting ritual would also be usable
if we would allow it to be possessed by God (as it was among the
Hebrews). When the people are used to acting out their deepest
feelings, whether they be of frustration, joy, uncertainty, or
dependence, a group prayer in the church may not be satisfactory.
If Christianity is to be maximally meaningful to the Kamwə, ritual
should be largely indigenous while the meaning is reinterpreted in
a Christian way so that what is expressed is both thoroughly satisfying and thoroughly Christian.

Strategy Built on Current Developments

As we have seen, times are changing and Christianity needs to be in touch with new developments and pressures. The government is emphasizing the need for literacy and the written word is used more today for communication purposes. In this section we will deal with literacy and tape programs as tools for Christian training and outreach.

Literacy

It has long been a major emphasis of missions to teach people to read so that they can learn directly from God's Word. However, the nationals often look on literacy as an abstract thing that is good in itself. But it takes much work for preliterates to learn to read and when they have learned, the skill is very little more than a foreign status symbol to most of them. There is a tendency for them to forget the skill when there is no continuing need for it. Foster suggests that "before we teach anything, we must be sure the new knowledge will fill a real need felt by the people; if this is not the case, we must first create the need" (1973:169). Concerning motivation to read, he says:

> ...literacy generally becomes important only when
> villages begin to see that those persons who are
> literate have extra advantages, or when they come
> to feel they are less likely to be cheated by city
> people if they can read (ibid).

The need for literacy must be felt by the national if a literacy program is to be successful. This is related to another problem: What is the value of competency in reading if the church does not supply reading material? A good literacy program must see that there is literature available to read.

The Kamwə Literacy-Literature (Lit-Lit) Training Center originated in 1971 for the purpose of training leaders to teach literacy and also to get reading materials out in the Kamwə language. A literacy campaign was launched in 1972. The missionary taught eight men to type and run the mimeograph machine. These men, then taught the next class of twenty. A simple primer was published. No further materials were published, the missionary went home, and the funds for the program were short. This may reflect an indifference on the part of the church, I don't know.

The Gospel of Mark was published in 1972 and the entire New Testament became available in Kamwə in 1976. The people were very enthusiastic about having God's Word in their own language, but I do not know how much reading of it is being done. There is a

definite need for easy-to-read materials for the people who know
how to read to get into the reading habit. Folklore and life
histories could be written up by laymen and leaders and then published through the Lit-Lit Center. A simple monthly news sheet
circulating through the churches would also be helpful. I see
a definite need for an Old Testament history or portions of the
Old Testament to be translated into Kamwə because the worldviews
of the Old Testament are so much like that of the Kamwə. In the
Old Testament, God is seen working with a family-centered group
who is familiar with sacrifice, dreams, proverbs, the spirit world,
nature, agriculture, etc.

Tippett (1967:306) points out that the Bible alone is not enough.
It needs a frame of reference such as a prayer book, catechism
creed, or aids to worship. When the people have the indigenous
Bible,the language of faith and practice becomes more stabilized
(as with German in Luther's day) but learning the meaning requires
adequate training. A Bible catechism is valuable at this point.
If these aids are not available, the people are vulnerable to
peculiar religious sects and nativistic philosophy. The Bible has
many difficult passages and any portion needs to be understood in
its own context and in relation to the themes that run through
the entire Bible. Bible study guide sheets would be helpful if
they were prepared with the Kamwə worldview clearly in mind. The
catechism used at present by the Kamwə church needs to be examined
with the Kamwə worldview in mind. Many times its teachings represent only the missionary's view of what is important. When the
catechism is relevant and has its roots in the Bible itself the
new convert can stand firm against syncretistic beliefs.

The kind of teaching that is done from the Bible is significant
in the way the church grows both quantitatively and qualitatively.
Tippett (1967:301-307) illustrates this with two separate groups
in the Solomons. The Methodists emphasized the didactic passages
of Scripture and overlooked those that show the love, power, and
glory of God. They viewed the Bible more as a norm for living
than as an aid to devotion. The dynamic passages were usually
avoided. The Anglican Church, however, follows a lectionary for
scripture selection. This provides a systematic reading to the
people at worship. It also gives a feeling of corporateness,
since the whole church in the diocese studies the same Scripture
each week. But, again, it does not emphasize the great passages
of dynamic encounter and of God in action. In the light of these
illustrations, I would suggest a local preaching schedule based
on the worldview and needs of the Kamwə and focused on the dynamic
passages of the Bible emphasizing the greatness of God, His good-
ness, His love, His compassion, spiritual experience, and the
Holy Spirit. These emphases would also be obvious in the preparation of teaching aids to be used in Bible study time in the home.

The church needs to be supportive and help the parents teach their children in the home.   There is much to be done in literacy that will affect the depth of Christian experience in the church.

Tape Program

Tape recorders are now found in some of the homes in the Kamwə area. So it is suitable that the church use this means of teaching as well. Taped training is both a way of reaching the illiterate who cannot read God's Word and a way of stimulating him to desire to read. Several kinds of materials could be put on tape: the Bible itself, study programs based on Scripture and with the Kamwə worldview as a backdrop, and whole worship services with singing, Bible reading and exposition, and prayer for outreach. Care must be taken, however, to be sure the Gospel remains personal by having face-to-face interaction after the tape is played. The non-reading Christians could play an important part in preparing tapes and leading in discussions after playing them to a group. The use of the tapes could be on a rotating loan basis. Much experimenting needs to be done with this program. The Kamwə Church already has over fifty tape players given by Bible Translations on Tape, but materials available on tape are very limited. It is time-consuming to make these tapes, but it is another way the individual Christian can participate in the program. Many of the suggestions for literacy made above are relevant for a tape ministry as well.

16

Strategy:

Indigenous Theology

The Kamwə Church has many rich resources from which to draw. We have already discussed the indigenous culture and indigenous communication as a means of employing worldview-based and hearer-oriented communication of the Gospel. The Kamwə now have the New Testament in their own language through which they can learn more about God. Sundkler, in discussing a Christian theology in Africa, refers to theology as translation:

> Theology is, in the last resort, translation. It is an ever-renewed re-interpretation to new generations and people of the given Gospel, a re-presentation of the will and way of the one Christ in a dialogue with new thought-forms and culture patterns. Translation to Africa, on this level of theological encounter, has hardly begun (1960:281).

As we have seen by our investigation of the Kamwə worldview, God has been at work preparing them for Himself. The belief in the supernatural, the use of mediators to interact with the supernatural beings, the belief in God's involvement with their origins, the values of the society, the myths, etc., all serve as a basis for Christianity. In this final chapter on strategy we will define theology, focus on the need for indigenous theology, and give some specific suggestions for Kamwə indigenous theology.

Theology Defined

In order to understand this strategy, it will be necessary to focus first on the term "theology." To many it refers to a discipline of study which sets forth systematic doctrines based on the

historical, critical and exegetical study of the Bible. This discipline I prefer to call western theology, as it was formulated
as a result of western man's studying the Scriptures to find
answers to his questions. Western theology is a culture-bound
ethnic variety of theology. A more precise definition of Christian
theology is that of Harjula: "the critical reflection on, arti-
culation and translation of God's self-disclosure, expecially in
Jesus Christ, in and for a given historical and cultural context"
(1970:1, quoted in Kraft, 1977:558). This definition underlies my
use of the word as I deal with it here. The function of theology
according to Sundkler is "to interpret...Christ in terms that are
relevant and essential to African existence" (1960:211).

Kraft sees theologizing as a dynamic, continuous process engaged
in by human beings according to human perception. It is not the
passive acceptance of a prepared doctrinal product, but rather
involves Spirit-led human interaction with God.

> Theology, then, must always be seen as the result of
> a dynamic process of human theologizing. It should
> not be confused with the changeless, absolute Truth
> that remains in the mind of God. That divine Truth
> is beyond our reach in any total sense (I Cor. 13:12),
> even though God has seen fit to reveal an adequate
> amount of insight into it via the Spirit-led percep-
> tion of that Truth recorded by the authors of the Holy
> Scripture (1977:529).

So as we talk of the Kamwɔ developing indigenous theology we
are dealing with their perception of the divine Truth based on
God's Word and their language framework for organizing the concepts so that it is regarded as relevant by the hearers. The world
view of the hearer is the matrix in which biblical theology must
be expressed.

The Need for Indigenous Theology

Bernard Ramm, in an article dealing with the relationship of
evangelical theology to technological developments in the secular
world, sees a need for rethinking the present concept of the authenticity of the Holy Scripture and the present theology of the Holy
Spirit. He suggests that maybe the processes we have assumed as
necessary to go along with our concepts are products of our own
cultural conditioning and not of Scripture itself (1971:55). This
recognition from a noted evangelical biblical theologian is an
encouragement to Christian ethnotheologians who have sensed this
to be evident in their cross-cultural mission work. The need for
indigenous theology is evident and should prove useful to western
theology as well.

Ezeanya urges the church to adapt herself to different environ-
ments:

> Adaption...has nothing in common with liberal syn-
> cretism which would embrace indistinctly all dogmas,
> all rites and every superstition to make an amalga-
> mation out of them. It is not then a question of
> trying to preserve everything in traditional religion
> and cultures of African people simply because it is
> theirs, and trying to foster them side by side with
> Christianity...The Gospel message must remain the
> focal point and must be presented in its full splendor
> and not weakened in any way but rather adorned, enriched
> and made more intelligible and attractive by the use
> of whatever is good, just and beautiful that is found
> in the cultural heritage of a people.
>
> The Gospel, therefore, must always remain to be made
> to appear as a message of salvation from God himself
> a message destined for every nation, a way of life which
> people can and should live while remaining authentic
> citizens of their own nations (1969:34).

Many of the problems of the church in Africa today are the
result of failure to adapt, and the importing of western theology
that has discouraged indigenous theologizing. Idowu pinpoints the
problem of the church in Africa today as one of divided loyalties
of most of the members between Christianity with western categories
and practices on one hand, and the traditional religion on the
other (1973:205). Mbiti recognizes the present belief in magic,
sorcery, and witchcraft among Christians and says, "The people
have not been sufficiently armed to fight against witchcraft and
sorcery, in spite of many years of contact with Christian teaching
and western education" (1971:9).

The pre-Reformation Catholic Church had rituals and other aids
to help the faithful deal with the powers of darkness. However,
the Reformation deprived the people of these aids (i.e., chants,
holy water, sacred objects, cross) and gave no functional substitutes. They kept the demons but left the people defenseless.
Thomas comments on this situation:

> Before the Reformation the Catholic Church has pro-
> vided an elaborate repertoire of ritual precautions
> designed to ward off evil spirits and malevolent
> magic...A good Christian who used holy water, the
> sign of the cross, and the aid of the priest ought
> not to be so afflicted at all. After the Reformation,
> by contrast, Protestant preachers, strenuously denied

that such aids could have any affect. They reaffirmed
the power of evil, but left believers disarmed before
the old enemy (1970:58).

At this point power encounter is essential. It is important for
the Christian to understand what Christ meant concerning power
encounter. "Behold I give you power...over all power..." (Luke
10:19). This power must be usable on the level of daily life
against the evil spirits. Tippett deals with the problem of
encounter, showing how this battle with evil must be fought in the
framework and understanding of the local people (1967:100-111).

Crane, in an article on the "Indigenization of the African
Church," states that in the past the confrontation between the
Gospel and the African worldview has been conditioned by western
value judgments on that worldview (1964:409-410). Western Christianity has been guilty of the almost wholesale rejection of the
African worldview with its understanding of the wholeness and
continuity of life, its primal understanding of nature as alive
and worthy of respect, its closely knit family ties, its understanding of personality in the context of community, and the
importance that it attaches to myth and ritual. Crane suggests
six points of contact in which Christ can be understood in African
worldviews: 1) the rediscovery of selfhood, 2) the relation of
man and nature, 3) man in community, 4) initiation and baptism,
5) continuity between the living and the dead, and 6) the gifts
of the Spirit. He suggests that too often the tendency is to
reduce "the powers of darkness" either to scientific categories
or to figments of the imagination. Failing to deal with them
results in a religion that is powerless and not satisfying to
the African need (ibid:412-418).

Welbourn, in his discussion of "the importance of ghosts"
(ancestral spirits),sees it necessary to accept the existence of
ghosts and witchcraft, recognizing that neither this system nor
ours is irreproachable. He sees the ghosts as representing the
personal touch and being emotion-centered and an important part
of life. However, he sees the technological age as an essential
in the modern world. His conclusion is, "If we have [Christ], we
do not need ghosts" (1963:26).

In discussing independent churches Sundkler describes the missionary approach, the related doctrines that were selectively
given to the African, and the resulting problem.

Malinowski has shown that in the culture contact
between White and Black in Africa there is not only
"selective conservatism" on the part of the African--
who accepts and adopts mainly those elements of the
new culture which fit into his old system--but also

> a selective giving on the part of the European.
> This is the case also in Mission work. Each denom-
> ination and missionary organization from overseas
> brought its characteristic denominational one-sided-
> ness, its own peculiar kind presented as a preaching
> and teaching institution only, whereas the rich devo-
> tional heritage of the Church Universal was not trans-
> mitted to the young African church in the same degree
> (1961:296).

The strong western influence, though unconscious and unintentional
has left the African Church generally with a foreign theology.

It is important for the Kamwə Church to seek for herself answers
from the Scriptures to meet her own needs under the guidance of
the Holy Spirit. Understanding what I do of the worldview I would
like to suggest some possible ways that the teachings of Scripture
might appropriately meet the Kamwə in order to set in motion the
process of theologizing from their own perspective.

Suggestions for Kamwə Indigenous Theologizing

Kamwə indigenous theology might very well give a prominent place
to the mountains, for Scripture reflects God's use of the mountain
in communicating meanings to the Hebrews. To the Hebrews and
neighboring tribes, mountains were naturally places where sacrifices were made to the Supernatural. Abraham took Issac to the
mountain to offer him as a sacrifice to God (Gen. 22:1-14), Jacob
made a sacrifice on the mountain (Gen. 31:54), Moses talked to
God on the mountain (Ex. 2 and 3) and Moses also received instruction from God and the tablets of stone with the commandments of
God on them on the mountain (Ex. 19, 24, and 34). It was on a
mountain where Elijah confronted the prophets of Baal and demonstrated God's power over them (I Kings 18:19-40). The mountain
spoke to the Hebrews of God's presence (Ps. 121:1, 2), God's
possession (Ps. 15:1, 2; Ps. 24:3), a place of meeting God with
sacrifice (I Sam. 9:8-25), and security (Ps. 91:14). Certain
Psalms are labeled Psalms of Ascent because they were used by
pilgrims going up to Jerusalem for the annual festivals.

In the New Testament it was on a high mountain that the trans-
figuration took place (Matt. 17:1-8) and on the mountain Jesus
taught His disciples (I Pet. 1:18) and talked to God (Matt. 26:30).
On a high mountain Jesus was tempted by the devil (Matt. 4:8-11).
The longest sermon reported in the Gospel from the mouth of Jesus,
according to Matthew (5-7), was presented on the mountain (or
hillside). Because of the meaning of the mountain already in the
Kamwə worldview, God may wish to speak the meanings in Scripture
through this channel.

I would imagine that the doctrine of God as Creator would be
essential and full of meaning for the Kamwə. Sawyerr, an African
theologian, sees the African attitude toward God as a reflection
of his experience in relationship to his chief and to the ancestral
spirits.

> First, He is thought to be the Creator of the world
> and of man. He is therefore the oldest imaginable
> Being. Like grandfather then, He must be the one
> person who feels a concern for His children. He is
> accordingly man's <u>ancestor</u>. He is therefore a God
> of justice and mercy, who affords protection to all
> His children...Second, He, like the early ancestors
> of man, is now far removed by time and space from
> man and, therefore, is not closely associated with
> their everyday affairs...

> God is like a chief and is, indeed, the chief sover-
> eign. He rules the world and administers justice and
> equity. He is a distant ancestor who has a direct
> interest in the well-being of man and could be directly
> approached by anyone in times of danger or crisis...

> His omnipresence is assumed in every rite, whether in
> offering sacrifice to the dead, or blessing a devoted
> son, or uttering a curse against a witch or a thief; so
> also when, in an attitude of fatalism, men resignedly
> accept loss of property or of life of a dear one by
> death, because they believe that the tragedy is of God.
> He is always man's vindicator and plays that role like
> a <u>kinsman</u>. So all man's hopes and aspirations are
> anchored in God. He is not just a philosophical con-
> cept but a reality...(1970:8-10).

Since God created man He would be man's ancestor. As the Kamwə
reflect on God as ancestor, He takes on understandable characteristics: protecting, loving, just, concerned. But being the
earliest ancestor places Him very far away, as does his association with chief. The Kamwə chief uses an intermediary to reach
the people. The Kamwə feel that the spirit beings (<u>hyala</u>) represent God and are to be dealt with rather than going direct to God.
However, the Kamwə do recognize God's presence by addressing Him
before addressing the spirits when sacrificing. This is all
beautiful preparation for Christianity and also provides the
basis of an indigenous theology. The distance the Kamwə feel
between themselves and God is a very real problem.

We have seen in the Kamwə perspective how important the corporate life of the clan is. The fact that the Christian is a
<u>family man</u> with both privileges and important responsibilities

to his clan will affect how God speaks to him through the Word. It is in the clan that the fundamental facts of life are presented: the vitality and fertility of the individual and the family, marriage, procreation, birth and death (Sundkler 1960:287). Theology, growing out of where the Kamwə are and the needs they have, most likely will reflect this family emphasis.

> There is a possibility...that the African Protestant theologian of the future will build on this fact of the family as one of the main pillars of his theology, particularly of his ecclesiology. He may come to regard it as his particular task to see the Church in terms of the Great Family (ibid:289).

The Incarnation of Christ, a historical fact, speaks to God's plan for nearness and communication. Christ also is the Mediator and this is real, not just metaphorical. He represents God and man deals with him even as he used to deal with the spirits. Christ, the true God and true man came to reveal God to man and to represent man before God. This provides a way for bringing a far-away God into close and essential daily interaction. The mediatorial work of Christ should be an important focus of Kamwə indigenous theology.

The Kamwə might well transform from a Christian perspective their doctrine of an active spirit world. The world of man and the world of spirits are not two independent worlds. One has no meaning without the other; they are complementary. The world of men is directed by the spirits and there must be order and harmony. The Bible has much to say about this spirit activity, but it is largely lost in western theologizing. In order for the Kamwə Christian to experience the relevance of Christianity in daily living, he needs much teaching and guidance to work out his new relationship in Christ as it relates to the spirit activity around him. Church leaders need to focus on this and begin theologizing in this area. Billy Graham's recent book on *Angels* (1975) recognizes this deficiency in our theology.

The Kamwə might well develop a theology that stresses the rhythm of nature and the rhythm of man as he interacts with nature. The Jews lived close to the soil and viewed their cultivation of the soil as tied up with their service to God. They made each respective phase of their agriculture an act of worship to God. We read of seedtime (Joel 2:23, Lev. 16, 23:34), harvest (Ex. 12: 1-51, Lev. 23:10f, Josh. 3:15), summer (Lev. 26:5, II Kings 5: 18-20). Since the Kamwə have a similar soil-closeness in their lives, there is a need for worship through agriculture and the cultivation of the soil. The universe and man both throb with rhythm. Man has the rhythm of sleeping and working; hunger and

eating; breathing and pulse; birth and death. Many Kamwə values
indicate how keenly he is aware of his surroundings in nature.
Tippett recognizes the need for studying how best to communicate
a New Testament message by means of an Old Testament form or
method. "A race of people living close to the soil and coming
suddenly out of a pagan world into an experience of God, is faced
with a situation very similar to that which existed between Hebrew
and Canaanite, and needs rite and rubric as we have learned to
use the creed" (1958:104). The Bible speaks to this need and
when we have revelation, then reflection on that revelation, the
result can be indigenous theology.

Sundkler emphasizes and illustrates the centrality of the Old
Testament to the whole theological conception of African preachers

> The Old Testament in the African setting is not just
> a book of reference. It becomes a source of remem-
> berance. The African preacher feels that Genesis
> belongs to him and his Church, or rather vice versa--
> that he and his African Church belong to those things
> which were in the beginning. From this sacred charter
> in the Book, his own people and Church receive their
> recognition...They belong to the original tree of Life,
> being grafted into it and receiving its reviving sap
> (1960:285).

He sees the African re-interpreting the Hebrew myths and the
stories of the Patriarchs and the Exodus in the light of their
own fate and aspirations. Because of the Kamwə stress on tradition and "remembering," and because of cultural similarities
between them and the Hebrews, the Old Testament may offer more to
them than to the Westerner and prove to be a very useful instrumen
for Christian growth and theological perception.

Another area where a theology is needed is that of healing and
sacrifice. The Kamwə in their worldview see this as a theological
matter. Western theology, however, is silent, even though the
Bible speaks on the issue, because the west has divided the sacred
and the secular. According to the Kamwə interpretation and
experience, disease is not just a physical condition. It is also
a religious matter, and the spirit world is involved. To handle
sickness, then, the man who deals with the spirit world must be
contacted to find out the precise cause, who is responsible, and
the right cure.

The Navaho also see all ailments, mental or physical, as of
supernatural origin. Treatment involves appeasement of the super-
naturals. Kluckhohn and Leighton comment on the values of native
medicine and western medicine:

> The answer is that native practice brings good
> results--in many cases as good as those of a white
> physician or hospital. Admittedly there are types
> of ailments which must be made much worse by the
> Singer's treatment. On the other hand, the evidence
> is good that individuals who obtained no relief from
> white medicine have been cured by chants (1946:230-231).

> ...Skillful physicians have long known that the will
> to get well, the belief that one is going to recover,
> and other attitudes can be more than half the battle.
> Moreover, the fact that many "physical" disabilities
> have "psychic" causes is being increasingly recognized
> (ibid:231).

The Navaho ceremony with the Singer has definite value:

> Then there is the prestige and authority of the Singer
> assuring the patient that he will recover...The pres-
> tige, mysticism, and power of the ceremonial itself
> are active, coming directly from the supernatural
> powers that build up the growing earth in spring,
> drench it with rain, or tear it apart with lightning.
> In the height of the chant the patient himself becomes
> one of the Holy People, puts his feet in their moc-
> casins, and breathes in the strength of the sun. He
> comes into complete harmony with the universe and must
> of course be free of all ills and evil. Finally, it
> is very likely that he has seen the ceremonial work
> with others and may have had it before himself...
> (ibid:231-232).

The Kamwɘ would have much the same attitude toward native medicine and western medicine. The Church, by ignoring the physical
and focusing on man's spiritual welfare only, is leaving a void
that drives/draws the people back to dealing with the spirits.
It is time that the Church look to the Bible itself to find
answers regarding sickness and sacrifice. It may be that confession of sin should be a prerequisite to healing. Loewen
presents the goals of confession as follows: 1) to restore proper relationship with the supernatural (as in Lev. 16), 2) to
restore social and moral equilibrium, and 3) to restore physical
health (1975:292).

At any rate, it is imperative for the Church to develop a
meaningful way to solve tensions and problems arising between
Christians. Many questions have not yet been answered concerning
faith, illness and sacrifice. The Church will need to devise
means to express God's concern for the whole person, lest the

Gospel become a partial message that is valid only for times of
health. Often "in times of personal crisis, such as barrenness
and sickness, when many baptized believers, thinking that Jesus
Christ did not have any interest, or worse, the power to improve
their state of affairs, felt they had to visit the traditional
healer" (Mitchell, 1963:50). The question Mitchell poses is:
Does Christ's victory over sin involve direct deliverance by
Divine healing from physical and emotional as well as spiritual
sickness? (ibid:51).

There is a great deal of similarity between the ideal personal
qualities taught by the elders and valued by the Kamwə society
and those taught in the Scriptures. Since the understanding of
what it means to be kind, generous, loving, peaceful, respectful,
etc., are all defined by the culture, the Scriptures will be
interpreted in this light. For example, the Kamwə emphasis on
harmony and peace would give rich meaning to James 3:17, 18 and
Rom. 14:19; their emphasis on honor and respect would give insights
into Rom. 12:10-13 and I Pet. 2:17; their understanding of generosity would provide the grounds for interpreting II Cor. 8:7-14
and I John 3:17. The understandings that the people already have
in their personal values provide a fertile field for an indigenous
theology to develop from the Scriptural teachings. God's communication with man through His Word is open to direct and careful interpretation and application by the Kamwə people themselves.

Summary

These are only a few of the possible areas where indigenous
theology would be valuable. To theologize from a Kamwə perspective is urgent, since only when this is done will the people have
the help they need from God's Word and a relevant Christianity.
Only as the Bible speaks specifically to the African worldview
will Christianity have power and defense in its surrounding.
Tippett states, "A healthy church should grow organically, quantitatively, and qualitatively. It should be culturally relevant,
and bringing its younger members into a vital experience" (1967:
283).

When the Kamwə seek answers to their problems in God's Word
and develop an indigenous theology, they will be making a contri-
bution to the cause of Christianity. God has given them special
insights that need to be freed to be used in developing an indigenous theology. Monica Wilson suggests several insights from
traditional religions for Christians to learn from Africa:
1) the focus on the relationships between human beings, the closeness of community (including the responsibility man has for the
dead and the unborn), 2) an awareness of evil and the need to
confess it, 3) the bridling of competition, the need and know-how

for cooperation, and 4) the "apprehension of reality through
ritual" rather than through intellectual dogma (1971:137-142).
As the Kamwə Church expresses theology in her indigenous thought
forms and with varying accents and emphases, there may appear
hidden treasures of truth which will enrich the Church.

Von Allmen attempts to show how it is possible to have an
indigenous theology based on a true fidelity to the New Testament.
He emphasizes the fact that Pauline theology was the developing
of an indigenous theology for Greek Christians. It was necessary
for the "native" preachers to be "bold enough to be themselves,
bold enough, while remaining faithful to the foundations of the
faith they had received, to sift critically the received vocabu-
larly in order to express themselves intelligibly to their linguistic brothers" (1975:41). The result of this early preaching
was a response to Christ:

> These Greek-speaking Christians, in their turn,
> gave expression to the faith received. One can,
> of course, try to list the themes thus treated
> and arrange them into a treatise on the theology of
> the primitive church as expressed in its confessions
> of faith. But recent study has become sensitive to
> the fact that what the first Christians precisely did
> not begin by doing was to express their faith in the
> form of a systematically worked out theology...a
> simple historical observation ought to be sufficient
> starting point: the first Christans did not express
> their faith in a speculative way, in a strictly the-
> ological way. They responded to the preaching by
> worship; they sang the work that God had done for
> them, in hymns. That was the way in which the first
> Christians gradually discovered the implications of
> their faith in Jesus Christ (ibid:41-42).

He goes on to say that the theologian has no right to fear the
spontaneous manner in which the Church sometimes expresses its
faith. Missionaries are not to preach a theology but the Gospel
of Good News. The response will be in the form of worship or
hymns. Theology comes later and must be such as not to squelch
the life of faith in the Church.

The Kamwə have been responding to Christ in singing and worship. It is my hope that one of the results of this book will
be to challenge some of the Kamwə Christians to be bold enough
to be themselves and remain faithful to the foundations of the
faith and begin developing an indigenous theology that is an
outgrowth of the experience and needs of the Kamwə Church.

17

Conclusion

We have been concerned with the effective communication of the Gospel. With this in mind, we have examined worldview and how an understanding of the worldview provides a foundation for hearer-oriented communication. Our focus has been on the Kamwə of Northern Nigeria. After describing their worldview we based our strategy for future Church work on the insights we have gained.

Ethnoscience has provided the theoretical perspective in terms of which we have analyzed worldview. We have worked on the assumption that language reflects culture and by becoming familiar with the sameness, distinctives, and relationships of linguistic structures we can be enlightened as to the worldview. We have recognized at certain points the limitations of this model and have felt free to group terms even though there was no cover term for them. By coming to grips with the Kamwə terminology that is used, we have gained a deeper understanding of the meaning--referential, conceptual, and emotive. Studying the language is seen as the most effective way to get into the conceptual framework, since it gives us a basis for understanding their experiential world.

The Kamwə are a mountain people who find their self-awareness in the clan group. Historically there has been much warfare between clans. The language illustrates the divisions among the total Kamwə tribe as there are eight different dialect areas. The family unit which is patrilineal and patrilocal is a tight-knit group, providing for all the needs of its members. The individual has little identity apart from his family. Within each clan the divisions include: 1) two castes: tradesmen and commoners, 2) men's community and women's community, 3) the youth and the elders. These homogeneous social units are inter- dependent as opposites. This social structure which explains the Kamwə group self-awareness provides a backdrop for understanding the worldview.

The Kamwə Worldview

The mountain is special in the Kamwə perspective and their language reflects this. Each clan group associates with a par- ticular mountain of their forefathers. This particular mountain speaks of security, safety, supplies, a visual tie to the past, burial grounds for the ancestors, and a closeness to God. The language reflects the mountain orientation in the terms used for the parts of the compound, locational prepositions, and certain verbs of motion. The meaning of the mountain is important in the Kamwə worldview.

Guinea corn is special in the Kamwə perspective. It is a gift of God for the welfare of the Kamwə. Its growing season is the reference point for all other activities. The people personify the guinea corn and use it for all the ceremonies in the form of mush, beer, or sweet drink. It symbolizes a oneness of the supernatural and the human as man cultivates and uses what God gave.

The supernatural is very much in focus in daily living, accord- ing to the Kamwə worldview. The Creator God is far away but He can be contacted in times of crisis. But the spirits are the ones who may cause difficulties for the Kamwə, so the focus is more interacting with the spirit world. The ancestors are a part of the spirit world, too. As we have seen, the Kamwə have several kinds of practitioners who are responsible for peace and balance with the spirit world. The household head is respon- sible for carrying out the ritual performance and for seeking the services of specialists when needed. He also is responsible for the welfare of his family and represents his family when the elders meet. Some of the specialists deal with the spirits and others are herbalists. The various spirits are the cause of illness, and charms are used as protective devices against them. Survival and social equilibrium are dependent on learning to call on the invisible forces to deal with the visible world.

According to the Kamwə worldview, the personal qualities that are valued are kindness and good character, generosity, good health, hard work, discipline, living in harmony, possessing riches, and showing proper honor and respect. These are the values that are taught the children in the enculturation process.

These values are exemplified in the lives of the elders. Proverbs are one of the means of teaching and together we looked at a few selected Kamwə proverbs. The values are also taught by the singing of songs by the young girls as they make up songs about individual behavior. It is important to be a part of the group as these qualities can only be developed in the group arena.

In Chapter 7 we focused on the current Kamwə situation which is "a new autonomous entity" with an interpenetration of the traditional and the western. Even though the environment is undergoing much change, the worldview is slower to change. Most of the people live on the plains but the mountain orientation is still evident. New crops are being grown but guinea corn is still essential and very much in focus. Even though a professional (e.g., teacher)is allowed to buy his guinea corn today, he must produce a small amount on his own land. Because of the scattering of the family for school and work purposes, the ceremonial ritual use of guinea corn is not so important. The ceremonies spoke of the unity of the family and to perform them when the family is divided would be dangerous. So we are seeing a slow breakdown of the traditional religion. However, the spirit world is still very active among the Kamwə. The authority that was a part of family life is breaking down slowly as is the dependence on the family. However, family relationships are still very important and when there is trouble the family comes to the rescue. We have seen **how the interdependent systems are slowly being adjusted to accom**modate modern man. The government and Christianity have brought many new terms into the Kamwə language.

We recognized the existence of culture change but also the stability of values even though the cultural forms are new. The worldview lives on acting as a governor of change and provider of the building blocks for maintaining equilibrium in the society.

Worldview and Communication

In part III we dealt with worldview and communication. Recognizing that communication is a dynamic process, we attempted to better understand it through examining the parts: communicator, message, and receptor. Our special emphasis was on the receptor and how understanding his worldview can improve communication.

We have recognized the limited value of words as they can and do obscure as well as reveal meaning. Since a message must be reconstructed by the receptor after being encoded by the communicator we pointed out that meanings are in people. Only information can be transferred between people. The reactions of the receptor to the message give significant clues to the communicator for the encoding process. Cultural perception plays an important role in the communication process. We see, therefore, what we've been trained to see and choose terms for expressing our concepts according to the classification of our language forms.

The social system is to be considered in understanding the communication process. Words have meaning in a precise context and one cannot simply translate from one culture to another with isolated words. The meaning is derived from the interaction between information and context. Communication to a specific need of the receptor is likely to be perceived by the receptor and to challenge the receptor to discovery. Such communication, therefore, will be more apt to bring about life-changing effects. The receptor is the decision-maker in both how the intended message is to be acted out and the ultimate meaning it receives in the society.

We examined the three (or more) crucial worldviews involved in communicating the gospel recognizing that the differences between worldviews are the greatest barriers to intercultural communication. The meanings we have for the Christian content are permeated with our own worldview, the Scriptures are permeated with the worldview of that day, and the receptor only understands the message in light of his own worldview. We have illustrated this difference by looking into God's commandment found in Ex. 20: 12 and by examining the role of music in the three cultures. If the various worldviews are not understood, the chances of clear communication are very low.

Since the communication process involves eliciting or constructing meanings rather than transmitting them, understanding the worldviews involved is of major importance. Chapter 11 focused on the results of understanding worldview in relation to the receptor, communicator, message, communication forms, worship forms, church structure, and leadership roles. We see that God has not approved of any single worldview system but is apparently willing and anxious to work through each culture.

Strategy for the Church

In the final section we have examined the existing Kamwə Church in order to see what God has done and to understand the origin and development of the work, so that we might suggest strategy for the future. We dealt with outside advocates, inside advocates and innovators as we watched the Church grow. We observed the cell-like division of the Church, the development of meaningful organization, the coming of literacy, the translation of the New Testament, and the withdrawal of the missionary. We have described the existing indigeneity and expressed the need for greater freedom from western forms so that the Church will be what missiologists are currently calling "dynamically equivalent" to the New Testament Church (Kraft 1973a).

We focused on the need for the Kamwə Church to consider the worldview in order to meet individual and groups needs, to bring about meaningful change, and to use indigenous cultural forms. Faith and practice, outreach, and service ministry all need to be based on the Kamwə worldview, too.

Specific strategy has been suggested to provide stimulus for discussion and consideration by the Church leadership, for the innovator comes from within the group. The foci of the strategy included homogeneous units, an integrating Gospel, and indigenous leadership. The use of Kamwə terms, indigenous communication forms, and ritual also provide the basis for hearer-oriented communication and the suggested strategy. The use of tapes and literacy in my suggested strategy reflects current developments in the area. The strategy suggested for developing an indigenous theology is essential for the future of the Church. The Church is still in the "destiny period" and there are resources that they have yet to discover and exploit. There are experiences of faith that need to be consolidated and interpreted. I am anxious that the Kamwə Church discover the manner and means by which they can most effectively worship God and receive comfort and guidance commensurate with their needs and aspirations. If I have been able to contribute even a little to bring this about, I will be satisfied.

The Kamwə Church has shown me that Christ can be the Saviour in an African worldview. John V. Taylor has said:

> Christ has been presented as the answer to the
> questions a white man would ask, the solution to
> the needs that Western man would feel, the Saviour
> of the world of the European world-view, the object
> of the adoration and prayer of historic Christendom.
> But if Christ were to appear as the answer to the
> questions that Africans are asking, what would he
> look like? If he came into the world of African
> cosmology to redeem Man as Africans understand him,
> would he be recognizable to the rest of the Church
> Universal? And if Africa offered him the praises
> and petitions of her total, uninhibited humanity,
> would they be acceptable (1963:24)?

As has been outlined, the Kamwə approach to Christianity includes both indigenous and foreign elements. The Church stands at a fork in the road--one fork taking them on into a more foreign expression that will involve conversion to a foreign worldview, and the other fork taking them into greater elaboration and development of the indigenous aspects of their Christianity. As I see it, the future vitality of Christianity among the Kamwə depends

on their decision as to which path they follow. My conviction is
that tne better path is that of indigenous Christianity. My hope
and prayer is that their choice would be to bring Christ into
their "African cosmology," to more fully experience Him as their
Redeemer, that from within their frame of reference they may
offer Him their "praise and petitions," their "total uninhibited
humanity."

Appendix A

Glossary of Kamwə Words

argi	-	distilled alcohol
badle	-	guinea corn beer
bathyə	-	little
ɓwagə	-	two
calyi	-	a place over close--parallel to mountain
cicitlə	-	stinginess
ɗa məlyə	-	ceremony at the sacred household pot
daɓəghi	-	harmony, peace and unity
dəgwəma	-	brothers born of same mother
dəgwəta	-	brothers born of same father, sons of father's brothers
ɗiɗiwi	-	evil spirit who lives in forest
dlera	-	crab
dzatə	-	go up close
dzəgə	-	go (general term and non-specific if direction--unknown)
dzəgwa	-	go down far
dzəmə	-	go up far
galipə	-	wealthy person
gədla	-	special thorn with magical power used for protection
guri	-	special charm worn around waist
gwaguləngə	-	good health

ha	–	guinea corn (general term for grain)
həwəshe	–	honor or respect
hyala	–	spirits (good and evil)
Hyalatəmwə	–	God
ja	–	go down close
jalyi	–	go over close
jige	–	go outside, go to bush
ka	–	people from
kadibili	–	cloth clothes
kakye	–	stranger, outsider, baby daughter
kata	–	descendents of a single known ancestor
katsala	–	an expert
kələngi	–	ceremony of the elders
kutə	–	one
kulakwacə	–	ground nuts (peanuts)
kwa	–	(locational preposition) a place down far
kwantəkwa	–	chicken
la	–	(locational preposition) a place down close
lafwe	–	herbs
latə	–	(locational preposition) a place up close
laya	–	charm--a small leather case worn hanging on the body
lighe	–	tradesman
ma həwə	–	disrespectful person
makwa	–	daughter-in-law
maraza	–	mother of my husband
mari	–	lazy person
mə	–	(locational preposition) a place up far
məɓa	–	the world of death
məɓatamwə	–	sky
məhələ	–	good character and kindness
məkwe	–	mother-in-law, father-in-law, son-in-law
mələ	–	commoner
məlyə	–	special ceremonial pot in the compound
məmbali	–	spirit of a person which goes to spirit world eventually
mbəlyi hankə	–	those living in the compound
mbəlyi kwahye	–	ancestor spirits
mdi kə lafwe	–	medicine man
mdi kə nə dlera	–	diviner who works with crabs
mdi kə nə kwahye	–	diviner who uses paraphenalia bag
mdi kə zəmə hyala	–	spirit man or man who rids people of spirits
mdi məlimi	–	member of core group, man of the town
mpya	–	hut
mtə	–	death

ngwalyime	-	married or unmarried daughters
nkwa mə thala	-	up-side of the compound (men's)
nkw məkulə	-	burial grounds
ntivəntə	-	forgiveness
ntuntuli	-	evil spirit
pəlyə	-	(locational preposition) a place far parallel to mountain outside a boundary
pi	-	the blessing of the supernatural
pisi malə	-	a special tsawhi ceremony for the bride
sarəka	-	community ceremony
satə	-	come up close toward speaker and mountain
səkə	-	come (general term and non-specific if direction is unknown)
səmə	-	come up far toward mountain
səkwa	-	come down far from mountain side
sha	-	come down (close) from mountain toward speaker
shafa	-	leaf with special power used for ordeals
shalyi	-	come over close
shetari	-	an evil spirit
shika	-	come inside, come from bush
shikəkulə	-	libation ceremony at the graveside on behalf of the deceased
shilyə	-	come over far
shishi	-	jealous person
shi	-	grandparent, grandchild
ta	-	biological father and his brothers
taraza	-	father of my husband
tərənkwə	-	down-side of the compound (women's)
tiki	-	poor man
tlamda	-	the one in charge of the house, master, owner
tlənə	-	work
tsawhi	-	forgiveness ceremony involving guinea corn
tya	-	sweet drink made from germinated dry shoots of guinea corn
vasa	-	failing to obey the ancestor teaching
vəcəmwə	-	the Kamw language
vwə	-	spirit that is inherited and lives inside a person
wasə pəla	-	openhanded, generous
we	-	(negative)
wsi	-	thing
wsi wshi	-	things of the ancestors, tradition
wshəntə	-	one who has no regard for others

wtsəgə	—	mother's relatives and children of daughters (who are married into another clan)
wzha	—	daughters of everyone in dəgwəma and dəgwəta group
wzharma	—	sister born of same mother
wzharta	—	sister born of same father, father's brother's daughters
yemyi	—	water
zahuli	—	seer
zaya	—	household head
zəmə	—	ritual performance
zigwi	—	son of all whom one refers to as dəgwəta or dəgwəma
'ini	—	greediness
'intəghi	—	selfishness
'yagare	—	cruelty
'yə	—	discipline

Appendix B

Orthography

The Kamwə words cited in this book follow the orthography described and used by linguist-translator, Roger Mohrlang, who reduced the language to its written form and translated the New Testament (within the last eight years). My description of the symbols will be from a technical perspective based on his material on Kamwə (Higi) phonology (1972). At this date there are not many written materials in the language and those who can write are still more apt to do so in Hausa as they have been taught. For this reason there may be spelling discrepancies in the Kamwə words and phrases used in this material. As I was gathering data, there was often hesitation in how it should be spelled. Figure 20 explains the consonant symbols used. In all of the instances (except for r and ') on the chart where there are two phonetic pronunciations for a symbol, the first is the pronunciation used in palatalized syllables and the second is the pronunciation used in the non-palatalized syllables. The distinguishing rules for the pronunciation of /'/ are: [g] in post labialized syllables, [g̶] in palatalized syllables, and [ʔ] elsewhere. The /r/ is always flapped when it occurs before vowels and may be lightly trilled or flapped elsewhere.

The vowel system is made up of only four contrastive vowels in word-final position preceding a pause and three in word medial position (Mohrlang, 1972:45). The static values of vowels in final position include:

$$i - \text{front high vowel}$$
$$e - \text{front mid vowel}$$
$$\varepsilon - \text{front mid-low vowel}$$
$$a - \text{central low vowel}$$

KAMWƏ ORTHO-GRAPHY	DESCRIPTION OF SOUND	PIKE'S PHONETIC SYSTEM	INT'L PHONETIC ALPHABET
p	voiceless lightly-aspirated bilabial stop	pʰ	pᶜ
t	voiceless lightly-aspirated alveolar stop	tʰ/t̪ʰ	tᶜ/t̪ᶜ
k	voiceless lightly-aspirated velar stop	k̂ʰ/k̩ʰ	k̩/k̩
b	voiced bilabial stop	b	b
d	voiced alveolar stop	d/d̪	d/d̪
g	voiced velar stop	g/g̩	g/g̩
ɓ	voiced bilabial implosive	bˤ	ɓ
ɗ	voiced alveolar implosive	dˤ/d̪ˤ	ɗ/d̪
'	voiced velar stop/voiceless glottal stop	gˤ/g̩ˤ/ʔ	ɠ/ɠ̩/ʔ
ts	voiceless lightly-aspirated alveolar affricate	tsʰ(ȼʰ)	tsᶜ
c	voiceless lightly-asp. alveopalatal affricate	tš̌ʰ(č̌ʰ)	tʃᶜ
dz	voiced alveolar affricate	dz(ʒ)	dz
j	voiced alveopalatal affricate	dž̌(ǰ)	dʒ
f	voiceless labio-dental fricative	f	f
v	voiced labio-dental fricative	v	v
s	voiceless alveolar fricative	s	s
sh	voiceless alveopalatal fricative	š	ʃ
z	voiced alveolar fricative	z	z
zh	voiced alveopalatal fricative	ž	ʒ
h	voiceless velar fricative	x̂/x̩	x̩/x̩
gh	voiced velar fricative	g̣/g̩	ɣ̩/ɣ
tl	voiceless alveolar lateral fricative	ƛ̩ᵗ/ƛ̩	ɬ t/ɬ
dl	voiced alveolar lateral fricative	ƛ̩ᵈ/ƛ̩	ɦᵈ/ɦ
ly	voiced alveolar lateral flap	ł̌	ɭ
l	voiced dental-alveolar lateral	l̂	l̩
r	voiced alv. flapped or lightly trilled vibrant	ř/r̃	ɾ/r
m	voiced bilabial nasal	m	m
n	voiced alveolar nasal	n/n̂	n/n̩
ng	voiced velar nasal	ŋ/ŋ̩	ŋ/ŋ̩
w	voiced labio-velar semivowel	w	w
y	voiced alveopalatal semivowel	y	j

*Figure 20.   Chart of Kamwə Orthography

* (Pike, 1947:5, 7, 46, and "Phonetics," in the Encyclopedia Britannica, 1962:771)

The three vowels in medial position are fluid with each vowel symbol comprising a wide horizontal range of phonetic values:

Tongue Height	Position on Tongue		
	front	central	back
high	i	ɨ	u ʊ
mid	e	ẹ	o
low	ɛ	ʌ a	ɔ

Thus the specific phonetic value of a medial vowel at any point is largely determined by the combination of prosodies influencing the vowel at that point. The prosodies found in Kamwə include: 1) labialization (written with w or p before bilabials or m when combined with pre-nasalization), 2) palatalization (written with y), 3) pre-nasalization (written m before bilabials and n elsewhere). Labialization tends to move the vowel to the backed form, palatalization tends to use the front forms and when neither prosody is present, the central forms are used. Back-velarization, the presence of a velar consonant in a non-palatalized syllable, pulls the higher-range vowel down and the lower-range vowel up. "The exact value [for word-medial vowels] depends on (1) the speed of utterance; (2) the particular combination of prosodies acting at any given point; (3) the consonants contiguous to it; and (4) the degree of stress on the syllable." (Mohrlang 1972:57).

The vowel symbols used in the Kamwə orthography are:

    i - front high unrounded
    u - back high rounded
    e - front mid unrounded
    a - central low unrounded
    ə - central high and front mid-low unrounded

Each syllable in Kamwə carries one of the three contrastive tones which occur in the language: high ['], low [ ], low-high [ᵛ]. However, tone is not regularly written in the orthography except to distinguish minimally contrasting word pairs. /'/ usually represents high tone, but may represent low-high glide as well; it always contrasts with a low-tone version of the same spelling. Examples of words requiring tone marks are: /ná/ 'you singular (subject, completive aspect)', and /na/ 'you singular (subject, incompletive aspect)'; /má/ 'hunger' and /ma/ 'mother'; /fá/ 'to hear' and /fa/ 'to touch'.

Appendix C

Kamwə Myths

The myths or origin stories included here explain inter-community relationships, relation to the mountain, the importance of guinea corn, the origin of the tradesmen caste, the origin of the vwə spirit, the problem of death and the origin of burial of the dead. These are reflected in the worldview and validate the beliefs of the Kamwə.

Origin of Bazza Clan

(Takwale 1967)

The history of the origin of Bazza can be traced to Mcakali and then to Kirawa in the Cameroon Republic like other clans of Kamwə. In the history of Kamale clan, (Ka Wstəka), we read that Kamale and Bazza (Dakwa) are brothers.

They left Mcakali in search of farmland. They travelled southwards across the Mandara Mountains. They came to one of the spurs of the Mandara Mountains called Sukur. Here we do not know whether Bazza people first went across Sukur before the Sukur people came and settled or the Sukur people were there before the Bazza people came. It might be also that they came together as one group. The Bazza people favor this statement that they were in one group, but the Sukur people are against it. The people of Sukur say that from the beginning when they were still at Mcakali there was enmity between them and the people of Kamale (of whom the people were a part). But Bazza people say that when the father of the

Bazza people decided to leave Sukur, he told one of his cousins
to remain at Sukur. This person then became the father of all
the people of Sukur.

At Kamale the group of Bazza people stayed for many years.
They were all together known as the people of Kamale. The farmland, however, became exhausted and there was famine. The father
of the Bazza people and his group went to the south from mountain
to mountain because of fear. They came to the Futu Mountain.
They wanted to settle there but due to the lack of drinking water
and flat land for farming they left. From Futu they did not stop
until they came to Mwekule Mountain which is the spiritual center
of Bazza. There they settled on this mountain. Later on some
of their relatives from Kamale, Sukur, and Mcakali followed their
route until they came and joined them at Mwekule.

When the Bazza people arrived on the top of Mwenkule Mountain,
they found a valley with a stream of water, a forest, and wild
fruit trees. They found the ground to be suitable for farming
and grazing. There were many animals also for hunting. The Bazza
people settled here. They planted some of the crops that they
had brought along with them. Their farm products did well and
their animals increased in size and number. They became very
prosperous and they enjoyed this place very much. But after some
years the forest was cleared, the land became exhausted and they
once again found themselves in a difficult condition.

When the land of Mwekule was exhausted, the Bazza people came
down to the foot of the mountain to plant their crops. They came
to the foot of the mountain for farming but they continued to
live on Mount Mwekule.

The Meaning of Ghumci

(Takwale 1967)

The people of Metla came from Sukur. They came in a group.
On their way to Metla some of them settled at Mogodi and the rest
proceeded to Nkala. When they came to Nkala they settled and
increased in number. They had three groups: Tizhe, Zira, and
Tumba. The group of Tizhe stayed at Nkala but the group of Zira
and Tumba went to Metla and Ghumci, respectively. Before the
groups of Zira and Tumba left, they called on the one who was the
high priest to divide the family properties as there were two
sacred stones, called birth stones. The high priest put one of
the sacred stones among the smallest part and the other stone in
the second to the smallest part, thus, the biggest part had no
birth stone. The three groups were called to make the choice.
The group of Tizhe, being the eldest group, was asked to make

his choice first. The group took the biggest part, and the group of Zira and Tumba had to take the smaller portions. The group of Tumba, who took the smallest part, became angry with the rest of his brothers. When he came to Ghumci he said, "Good-bye for ever," to his brothers. And this is the meaning of Ghumci.

The group of Tumba, who stayed at Ghumci, cut themselves completely from the rest of his brothers. Even during the time of war, the group of Tumba got no help either from Tizhe or Zira. However, Tumba was able to drive the people of Kamwendiva away from the present area of Ghumci. The people of Kamwendiva went towards northwest and settled.

The Origin of Guinea Corn

(Informant Nggida 1974)

God sent a dog with grain on its tail. A boy saw it and pulled it off. He dug a hole and put the grain in the ground. It sprouted. It grew and grew. It was a thing of wonder. As it matured, it formed a head on the top. Then it became ripe.

The people saw it and said, "Let's go and take it." They got the head and planted the grains again. They grew and formed heads again. This time the people took it and ground it up so they could make porridge. They drank it and their bodies were healthy and strong. Each time the people set aside some of the grain to plant again.

The Origin of the Tradesmen

(Informants Daniel and Bugi 1974)

In the beginning there were no tradesmen. Everybody was brothers and sisters to each other. The custom was to kill a goat when a person dies. The goatskin was used for making a loin cloth for the corpse. The meat was hidden in a tree and not eaten until after the corpse was buried in the grave.

One night after there had been a death, a greedy man came and took the meat out of the tree and ate it. When there was another death the greedy man came at night again. He took the meat and ate it. When a third man died, the people caught the greedy man and told him that if he was going to eat the meat, he was going to work for it. "If it is going to be this way, you will become a tradesman. When someone dies you will be called to make the loincloth, to prepare the corpse, and to carry the corpse to the gravesite."

Since that time, the tradesmen have been a distinct group who earn their living by serving the community.

The Coming of the Vwə Spirit

(Takwale 1967)

Long ago, when the people were created, there was nothing called vwə. But there was a man who had three sons: Tizhe, Zira, and Tumba. When the last-born was still young, the man died leaving the mother with her three sons. Not long after this the mother died, leaving the three children by themselves. Nobody came and took care of these children. They stayed by themselves and grew to be men. They worked hard all their lives.

When Tizhe was twenty years old they were able to collect enough money for marriage and Tizhe married. After two years Zira also got married. They were living very happily and their prosperity increased rapidly. Two years later Tumba got married. All were happy.

But one morning the wife of Tumba came out mourning and crying. She told the two brothers that Tumba had died. The two brothers could not believe her. Tizhe said, "What! Death cannot do that." Zira said to Tumba's wife, "Woman don't trouble yourself by crying. It can't be true that our beloved brother is dead. Even if it is true death must pay for it." These three brothers loved each other very much and were ready to sacrifice their lives for each other. Tizhe went to the door of Tumba and shouted, "Tumba, wake up!" There was no answer. Zira rushed into the room and tried to raise Tumba to get him to sit up, but Tumba was really dead and could not be gotten up. Zira came out and told Tizhe that Tumba was really dead.

The brothers who remained armed themselves saying they would go to fight Death. After they traveled one mile, Tizhe stopped and said, "Zira you better go home in order to take care of our family. This journey may take us a long time. I will be able to kill Death if I see him." Zira went back home and Tizhe continued his journey.

He walked and walked for several days in the bush without eating and drinking. One day at noon he met a very old man sitting alone in the forest. The old man asked what brought him to that forest. Tizhe told him to get out of his way or he would kill him. The old man kept on asking him. Tizhe tried to hit him with his stick but he could not hit the man. At last Tizhe found out that this old man was supernatural. He then told the old man about the death of his brother Tumba. He told him how he must go and kill Death for revenge. The old man told him that it was not easy to kill Death. Tizhe said, "Just take me to the place and show me Death. If I do not kill him I don't care if you kill me."

The old man took him to a big flat rock. They walked to the
center of the rock and there was a big tamarind tree under which
there was a big hole through the rock. The old man stopped and
pointing to the hole said, "This is the home of Death." Tizhe
told him to call Death out. The old man did and Death came out.
Death said, "Why have you brought this goat?" Tizhe was frightened
and asked the old man to hide him. The old man prevented Death
from killing Tizhe.

When Tizhe went home and told the news, Zira was about to kill
him saying that Tizhe did not love their brother Tumba or he would
have killed Death when he saw him. Zira then went to the old man
who took him to the place of death. The old man called Death.
When Death came out he was preparing the skin of Zira's brother
Tumba.

When Zira saw him, immediately he attacked Death. He hit him
with his big club and Death started to run away. The description
of Death was as follows: he was very tall (about eight feet),
one of his legs was cut right on the knee, his teeth were on the
surface because they were too long to be covered with lips (about
six inches). Zira had already hit Death on his long teeth and
all of them fell out except one. Zira took the skin of his
brother Tumba and tied his abdomen with it. He started to chase
Death. They ran for a hundred miles without stopping to eat or
drink. Death became very tired.

Everybody Death went to for help ran away from him. At last
Death came to a woman who was drawing water from a well. He asked
the woman to hide him and she hid him under her big calabash and
sat on it. Zira came more than ten times to the woman asking her
whether she had seen the direction that Death took. The woman
lied to him saying that she had not seen Death.

When Zira went away she let Death come out so that he might
leave. But before Death left, he took his remaining one tooth
and gave it to the woman. He said, "This I give you to help you
in time of trouble. You can also use it to obtain anything that
you want. This gift that I have given you will be as a brother
to you. You have saved my life and I thank you for it." Death
left and the woman pushed the tooth into her abdomen. This has
become what is today called the vwə spirit. From that time on,
the offspring born to that woman during the night became witches.

The First Death

(Takwale 1967)

When the first man died, the people thought he was asleep. But
after many hours trying to awaken the person they could not. This

was amazing. God their ruler or father, when he was with them,
did not teach them about this. And now they could not go to God.
However, the home of God at that time could be reached from certain high mountains that men could not climb.

The people sent two messengers--a chameleon and a lizard--to
ask God what they should do with the person. God sent the mes-
sengers back with a medicine that would cure the man. The lizard
left the chameleon and ran to the people. He came and told the
people that they should dig a hole in the ground and bury the
man in it. The people did not waste time in doing it.

Finally, the chameleon came with the medicine. It was too
late, for the person had been buried already. The medicine was
thrown away and whenever someone died he was buried like the
first person. Starting from this time, people have been looking
for someone who can make contact between them and God.

Origin of Kamwə

(Tili Clan Origin)

God created the heaven and the world. He lived in the heaven
but the world was empty. After many years, woman was first
created by God. God saw from heaven that woman was very lonely.
He came down and asked the woman to go to heaven to live together
with him. The woman refused saying that she preferred to live
in the world rather than to go to heaven to live with God. Of
course she had much trouble. She had nobody to converse with,
she slept on grass under a big tree, and she had to live on roots
and fruits of trees. However, God did not force the woman to
go and live with him, but instead he made the woman to become
his wife. He always came down and slept with her. The woman
gave birth to ten children, five boys and five girls. God came
down and made shelter for his children, he also came with food
for them. When the children were still young, God told the woman
that he would take the children and would rear them in heaven
together with him. The woman refused saying that none of her
children would go to heaven. She said that the world belonged
to her and the heaven belonged to God, therefore her children
would stay in the world to multiply to fill the world. God then
asked her to divide the children between them. He would put his
share in another part of the world. To this the woman agreed.
She took three boys and two girls and gave them to God and she
had two boys and three girls for herself. She took more females
for she knew that males do not give birth. God received his
share, the three boys and two girls. He went away to a different
part of the world with these five children. He blessed them with
many good things that he refused to give to the children taken
by the woman.

The place where the woman lived is believed to be Mcakali which is known as Godir in the Cameroon Republic. All the people of the world came from this woman who lived at Mcakali. The children of God were blessed with many good things including the power to rule the children of the woman. They were given horses and spears to fight the children of the woman. But to the children of the woman God gave axes, hoes, and sickles for tilling the ground. Thus, even today it is a popular conception that the Kamwə should be farmers and the Fulani should be the rulers. Anybody who opposes this opposes the law of God.

Appendix D

Growth of the Kamwə Church, 1958-1976

Figure 21 indicates the growth of the total Kamwə Church from 1958 to 1976. Figure 22 indicates the origin dates and growth of each of the eleven churches which represent specific geographical areas within the Kamwə Church from 1958 to 1975. In these figures I have used a dash for representing the years in which no data was available. These figures are followed by tables which give the numerical data. This material was obtained through the Brethren Church Missions Office, Ashland, Ohio, and through personal correspondence with John Guli in Nigeria.

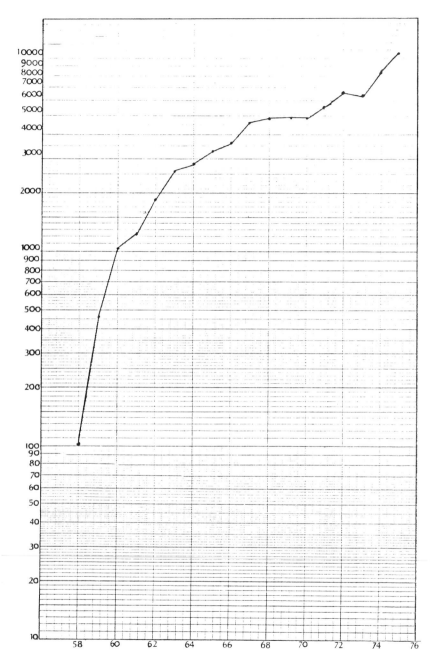

Figure 21. Kamwə Church Growth (See Table 1)

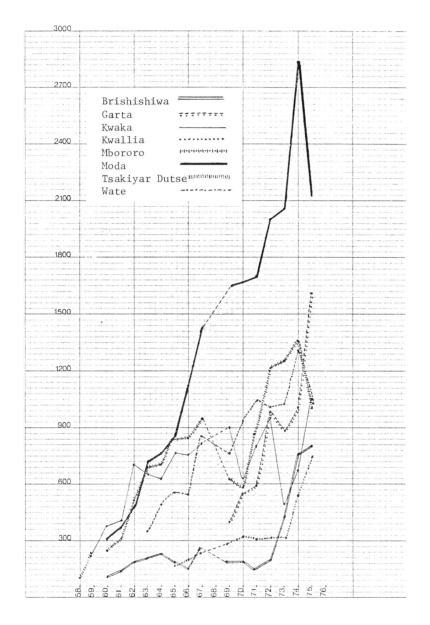

Figure 22. Church Growth for Geographic Units   (See Table 2)

Table 1. Kamwe Church Growth

Year	Members		Year	Members
1958	102 members		1967	4606 members
1959	465 "		1968	4836 "
1960	1054 "		1969	4935 "
1961	1204 "		1970	4884 "
1962	1884 "		1971	5498 "
1963	2605 "		1972	6670 "
1964	2814 "		1973	6488 "
1965	3337 "		1974	8442 "
1966	3616 "		1975	10684 "

Table 2. Kamwe Church Growth According to Geographic Units

	1958	1959	1960	1961	1962	1963	1964	1965	1966	1967	1968	1969	1970	1971	1972	1973	1974	1975
Brishishiwa			112	128	173	204	233	179	165	285	--	188	189	163	198	430	751	800
Kwaka		220	397	412	708	644	636	752	744	838	--	900	633	800	957	498	680	1027
Garta											--	399	551	595	989	894	1000	1611
Kwallia								172	201	230	--	289	313	306	308	309	542	742
Mbororo			243	304	510	686	701	825	832	955	--	622	594	878	1210	1251	1343	1000
Moda			302	360	493	726	751	846	1125	1421	--	1656	1672	1690	2001	2080	2822	2125
Tsakiyar Dutse	102	245																
Wate						345	493	563	549	877	--	781	932	1066	1007	1026	1304	1025
Boka																		773
Mentihwi																		431
Futu																		600
Mbelimeya																		550

Bibliography

ADEGBOLA, E.A. Adeolu
    1976   "In the History of Thought," in Taylor pp. 63-71.

ARENSBERG, Conrad M. and Arthur H. NIEHOFF
    1974   *Introducing Social Change*. Chicago: Aldine Atherton,
           Inc.

ARINZE, Francis A.
    1970   *Sacrifice in Ibo Religion*. Nigeria: Ibadan University
           Press.

BAKER, Archibald
    1934   *Christian Missions in a New World Culture*. New York:
           Willett, Clark and Company.

BAKER, Roger L. and Yola M. ZUBEIRU
    1955   "The Higis of Bazza Clan," *Nigeria*, 47:213-20.

BALDWIN, Elmer R.
    1953   "The Establishment of the Church of the Brethren
           Mission in Africa," unpublished thesis for Bethany
           Biblical Seminary, Chicago.

BARNETT, H. G.
    1953   *Innovation: The Basis of Cultural Change*. New York:
           McGraw Hill Book Company, Inc.

This list is confined to sources consulted and references cited.

BARNLUND, Dean
    1968   "Communication: The Context of Change," *Perspective
            on Communication* by C.E. Larson and F.E.X. Dance, (eds.)
            pp. 24-40 Madison, Wisconsin: Helix Press. References
            cited from reprint in Mortenson (1973:5-27).

BARR, James
    1961   *The Semantics of Biblical Language*. Glasgow:
            Oxford University Press.

BARRETT, David B.
    1971   *African Initiatives in Religion*. Nairobi: East
            African Publishing House.

BEALS, Alan R. and George and Louise SPINDLER
    1973   *Culture in Process*. New York: Holt, Rinehart and
            Winston.

BEDE, The Venerable
    1955   *A History of the English Church and People* (translated).
            (chapter 24, pp. 245-48) Baltimore: Penguin Books.

BELSHAW, Cyril S.
    1954   *Changing Melanesia*. Melbourne: Oxford University Press.

BERGSMA, Harold M.
    1970   "Tiv Proverbs as a Means of Social Control," *Africa*,
            40:151-163.

BERLO, David K.
    1960   *The Process of Communication: An Introduction to Theory
            and Practice*. San Francisco: Rinehart Press.

BERNDT, Manfred
    1961   "Adaption of the Religious Dance and Similar Physical
            Movements in the Indigenous Church," unpublished
            S.T.M. thesis, Concordia Seminary, St. Louis, Missouri.

BITTINGER, Desmond W.
    1941   *Black and White in the Sudan*. Elgin: Brethren
            Publishing House.

    1941   *An Educational Experiment in Northern Nigeria in Its
            Cultural Setting*. Elgin: Brethren Publishing House.

CARROLL, John B. (ed.)
    1956   *Language, Thought, and Reality*. New York: John
            Wiley and Sons, Inc.

CHRISTENSEN, Thomas G.
    1971   "Gbaya Value Orientations As Opportunities for Dialogue
            with the Christian Mission," unpublished S.T.M. thesis,
            Lutheran School of Theology, Chicago, Illinois.

COHEN, Arthur R.
    1964   "The Communication," *Attitude Changes and Social
            Influence,* New York: Basic Books Inc.

CONKLIN, Harold C.
    1955   "Hanunoo Color Categories," *Southwestern Journal of
            Anthropology,* 11:339-44.

COSERIU, Eugenio
    1975   *Exploring Semantic Structures.* Munich: Wilhelm
            Fink Verlag.

CRANE, William H.
    1964   "Indigenization in the African Church," *International
            Review of Missions,* 53:408-422.

CURTAIN, Philip D.
    1968   "Oral Data, Field Techniques for Collecting and
            Processing," *Journal of African History,* IX:3 pp. 367-385.

DARK, Philip
    1957   "Method of Synthesis in Ethnohistory," *Ethnohistory,*
            4:3 pp. 231-257.

DICKSON, Kwesi A. and Paul ELLINGWORTH
    1969   *Biblical Revelation and African Beliefs.* London:
            Lutterworth Press.

DOUGLAS, Mary
    1970   *Witchcraft, Confessions and Accusations.* London:
            Travistock Publications.

DYA, Zira
    1967   "Higi Ethnography," unpublished manuscript, Pasadena.

EZEANYA, Stephen N.
    1969   "God, Spirits and the Spirit World," in Dickson and
            Ellingworth 1969:30-46.

FINNEGAN, Ruth
    1970   *Oral Literature in Africa.* Nairobi: Oxford University
            Press.

FISON, Lorimer
    1892   *The Proceedings of the Australasian Association for
           the Advancement of Science.* Anthropological section,
           "President's Address," pp. 145-151.

FORTES, M. and G. DIETERLEN
    1965   *African Systems of Thought.* London: Oxford
           University Press.

FOSTER, George M.
    1973   *Traditional Societies and Technological Change* 2nd
           edition. New York: Harper and Row Publishers.

    1976   "Disease Etiologies in Non-Western Medical Systems,"
           American Anthropologist, 78:773-82.

GARCIA, Samuel R.
    1973   "The Incarnation of the Church in Indigenous Cultures,"
           Missiology 1:21-30.

GEERTZ, Clifford
    1966   "Religion as a Cultural System," *Anthropological
           Approaches to the Study of Religion,* Michael Banton,
           ed., pp. 1-46. London: Travistock Publications.

GOODENOUGH, Ward H.
    1957   *Cultural Anthropology and Linguistics.* Series on
           Language and Linguistics 9:167-173. Georgetown:
           Georgetown University Monograph.

GRAHAM, Billy
    1975   *Angels: God's Secret Agents.* New York: Pocket Books.

GRIMLEY, John B. and Gordon E. ROBINSON
    1966   *Church Growth in Central and Southern Nigeria.* Grand
           Rapids: William B. Eerdmans Publishing Company.

GULI, John
    1967   "Higi Ethnography," unpublished manuscript, Pasadena.

HALL, Edward T.
    1959   *The Silent Language.* Garden City: Doubleday and
           Company, Inc.

    1966   *The Hidden Dimension.* Garden City: Doubleday and
           Company, Inc.

HARJULA, Raimo
    1970   "Towards a Theologia Africana," unpublished paper,
           Kenyatta College, Dept. of Religious Studies, Kenya.

HASTINGS, J. (ed.)
1927   *Dictionary of the Bible*. New York: Charles
        Scriber's Sons.

HAYWARD, Victor E. W.
1963   *African Independent Church Movements*. London Research
        Pamphlets No. 11, London: Edinburgh House Press.

HIEBERT, Paul G.
1976   *Cultural Anthropology*. Philadelphia: J.B.
        Lippincott Company.

HOFFMAN, C.
1967   "A Higi Folktale," *Research Notes, Department of
        Linguistics and Nigerian Languages* 1:29-34.

HOWITT, Alfred William
1904   *The Native Tribes of South-East Australia*. London:
        The Macmillan Company.

HUNTER, David E. and Mary Ann B. FOLEY
1976   *Doing Anthropology*. New York: Harper and Row
        Publishers.

HYMES, Dell (ed.)
1964   *Language in Culture and Society*. New York: Harper
        and Row Publishers.

IDOWU, E. Bolaji
1973   *African Traditional Religion*. Maryknoll: Orbis Books.

IRVINE, S.H. and J.T. SANDERS
1972   *Cultural Adaptation Within Modern Africa*. New York:
        Teacher's College Press.

JACOBS, Donald R.
1961   "The Culture Themes of Puberty Rites of the Akamba,
        A Bantu Tribe of East Africa," unpublished Ph.D.
        dissertation, New York University.

KEARNEY, Michael
1975   "World View Theory and Study," *Annual Review of
        Anthropology*, 4:247-70.

KEESING, Roger M. and Felix M. KEESING
1971   *New Perspectives in Cultural Anthropology*. New York:
        Holt, Rinehart and Winston.

KIRK-GREENE, A.H.M.
    1958   *Adamawa Past and Present.* London: International
            African Institute by Oxford University Press.

    1959   "The Mba Ceremony of the Marghi," *Niderian Field,*
            24:80-87.

KLEM, Herbert Viele
    1977   "Toward the More Effective Use of Oral Communication
            of the Scriptures in West Africa." An unpublished
            D.Miss. dissertation, Fuller Theological Seminary,
            School of World Mission, Pasadena, California.

KLUCKHOHN, Clyde and Dorothea LEIGHTON
    1962   *The Navaho.* Garden City: Doubleday and Company, Inc.

KRAFT, Charles H.
    1973a   "Dynamic Equivalence Churches," *Missiology* 1:39-57.

    1973b   "God's Model for Cross-Cultural Communication--The
            Incarnation," *Evangelical Missions Quarterly* 9:205-216.

    1973c   "The Incarnation, Cross-Cultural Communication, and
            Communication Theory," *Evangelical Missions Quarterly*
            9:277-284.

    1973d   "Church Planters and Ethnolinguistics," in Tippett,
            ed. 1973:226-249.

    1974a   "Ideological Factors in Intercultural Communication,"
            Missiology 2:295-312.

    1974b   "Intercultural Communication," *Missiology* 2:295-312.

    1975   "Toward an Ethnography of Hausa Riddling," *Ba Shiru*
            6:17-24.

    1976a   "Intercultural Communication and Worldview Change,"
            unpublished paper, School of World Mission, Pasadena.

    1976b   "Cultural Concomitants of Higi Conversion: Early
            Period," *Missiology* 4:431-442.

    1977   "Theologizing in Culture," unpublished manuscript to
            be published by Orbis Books, 1978.

KWAST, Lloyd
    1973   "Ethnohistorical Research in West Cameroon," in
            Tippett, ed. 1973:295-307.

KWESI, Dickson and Paul ELLINGWORTH (eds.)
  1969 *Biblical Revelation and African Beliefs.* London:
        Lutterworth Press.

LA BARRE, Weston
  1964 "Paralinguistics, Kinesis, and Cultural Anthropology,"
        Approaches to Semitics, Thomas Sebeak, ed. pp. 198-202,
        216-220. The Hague: Mouton Publishers. Reference
        cited from reprint (Samovar and Porter 1972).

LESSA, William A. and Evon Z. VOGT (eds.)
  1972 *Reader in Comparative Religion: An Anthropological
        Approach* 3rd edition. New York: Harper and Row
        Publishers.

LINTON, Ralph
  1936 *The Study of Man: An Introduction.* New York:
        Appleton-Century.

LITTLE, Kenneth
  1970 *West African Urbanization: A Study of Voluntary
        Associations in Social Change.* Cambridge: Cambridge
        University Press.

  1971 "Some Aspects of African Urbanization South of the
        Sahara," a McCaleb Module in Anthropology, An Addison-
        Wesley Module, Philippines, Addison-Wesley Publishing
        Company, Inc.

LOEWEN, Jacob A.
  1967 "Lengua, Festivals and Functional Substitutes,"
        Practical Anthropology 14:15-36. Reference cited
        from reprint in Loewen 1975:156-77.

  1969a "Confession, Catharsis, and Healing," *Practical
        Anthropology* 16:63-74. Reference cited from reprint
        in Loewen 1975:287-98.

  1969b "Confession in the Indigenous Church," *Practical
        Anthropology* 16:114-127. Reference cited from reprint
        in Loewen 1975:299-312.

  1975 *Culture and Human Values.* South Pasadena: William
        Carey Library.

LOUNSBURY, Floyd G.
  1964 "The Structural Analysis of Kinship Semantics," from
        proceedings of the *9th International Congress of
        Linguistics.* The Hague: Mouton and Company.
        Reference cited from Tyler 1969.

LUCAS, J. Olumide
    1948   *The Religion of the Yorubas*. Lagos: C.M.S. Bookshop.

LUZBETAK, Louis J.
    1963   *The Church and Cultures*. Pasadena: William
            Carey Library.

MALINOWSKI, Bronislaw
    1925   "Magic, Science and Religion," in Needham, J. (ed.)
            Science, Religion and Reality. London. (Reissued
            1948 as *Magic, Science and Religion*. Boston:
            Beacon Press).

    1927   "The Problem of Meaning in Primitive Languages," in
            The Meaning of Meaning, Ogden, C.K. and I.A. Richards,
            pp. 296-336. New York: Harcourt, Brace and Company,
            Inc.

    1945   *The Dynamics of Culture Change: An Inquiry into Race
            Relations in Africa*. New Haven: Yale University Press.

MALINOWSKI, Bronislaw (ed.)
    1938   *Methods of Study of Culture Contact in Africa*. London:
            Oxford University Press.

MALLERY, Garrick
    1880   *Introduction to the Study of Sign Language Among the
            North American Indians as Illustrating the Gesture
            Speech of Mankind*. Washington, D.C.: Smithsonian
            Institute, Bureau of Ethnology.

MARETT, R.R.
    1909   *The Threshold of Religion*. London: Methuen and Co.

MARRIS, Peter
    1962   *Family and Social Change in An African City*. Great
            Britian: Northwestern University Press.

MAURIER, Henri
    1958   *The Other Covenant: A Theology of Paganism*. New York:
            Newman Press.

MBITI, John S.
    1969   *African Religions and Philosophy*. New York:
            Praeger Publishers.

1970   *Concepts of God*. New York: Praeger Publishers.

1971   *New Testament Eschatology in an African Background*.
       London: Oxford University Press.

MCGAVRAN, Donald Anderson
   1970   *Understanding Church Growth*. Grand Rapids: William
          B. Eerdmans Publishing Company.

MEEK, C.K.
   1930   "A Religious Festival in Northern Nigeria,"
          Africa 3:323-345.

   1931   *Tribal Studies in Northern Nigeria*. Vol. I, London:
          Kegan Paul, Trench, Trubner and Company, Ltd.

MILLER, Madeline S. and J. Lane MILLER
   1954   *Harper's Bible Dictionary*. New York: Harper and
          Brothers Publishers.

MITCHELL, Robert C.
   1963   "Christian Healing," in Hayward 1963:47-51.

MOHRLANG, Roger
   1972   *Studies in Nigerian Languages*. No. 2 Higi Phonology,
          Institute of Linguistics, Zaria.

   1975   *Vacə Yesu Kristi* (The New Testament in Higi). World
          Home Bible Lesgues, Jos, Nigeria.

MORTENSEN C. David (ed.)
   1973   *Basic Readings from Communication Theory*. New York:
          Harper and Row Publishers.

MULHOLLAND, Kenneth B.
   1976   *Adventures in Training the Ministry: A Honduras Case
          Study in T.E.E.* Nutley, New Jersey: Presbyterian
          and Reformed Publishing Company.

NAROLL, Raoul, and Ronald COHEN (eds.)
   1970   *Handbook of Method in Cultural Anthropology*.
          Garden City: The Natural History Press.

NEHER, Gerald
   1963   "Chibuk Face Marks," *Nigerian Field* 28:27-78.

   1964   "Brass Casting in North-East Nigeria," *Nigerian
          Field* 28:16-27.

NGGIDA, Tumba
    1967   "Higi Ethnography," unpublished manuscript, Pasadena.

NICOLL, W. Robertson (ed.)
    1951   *The Expositor's Greek Testament* Vol. IV. Grand Rapids:
           William B. Eerdmans Publishing Company.

NIDA, Eugene A.
    1947   *Bible Translating*. New York: American Bible Society.

    1959   *Customs and Cultures*. Pasadena: William Carey Library.

    1960   *Message and Mission*. Pasadena: William Carey Library.

    1975   *Componential Analysis of Meaning*. The Hague-Paris:
           Mouton.

NIRMAL, A.P.
    1976   "Celebration of Indian Festivals," in Taylor
           1976:79-83.

NOSS, Philip A.
    1972   "An Interpretation of Ghaya Religious Practice,"
           International Review of Mission 61:244.

OPLER, Morris E.
    1946   "Themes As Dynamic Forces in Culture," *American
           Journal of Sociology* 51:198-206.

OTTERBEIN, K.F.
    1968   "Higi Armed Combat," *Southwestern Journal of
           Anthropology* 24:195-213.

    1969   "Higi Marriage System," *Bulletin of the Cultural
           Research Institute* 8:16-20.

PARRINDER, Geoffrey
    1949   *West African Religion*. London: Epworth Press.

    1951   *West African Psychology*. London: Lutterworth Press.

PERCHONOCK, Norma and Oswald WERNER
    1969   "Navaho Systems of Classification: Some Implications
           for Ethnoscience," *Ethnology* 8:229-42.

PIKE, Kenneth L.
    1947   *Phonemics*. Ann Arbor: University of Michigan Press.

1962   "Phonetics," *The Encyclopedia Britannica* Vol. 17:770-772.
        Chicago: William Benton, Publisher, Encyclopedia
        Britannica, Inc.

1967   *Language in Relation to a Unified Theory of the
        Structure of Human Behavior*, 2nd edition. The Hague:
        Mouton and Company (1st ed. 1956-58).

RAMM, Bernard
1971   "Evangelical Theology and Technological Shock,"
        American Scientific Affiliation Journal June 1971,
        p. 52-56.

REDFIELD, Robert
1947   "The Folk Society," *The American Journal of
        Sociology* 52:293-308.

REYBURN, William D.
1957   "Conflicts and Contradictions in African Christianity,"
        Practical Anthropology 4:161-169.

SAMOVAR, L.A. and R.E. PORTER (eds.)
1972   *Intercultural Communication: A Reader*. Belmont:
        Wadsworth.

SAPIR, Edmund
1929   "The Status of Linguistics as a Science," *Languages*
        5:209-210.

SAWYERR, Harry
1970   *God: Ancestor or Creator?* Bristol: Longman Group, Ltd.

SCHRAM, Wilbur
1954   "How Communication Works," (p. 3-10), *The Process and
        Effects of Mass Communication*. Urbana: University
        of Illinois Press. Reference cited from Mortenson
        1973:28-36.

SCOTT, E.F.
n.d.   *Pastoral Epistles*, from *The Moffat New Testament
        Commentary*. New York: Harper and Brothers Publishers.

SERENO, Kenneth K. and David C. MORTENSON
1970   *Foundations of Communication Theory*. New York:
        Harper and Row Publishers.

SHINEBERG, Dorothy
1967   *They Came for Sandalwood: A Study of the Sandalwood
        Trade in the Southwest Pacific (1830-65)*. Melbourne:
        Melbourne University Press.

SMITH, E.W.
   1950   *African Ideas of God*.   London: Edinburgh House Press.

SNAITH, Norman H.
   1964   *The Distinctive Ideas of the Old Testament*.   New York:
           Schoken Books.

SPRADLEY, James and Michael A. RYNKIEWICH (eds.)
   1975   *The Nacirema: Readings in American Culture*.   Boston:
           Little, Brown and Company.

STOTT, John R.W.
   1968   *One People*.   Downers Grove: Intervarsity Press.

SUNDKLER, Bengt
   1960   *The Christian Ministry in Africa*.   London:
           SCM Press.

   1961   *Bantu Prophets in South Africa* 2nd edition.   London:
           Oxford Press (1st edition, 1948 Lutterworth Press).

TAKWALE, Joseph
   1967   "Higi Ethnography," unpublished manuscript, Pasadena.

TAYLOR, John B. (ed.)
   1976   *Primal World Views: Christian Involvement in Dialogue
           with Traditional Thought Forms*.   Ibadan: Daystar Press.

TAYLOR, John V.
   1963   *The Primal Vision*.   Philadelphia: Fortress Press.

TEMPELS, Rev. Father Placide
   1945   *Bantu Philosophy*.   Paris: Presence Africaine.

THOMAS, Keith
   1970   "The Relevance of Social Anthropology to the Historical
           Study of English Witchcraft," *Witchcraft, Confessions
           and Accusations* pp. 47-79.   London: Travistock
           Publications.

TIPPETT, Alan R.
   1958   "The Integrating Gospel," unpublished manuscript,
           Davuilevu, Fiji. (Bound copy at School of World
           Mission, Pasadena.)

   1963   "Ethnic Cohesion and Intra-configurational Involvement
           in the Acceptance of Cultural Change in Indonesia,"
           duplicated paper, Eugene, Oregon.

   1967   *Solomon Islands Christianity*.   Pasadena: William
           Carey Library.

1968   *Fijian Material Culture*. Honolulu: Bishop Museum
        Press.

1971   *People Movements in Southern Polynesia*. Chicago:
        Moody Press.

1973a   *Aspects of Pacific Ethnohistory*. South Pasadena:
        William Carey Library.

1973b   *Verdict Theology in Missionary Theory*, 2nd edition.
        South Pasadena: William Carey Library.

1975   "Christopaganism or Indigenous Christianity,"
        pp. 13-34; "Formal Transformation and Faith Distortion,"
        pp. 97-118; "The Meaning of Meaning," pp. 169-196 in
        Yamamori and Taber, eds. 1975.

TIPPETT, Alan R. (ed.)
1973   *God, Man and Church Growth*. Grand Rapids: William
        B. Eerdmans Publishing Company.

TURNER, Victor W.
1964   "Betwixt and Between: The Liminal Period in *Rites
        De Passage*," pp. 4-20; 338-47. *The Proceedings of the
        American Ethnological Society*. Symposium on New
        Approaches to the Study of Religion. References cited
        from reprint in Lessa and Vogt, 1972.

1967   *The Forest of Symbols: Aspects of Ndembu Ritual*.
        Ithaca: Cornell University Press.

TYLER, Stephen A.
1969   *Cognitive Anthropology*. New York: Holt, Rhinehart
        and Winston.

VAN GENNEP, Arnold
1960   *The Rites of Passage*. English translation by
        M. Vizedom and G. Caffee. Chicago: University of
        Chicago Press (originally published in French 1908).

VAUGHAN, J.H.
1962   "Rock Paintings and Rock Gongs Among the Marghi of
        Nigeria," *Man* 62:49-52.

1964a   "The Religion and World View of the Marghi,"
        Ethnology 3:4, pp. 389-397.

1964b   "Culture, History, and Grass-Roots Politics in a
        Northern Cameroons Kingdom," *American Anthropologist*
        66:1078-1095.

VINCENT, Marvin R.
    1946   *Word Studies in the New Testament* Vol. IV. Grand
            Rapids: William B. Eerdmans Publishing Company.

VON ALLMEN, Daniel
    1975   "The Birth of Theology," *International Review of
            Mission* 44:37-55.

WALLACE, Anthony F.C.
    1966   *Religion: An Anthropological View*. New York:
            Random House.

WEBER, H.R.
    1957   *The Communication of the Gospel to Illiterates*.
            London: SCM Press, Ltd.

WEBER, Max
    1947   *The Theory of Social and Economic Organization*.
            Translated by A.M. Henderson and Talcott Parsons;
            New York: The Free Press.

WELBOURNE, F.B.
    1963   "The Importance of Ghosts," in Hayward 1963:15-26.

WEMAN, Henry
    1960   *African Music and the Church in Africa*. Translated
            by Eric C. Sharpe; Uppala: ab Lundiqustrka Bokhonndilm.

WERNER, Oswald and Joann FENTON
    1970   "Method and Theory in Ethnoscience or Epistnoepistemology,"
            in Naroll 1970:537-578.

WESTERMANN, Diedrich
    1934   *The African Today and Tomorrow*. London: Oxford
            University Press.

WESTERMARCK, Edward
    1922   *The History of Human Marriage* Vol. III. New York:
            The Allerton Book Company.

WHORF, Benjamin Lee
    1942   "Language, Mind, Reality," Theosophist (Madras, India),
            January and April issues. Reference cited in reprint
            in Carroll 1956.

WIANT, Bliss
    1946   "Oecumenical Hymnology in China," *The International
            Review of Missions* 35:428-34.

WILLOUGHBY, W.C.
    1928   *The Soul of the Bantu*.   Garden City: Doubleday,
            Doran and Company, Inc.

WILSON, Monica
    1971   *Religion and the Transformation of Society*.
            Cambridge: The University Press.

WINTER, Ralph D. (ed.)
    1969   *Theological Education by Extension*.   South Pasadena:
            William Carey Library.

WOLFF, Hans Walter
    1974   *Anthropology of the Old Testament*.   Philadelphia:
            Fortress Press.

YAMAMORI, Tetsunao and Charles R. TABER (eds.)
    1975   *Christopaganism or Indigenous Christianity?*
            South Pasadena: William Carey Library.

Index

Marguerite G. Kraft was born in Philadelphia, Pennsylvania. After her father's death when she was five, the family moved to Lansing, Michigan. Later her mother was remarried to a minister. It was in this environment that she came to know the Lord and came into frequent contact with missionaries while they were entertained in her parents' home.

Her education includes a B. S. in Physical Education (1953) from Wheaton College, Wheaton, Illinois, and a Master of Arts in Linguistics from Hartford Seminary Foundation, Hartford Connecticut (1963).

She was married in 1953 to Charles Kraft and began specific preparations for mission work in studies at Ashland College and Seminary and Kennedy School of Missions, Hartford Seminary Foundation.

In 1957 she began her missionary work among the Kamwə of northeastern Nigeria. Her service in missions was a time of growth and insight into cross-cultural work. On returning to the U. S. she continued her studies and taught part-time while raising her four children.

When her husband joined the faculty at the School of World Mission at Fuller Seminary, she became interested in pursuing her doctoral studies. In 1973 she joined the faculty of Biola College, La Mirada, California, teaching Anthropology and Linguistics in the Missions program. She is currently an Associate Professor at that institution. She has also taught at Michigan State University, U.C.L.A., School of World Mission, Fuller Seminary, and Daystar's International Institute of Christian Communication, Nairobi, Kenya.

Books by the
William Carey Library

GENERAL

American Missions in Bicentennial Perspective edited by R. Pierce
Beaver, $8.95 paper, 448 pp.

The Birth of Missions in America by Charles L. Chaney, $7.95
paper, 352 pp.

*Education of Missionaries' Children: The Neglected Dimension of
World Mission* by D. Bruce Lockerbie, $1.95 paper, 76 pp.

Evangelicals Face the Future edited by Donald E. Hoke, $6.95
paper, 184 pp.

The Holdeman People: The Church in Christ, Mennonite, 1859-1969
by Clarence Hiebert, $17.95 cloth, 688 pp.

Manual for Missionaries on Furlough by Marjorie A. Collins, $4.45
paper, 160 pp.

*On the Move with the Master: A Daily Devotional Guide on World
Mission* by Duain W. Vierow, $4.95 paper, 176 pp.

*The Radical Nature of Christianity: Church Growth Eyes Look at
the Supernatural Mission of the Christian and the Church* by
Waldo J. Werning (Mandate Press), $5.85 paper, 224 pp.

Social Action Vs. Evangelism: An Essay on the Contemporary Crisis
by William J. Richardson, $1.95x paper, 64 pp.

STRATEGY OF MISSION

Church Growth and Christian Mission edited by Donald McGavran,
$4.95x paper, 256 pp.

Church Growth and Group Conversion by Donald McGavran et al.,
$2.45 paper, 128 pp.

Committed Communities: Fresh Streams for World Missions by
Charles J. Mellis, $3.95 paper, 160 pp.

*The Conciliar-Evangelical Debate: The Crucial Documents, 1964-
1976* edited by Donald McGavran, $8.95 paper, 400 pp.

Crucial Dimensions in World Evangelization edited by Arthur F.
Glasser et al., $7.95x paper, 512 pp.

Evangelical Missions Tomorrow edited by Wade T. Coggins and
Edwin L. Frizen, Jr., $5.95 paper, 208 pp.

Everything You Need to Know to Grow a Messianic Synagogue by
Phillip E. Goble, $2.45 paper, 176 pp.

Here's How: Health Education by Extension by Ronald and Edith
Seaton, $3.45 paper, 144 pp.

The Indigenous Church and the Missionary by Melvin L. Hodges,
$2.95 paper, 108 pp.

Literacy, Bible Reading, and Church Growth Through the Ages
by Morris G. Watkins, $4.95 paper, 240 pp.

A Manual for Church Growth Surveys by Ebbie C. Smith, $3.95
paper, 144 pp.

Mission: A Practical Approach to Church-Sponsored Mission Work
by Daniel C. Hardin, $4.95x paper, 264 pp.

Readings in Third World Missions edited by Marlin L. Nelson,
$6.95x paper, 304 pp.

AREA AND CASE STUDIES

Aspects of Pacific Ethnohistory by Alan R. Tippett, $3.95 paper, 216 pp.

A Century of Growth: The Kachin Baptist Church of Burma by Herman Tegenfeldt, $9.95 cloth, 540 pp.

Christian Mission to Muslims – The Record: Anglican and Reformed Approaches in India and the Near East, 1800–1938 by Lyle L. Vander Werff, $8.95 paper, 384 pp.

Church Growth in Burundi by Donald Hohensee, $4.95 paper, 160 pp.

Church Growth in Japan by Tetsunao Yamamori, $4.95 paper, 184 pp.

The Church in Africa, 1977 edited by Charles R. Taber, $6.95 paper, 224 pp.

Church Planting in Uganda: A Comparative Study by Gailyn Van Rheenen, $4.95 paper, 192 pp.

Circle of Harmony: A Case Study in Popular Japanese Buddhism by Kenneth J. Dale, $4.95 paper, 238 pp.

The Deep-Sea Canoe: The Story of Third World Missionaries in the South Pacific by Alan R. Tippett, $3.45x paper, 144 pp.

Frontier Peoples of Central Nigeria and a Strategy for Outreach by Gerald O. Swank, $5.95 paper, 192 pp.

The Growth Crisis in the American Church: A Presbyterian Case Study by Foster H. Shannon, $4.95 paper, 176 pp.

The Growth of Japanese Churches in Brazil by John Mizuki, $8.95 paper, 240 pp.

The How and Why of Third World Missions: An Asian Case Study by Marlin L. Nelson, $6.95 paper, 256 pp.

I Will Build My Church: Ten Case Studies of Church Growth in Taiwan edited by Allen J. Swanson, $4.95 paper, 177 pp.

Indonesian Revival: Why Two Million Came to Christ by Avery T. Willis, Jr., $6.95 paper, 288 pp.

Industrialization: Brazil's Catalyst for Church Growth by C.W. Gates, $1.95 paper, 96 pp.

The Navajos are Coming to Jesus by Thomas Dolaghan and David Scates, $5.95 paper, 192 pp.

New Move Forward in Europe: Growth Patterns of German-Speaking Baptists by William L. Wagner, $8.95 paper, 368 pp.

People Movements in the Punjab by Frederick and Margaret Stock, $8.95 paper, 388 pp.

Profile for Victory: New Proposals for Missions in Zambia by Max Ward Randall, $3.95 cloth, 224 pp.

The Protestant Movement in Bolivia by C. Peter Wagner, $3.95 paper, 264 pp.

Protestants in Modern Spain: The Struggle for Religious Pluralism by Dale G. Vought, $3.45 paper, 168 pp.

The Religious Dimension in Hispanic Los Angeles by Clifton L. Holland, $9.95 paper, 550 pp.

The Role of the Faith Mission: A Brazilian Case Study by Fred Edwards, $3.45 paper, 176 pp.

La Serpiente y la Paloma (La Iglesia Apostolica de la Fe en Jesuchristo de Mexico) by Manual J. Gaxiola, $2.95 paper, 194 pp.

Solomon Islands Christianity: A Study in Growth and Obstruction by Alan R. Tippett, $5.95x paper, 432 pp.

Taiwan: Mainline Vs. Independent Church Growth by Allen J.
    Swanson, $3.95 paper, 300 pp.
Tonga Christianity by Stanford Shewmaker, $3.45 paper, 164 pp.
*Toward Continuous Mission: Strategizing for the Evangelization
    of Bolivia* by W. Douglas Smith, Jr., $4.95 paper, 208 pp.
*Treasure Island: Church Growth Among Taiwan's Urban Minnan
    Chinese* by Robert J. Bolton, $6.95 paper, 416 pp.
*A Yankee Reformer in Chile: The Life and Works of David Trum-
    bull* by Irven Paul, $3.95 paper, 172 pp.

THEOLOGICAL EDUCATION BY EXTENSION

*The Extension Movement in Theological Education: A Call to the
    Renewal of the Ministry* by F. Ross Kinsler, $6.95 paper,
    304 pp.
The World Directory of Theological Education by Extension by
    Wayne C. Weld, $5.95x paper, 416 pp., *1976 Supplement only,*
    $1.95x, 64 pp. booklet
Writing for Theological Education by Extension by Lois McKinney,
 ⸱ $1.45x paper, 64 pp.

REFERENCE

*An American Directory of Schools and Colleges Offering Mission-
    ary Courses* edited by Glenn Schwartz. $5.95x paper, 266 pp.
Bibliography for Cross-Cultural Workers, edited by Alan R.
    Tippett, $4.95 paper, 256 pp.
*Church Growth Bulletin, Second Consolidated Volume (Sept. 1969-
    July 1975)* edited by Donald McGavran, $7.95x paper, 512 pp.
Evangelical Missions Quarterly, Vols. 7-9, $8.95x cloth, 830 pp.
Evangelical Missions Quarterly, Vols. 10-12, $15.95 cloth, 960 pp.
*The Means of World Evangelization: Missiological Education at the
    Fuller School of World Mission* edited by Alvin Martin, $9.95
    paper, 544 pp.
Protestantism in Latin America: A Bibliographical Guide edited by
    John H. Sinclair, $8.95x paper, 448 pp.
Word Study Concordance and New Testament edited by Ralph and
    Roberta Winter, $29.95 cloth, 2-volume set.
The World Directory of Mission-Related Educational Institutions
    edited by Ted Ward and Raymond Buker,Sr.,$19.95x cloth,906 pp.

POPULARIZING MISSION

Defeat of the Bird God by C. Peter Wagner, $4.95 paper, 256 pp.
The Night Cometh: Two Wealthy Evangelicals Face the Nation by
    Rebecca J. Winter, $2.95 paper, 96 pp.
The 25 Unbelievable Years: 1945-1969 by Ralph D. Winter, $2.95
    paper, 128 pp.
*The Word-Carrying Giant: The Growth of the American Bible
    Society* by Creighton Lacy, $5.95 paper, 320 pp.

BOOKLETS

The Grounds for a New Thrust in World Mission by Ralph D. Win-
    ter, $.75 booklet, 32 pp.
1980 and That Certain Elite by Ralph D. Winter, $.35x booklet,16 pp.
Penetrating the Last Frontiers by Ralph D. Winter, $1.00 book-
    let, 32 pp.
The World Christian Movement: 1950-1975 by Ralph D. Winter,
    $.75 booklet, 32 pp.